G000272779

TROUT AND SALMON LOUGHS OF IRELAND

A Fisherman's Guide

Also available from Unwin Hyman

A FLY ON THE WATER
Conrad Voss Bark

NEW ILLUSTRATED DICTIONARY OF TROUT FLIES
John Roberts

THE FORGOTTEN SKILLS Country Crafts Remembered
Norman Mursell

A FUTURE FOR GAME?
Colin McKelvie
Foreword by H.R.H. The Duke of Edinburgh

BOATFISHING FOR TROUT
Steve Parton

TROUT LOCHS OF SCOTLAND A Fisherman's Guide
Bruce Sandison

MY SMALL COUNTRY LIVING
Jeanine McMullen

COME DAWN, COME DUSK Fifty Years a Gamekeeper
Norman Mursell

THE CHANGING YEAR
Proteus of *The Field*

GREEN AND PLEASANT LAND A Countryman Remembers
Norman Mursell

FRANK SAWYER: MAN OF THE RIVERSIDE
Sidney Vines

DAYS AND NIGHTS OF GAME FISHING
W. B. Currie

NEW ANGLES ON SALMON FISHING
Philip Green

KEEPER OF THE STREAM
Frank Sawyer

EVER ROLLING STREAM
Bernard Aldrich
Foreword by H.R.H. The Prince of Wales

SEASONS OF CHANGE
Rural Life in Victorian & Edwardian England
Sadie Ward

TROUT AND SALMON LOUGHS OF IRELAND

A Fisherman's Guide

Peter O'Reilly

London
UNWIN HYMAN
Boston   Sydney

First published in Great Britain by Unwin Hyman, an imprint of Unwin Hyman Limited 1987

© Peter O'Reilly

All rights reserved. No part of this publication may be reproduced, stored in a retrieval system, or transmitted in any form or by any means, electronic, mechanical, photocopying, recording or otherwise, without the prior permission of Unwin Hyman Limited.

UNWIN HYMAN
Denmark House, 37–39 Queen Elizabeth Street,
London SE1 2QB
and
40 Museum Street, London WC1A 1LU

Allen & Unwin (Australia) Ltd
8 Napier Street, North Sydney, NSW 2060, Australia

Allen & Unwin New Zealand Ltd with the Port Nicholson Press
60 Cambridge Terrace, Wellington, New Zealand

ISBN 0 04 799036 8

British Library Cataloguing in Publication Data

O'Reilly, Peter
  Trout and salmon loughs of Ireland: a fisherman's guide.
1. Salmon-fishing – Ireland – Handbooks, manuals, etc.
2. Trout fishing – Ireland – Handbooks, manuals, etc.
3. Fly fishing – Ireland – Handbooks, manuals, etc.
I. Title
799.1′755   SH685
ISBN 0–04–799036–8

Set in 10 on 11 point Bembo by
Nene Phototypesetters Ltd, Northampton
and printed in Great Britain by Biddles Ltd, Guildford, Surrey

Contents

Illustrations

Maps

Acknowledgements

Derek Arnold, Arnold's Hotel,
Dunfanaghy, Co. Donegal.
Michael Barry, Manager, South
Western Regional Fisheries
Board, Macroom, Co. Cork.
Brendan Begley, 40 Lower Garden
City, Derry.
Andrew Bennett, Co. Library,
Navan, Co. Meath.
Sandy Bissett, Pontypridd, South
Wales.
Bosco Bonner, Dunfanaghy AC,
Co. Donegal.
Paul Bourke, Eastern Regional
Fisheries Board, Dublin.
Peter Brady, Kilnaleck, Co. Cavan.
Bertie Brennan, Clooncraff,
Ballymurry, Co. Roscommon.
Andrew Brown, 26 Farmleigh
Close, Stillorgan, Co. Dublin.
D. E. Brown, Hon. Sec., Carna
Anglers' Association, Carna, Co.
Galway.
Martin Butler, Delphi, Leenane,
Co. Galway.
John Campbell, Ballyveeney, Co.
Mayo.
Michael Chambers, Treenbeg,
Newport, Co. Mayo.
Trevor Champ, Central Fisheries
Board, Dublin.
Major N. F. Chance, Drumharnet,
Co. Donegal.
Michael Cleary, Corofin, Co.
Clare.
Michael Clesham, Kilbirnie,
Aasleagh, Leenane, Co. Galway.
Michael Conneely, Ballynahinch
Castle Hotel, Ballinafad PO, Co.
Galway.
Brendan Cooney, Carrickacromin,
Tunnyduff, Co. Cavan.
Padraig Corrigan, Lisadaly,
Croghan, Boyle, Co.

Roscommon.
Benny Courihan, c/o ESB,
Gweedore, Co. Donegal.
Vincent Courtney, 1 Glenard Road,
Omagh, Co. Tyrone.
Joe Creane, Roundstone, Co.
Galway.
Lt-Col. E. Cusack, Moycullen, Co.
Galway.
Carl Daly, Glencar Hotel, Glencar,
Co. Kerry.
Patrick Day, Headford, Co.
Galway.
Rory De Barra, 'Cornfield',
Hollymount, Co. Mayo.
Vincent Denning, Cavan Road,
Bailieborough, Co. Cavan.
John Diffley, Glenisland, Castlebar,
Co. Mayo.
Jack Dolan, County Hotel, Carrick
on Shannon, Co. Leitrim.
James Egan, Riverside, Boyle, Co.
Roscommon.
Des Elliott, 3 Ashdale Road,
Terenure, Dublin 6.
Lal Faherty, Lakeland, Portacarron,
Oughterard, Co. Galway.
Michael Faherty, Oughterard, Co.
Galway.
Michael Fitzgerald, Castlegregory,
Co. Kerry.
Dr Patrick Fitzmaurice, Central
Fisheries Board, Dublin.
Paddy Flaherty, Camus, Co.
Galway.
Miss Bridie Fleming, Central
Fisheries Board, Dublin.
Cormac Foley, Park
Superintendent, Muckross,
Killarney, Co. Kerry.
Patrick Foley, Lemaculla,
Ballinode, Monaghan.
Danny Fox, Northern Regional
Fisheries Board, Ballyshannon,

Co. Donegal.

Roger Gallagher, Valley House, Achill, Co. Mayo.

Very Rev. P. J. Canon Gargan, P.P., St Clares, Manorhamilton, Co. Leitrim.

Dr Patrick Gargan, Manager, Galway Fishery, Nun's Island, Galway.

Ian Geraghty, Cornamagh, Athlone, Co. Westmeath.

John T. Gibbons, Fair Green, Westport, Co. Mayo.

Seamus Gill, Buncrana, Co. Donegal.

James Gill, Buncrana, Co. Donegal.

Michael Gilmore, Anagry, Co. Donegal.

Danny Goldrick, St Martin's, Spiddal Road, Moycullen, Co. Galway.

Noel Hackett, Macroom, Co. Cork.

Seamus Hartigan, 17 Summerhill, Carrick on Shannon, Co. Leitrim.

Patrick Helmore, Crumlin Lodge, Inverin, Co. Galway.

Henry Hodgson, Currarevagh House, Oughterard, Co. Galway.

Billy Johnston, Quay Street, Donegal.

Joe Joyce, Dungloe, Co. Donegal.

Mary Kavanagh, County Library, Galway.

Michael Keane, Aasleagh, Leenane, Co. Galway.

Pat Keenaghan, 22 Hillside Drive, Mullingar, Co. Westmeath.

Edward Kelly, Stradone Garda Station, Co. Cavan.

John Kelly, North Western Regional Fisheries Board, Ballina, Co. Mayo.

Michael Kelly, Drogheda Road, Balbriggan, Co. Dublin.

Miss Eilis Kennedy, Department of Fisheries, Dublin.

Matt Kennedy, Youghalarra, Newtown, Nenagh, Co. Tipperary.

Garry Kenny, Portumna, Co. Galway.

Eoin Kerins, Ballynamona, Kells, Co. Meath.

Miss Carol King, Eastern Regional Fisheries Board, Mobhi Boreen, Dublin.

Sean King, Lettergesh PO, Renvyle, Co. Galway.

Michael Lennon, Kinard, Crossmolina, Co. Mayo.

Ron Lyttle, Foreglen Road, Killaloe, Co. Derry.

Patrick McAndrew, St Patrick's Avenue, Crossmolina, Co. Mayo.

Peter McCloone, 14 McMahon Villas, Letterkenny, Co. Donegal.

E. D. McClure, Gorse Lodge, Ards, Creeslough, Co. Donegal.

Philip McConnell, Friar's Quarter, Ballinrobe, Co. Mayo.

Andrew McCrea, Pettigo, Co. Donegal.

Brian McDermott, Ballybay Road, Carrickmacross, Co. Monaghan.

James McDonagh, Cashel, Co. Galway.

Michael McDonnell, Kylemore, Co. Galway.

Tom McEvoy, Bailieborough, Co. Cavan.

Alan McGurdy, Manager, Eastern Regional Fisheries Board, Mobhi Boreen, Dublin.

S. C. McMorrow, Central Fisheries Board, Balnagowan, Mobhi Boreen, Glasnevin, Dublin 9.

Patrick McNamara, Kildysart, Co. Clare.

Jack McNeely, Brackwansha, Ballina, Co. Mayo.

Mgr Gerard McSorley, P.P.,
Pettigo, Co. Donegal.
Kevin Macken, Rosmuck, Co.
Galway.
Peter Mantle, Delphi, Leenane, Co.
Galway.
Jim Minogue, Middle Line,
Scarriff, Co. Clare.
C. P. R. Mills, Burrishoole
Fishery, Newport, Co. Mayo.
John Mitchell, Mannions Town,
Strandhill, Sligo.
Gerry Moloney, Dalcassian Ave.,
Ennis, Co. Clare.
Ciaran Moran, Mulrany, Co.
Mayo.
Colm Mullarkey, Sligo Road,
Tubbercurry, Co. Sligo.
Owen Mullens, Manager,
Newport House, Newport, Co.
Mayo.
Gerry Murray, Eastern Regional
Fisheries Board, Virginia, Co.
Cavan.
Leslie Murray, Mount Murray,
Bunbrosna, Co. Westmeath.
William Murphy, Cahir,
Ballinrobe, Co. Mayo.
James Murphy, Cushlough,
Ballinrobe, Co. Mayo.
Patrick Murphy, Cork Street,
Macroom, Co. Cork.
Patrick Neylon, Corofin, Co.
Clare.
Sean Nixon, Cashel, Co. Galway.
Matthew Nolan, Ballagh,
Mullingar, Co. Westmeath.
Charles O'Boyle, Dungloe, Co.
Donegal.
Mrs E. O'Brien, Screebe Fisheries,
Camus PO, Co. Galway.
James O'Brien, Eastern Regional
Fisheries Board, Trim, Co.
Meath.
Daniel O'Connell, Anglers Rest,
Cork Road, Killarney, Co.
Kerry.
Hugh O'Connor, Garvary, Leggs

PO, Co. Fermanagh.
John O'Connor, Manager,
Ballynahinch Castle Hotel,
Ballinafad, Co. Galway.
Hugh O'Donnell, Killult,
Falcarragh, Co. Donegal.
William O'Donnell, 70 Glenowen
Estate, Derry.
Martin O'Donohoe, 110 Clonkeen
Road, Blackrock, Co. Dublin.
Dr Martin O'Farrell, Erriff Fishery,
Leenane, Co. Galway.
Dr Martin O'Grady, Central
Fisheries Board, Mobhi Boreen,
Dublin.
Patrick O'Grady, Hillside House,
Glenbeigh, Co. Kerry.
John O'Hare, Main Street,
Kenmare, Co. Kerry.
Ciaran O'Keeffe, Superintendent,
Glenveagh National Park, Co.
Donegal.
Michael O'Morain, Carna, Co.
Galway.
Brod O'Sullivan, Stella Maris,
Waterville, Co. Kerry.
Michael O'Sullivan, Lobster Bar,
Waterville, Co. Kerry.
Vincent O'Sullivan, South View
Terrace, Waterville, Co. Kerry.
A. B. Onions, Nobber, Co. Meath.
P. J. Padden, Northern Regional
Fisheries Board, Ballyshannon,
Co. Donegal.
Robert Pidgeon, Holly Lodge,
Glenvar Park, Blackrock, Co.
Dublin.
Dr D. J. Piggins, Salmon Research
Trust, Newport, Co. Mayo.
John Prendergast, Zetland Hotel,
Cashel, Co. Galway.
William Reidy, Eastern Regional
Fisheries Board, Carrickmacross,
Co. Monaghan.
P. J. Reynolds, Barrack Street,
Drumshanbo, Co. Leitrim.
James Rooney, Seatown West,
Swords, Co. Dublin.

John Scanlon, The Dowry, Manor Kilbride, Co. Wicklow.

Chris Shaw, Lisfahan, Buncrana, Co. Donegal.

Larry Sleator, Marlinstown, Mullingar, Co. Westmeath.

Frank Smyth, 30 Shop Street, Drogheda, Co. Louth.

John F. Smyth, Glenbrook, Loch Gowna, Co. Cavan.

Gerald P. Stanley, Clifden, Co. Galway.

Bill Stonehouse, Ross, Oldcastle, Co. Meath.

Tom Sullivan, Minaun, Cheekpoint, Co. Waterford.

Michael Tolan, Crossmolina, Co. Mayo.

Dr Kenneth Whelan, Central Fisheries Board, Mobhi Road, Glasnevin, Dublin 9.

Russell Whiteman, 28 Steelstown Road, Derry.

K. D. Wood, Manager, Costello & Fermoyle Fisheries, Costello, Co. Galway.

Christy Wynne, Boyle, Co. Roscommon.

Sean Young, 66 Main Street, Cavan.

Introduction

The purpose of this book is to provide a useful angling guide to the principal trout and salmon loughs of Ireland. I have set out where the loughs are situated and advise – where necessary – how to get there. For the enthusiast, anxious to identify more exactly the location of the more remote loughs, I suggest the usefulness of a half-inch or 1-inch Ordnance Survey map. While some fisheries are free, most are not, and so require permission of some kind. I have tried to indicate from whom permission can be obtained and give names and telephone numbers, as well as noting angling regulations, by-laws, etc. In the case of each lough, I have set out the kinds of game fish present, the average size of the trout, and in many cases I have given an indication of the size of the bigger trout. There is information too on bank fishing, whether a boat is necessary or available, the best seasons, successful angling methods and the best flies.

A word of explanation is necessary about licences and permits. In Northern Ireland, a licence is required by law for each fishing rod used by anyone over 18 years to fish anywhere except the sea. Under the age of 18 years, a rod licence is required if fishing for salmon or sea trout. In the Foyle Area (parts of Donegal, Derry and Tyrone), a rod licence is required by anyone fishing for brown trout, rainbow trout, sea trout or salmon. In the Republic of Ireland's seven fisheries regions, a rod licence is required for salmon and sea trout only. Anglers should not confuse a fishing licence with a fishing permit. A licence does not confer the right to fish anywhere. To obtain the right to fish, a fishing permit may be required. I say *may be required*, because in Ireland, there are loughs where a fishing permit is required, there are loughs where the fishing is free and there are many loughs where the owner of the fishing rights does not enforce them. A permit is a document issued by the fishery owner or his agent and it confers the right to fish on the owner's fishery. In the case of some developed and/or stocked trout loughs in the Republic of Ireland, I refer in the text to a Regional Fisheries Board Permit. This permission may be obtained by registering with any one of the Regional Fisheries Boards and paying the annual fee. It entitles the holder to fish on waters controlled by the Central Fisheries Board, and by the Regional Fisheries Board with which he or she is registered. The annual fee currently costs IR£9.50. Alternatively, there is a daily permit available for £2.

When I was asked to write this book, I cannot honestly say that I accepted the challenge immediately. I was all too well aware of the immense task the researching of the material would entail and the amount of factual information required regarding permission to fish, types of fish present, best seasons, best flies, availability of boats, the topography of the loughs, etc., etc. To me, it appeared a wellnigh impossible task, but one that badly needed to be done. As a keen angler all my life, who has derived such satisfaction and joy from fishing the loughs of Ireland, I felt I owed it to so many of those wonderful fisheries, their owners, my colleagues in the Regional and Central Fisheries Boards and my fellow anglers, to attempt to list and describe them.

Many of the loughs described here offer enormous scope and a fantastic challenge to the angler interested in lough fishing for trout and salmon. Those holding big populations of small fish have a special usefulness for the young and the novice angler and the not so young. The developed brown trout loughs, in many cases, hold stocks of trout that must surely rate as some of the best for quality and quantity to be found anywhere in Europe. The sea-trout fishing can be pure magic, in terms of action and excitement and the beauty of the setting in which most of the sea-trout loughs are situated can cast a spell on even the most fish-hungry angler. To hook a salmon on a fly from a boat on a lough, is, for me, the ultimate lough angling experience. The power of a fresh salmon as it storms for freedom towards the farthest shore is best described as hooking 'the proverbial train going through a station' and often you have about as much control over it. I fear it will take a much more brilliant writer than I to describe to the full the potential for drama afloat and the angling satisfaction that the Irish game-fish loughs can offer. I only offer you, dear reader, an introduction.

Stocks of wild trout and salmon are like any other natural crop. They thrive when conditions are right and are adversely affected by such natural phenomena as droughts, not to mention competitors and predators like coarse fish and over-exploitation of stocks. We all like to know that there is a high stock density in the lough we are about to fish. But research has shown that stock density of wild fish and numbers of fish taken by anglers are not directly related. There are other factors that must be taken into consideration, among them angling skill, local knowledge, the mood of sea trout or salmon and, in the case of brown trout, the season and daily fly hatches are of the utmost importance. There is nothing like a good hatch of fly to bring the trout to the surface and so at least within sight of the angler.

We live in an age of wildlife parks and zoos and put-and-take fisheries and in many countries these are necessary, but I fear they have bred a type of angler who measures his enjoyment by the number of fish he pulls out. But we also need our wild fisheries where the fish grow strong and learn to be survivors, fed only from Mother Nature's larder. Here the angler must learn many skills – boat handling, reading the water, watching the hatch, even inspired guessing, all of which add to the enjoyment of a day's lough fishing. I am convinced that we have some of the finest lough fisheries in the world. Come and enjoy them. Observe the country code and angling regulations, respect the rights of fishery owners and riparian owners, fish in a sporting manner, never using greedy or stock-damaging tactics and you will always find a Cead Mile Failte – a hundred thousand welcomes.

The map reference, after the name of each lough in the text, refers to the lettered subzones on the Ordnance Survey sheets.

Much as I would like, I cannot tell you how to catch our trout and salmon under all conditions and circumstances. In many instances, I have given a list of fly patterns that, from experience, have been found to work well on a particular fishery. This is done to help boost the angler's confidence. Where I refer to 'standard lough patterns' in the text, the flies that spring to mind (in sizes 8–14, depending on conditions) are Black Pennell, Butcher, Bibio, Green Peter, Claret, Murrough, March Brown, Invicta, Greenwell's Glory, Peter Ross, Watson's Fancy, Dunkeld, Sooty Olive, Wickham's Fancy, Silver Invicta and Connemara Black. But really no hard and fast rules can be laid down regarding flies and lures. Remember, two words we ought not use in relation to angling are 'never' and 'always'; neither should you discount local knowledge, experience and advice.

In the interests of being as comprehensive as possible, I have included some waters where permission to fish is not available to the general public. Included too are some that are simply not worth fishing, but I think I have made this abundantly clear, in such cases, in the text, lest the visiting angler be tempted to spend his time fruitlessly.

The open and close seasons vary greatly from region to region and even within a region. In most cases, I have tried to give the statutory open season for rod and line in the introduction to each chapter and closing and opening dates peculiar to certain fisheries are mentioned in the text.

The cost of permits/boats/boatmen varied greatly from fishery to fishery in 1986. On brown-trout loughs, the average price of a boat was IR£7. A boat and outboard motor averaged IR£13 and a boat, outboard and boatman averaged IR£26. On salmon and sea-trout fisheries, a boat/fishing cost IR£5–IR£25 and a boat and boatman IR£40–IR£50. An Irish lough angling boat can generally take three persons – three anglers or two anglers and a boatman, and the costs are divided accordingly.

A word of explanation is necessary about telephone numbers. Most telephone numbers in the Republic of Ireland are now on the automatic system and this can be called from any country with international dialling facilities to Ireland. For example: to call a Dublin number from Britain, dial 0001 and the number, e.g., 0001-379206. To call anywhere outside the Dublin area, dial 010-353, followed by the STD code (minus the initial 0) then the remainder of the number, e.g. 010-353-46-28210. For telephone numbers not yet on the automatic exchange, call the operator.

Collecting the details and information in this book has been a great source of joy and satisfaction for me. I received the utmost encouragement, kindness and assistance wherever I went. A special word of thanks is due to my fellow anglers for so much useful information, unselfishly given.

I gratefully acknowledge the assistance given to me by the Central and Regional Fisheries Boards and their staffs. I would also like to express my sincere thanks to Des Brennan, Angling Manager of the Central Fisheries Board, for the wholehearted encouragement he gave me in the writing of this book and for his valued advice and assistance in so many ways.

A special word of appreciation to R. J. D. Anderson, Fisheries Division, Department of Agriculture for Northern Ireland, and to W. G. Crawford, Secretary, Foyle Fisheries Commission, for their valued assistance.

My thanks to John Wilshaw, former Editor of *Trout and Salmon* and Mrs Margaret Vaux of the Salmon & Trout Association for suggesting to Unwin Hyman that I should undertake this work and to Merlin Unwin for his patient guidance during the course of its preparation.

I would like to pay tribute to Mick Finnegan, my fishing partner over many years, whose example and skill helped make me a better angler. May his leader never get a wind knot nor his Buzzers sink.

A special word of thanks to my wife, Rose, whose diligence, patience and ability to find lost pieces of information contributed in no small manner to the completion of this book.

In a work of such detail and having such a wide brief, there will undoubtedly be inadvertent errors and omissions, and indeed additions sometimes. We all, my informants included, have to rely upon memory in regard to some particulars and then there was the difficulty of ascertaining, in some instances, from whom permission to fish should be sought, but I have done my best, and know I can rely on the well-known mildness of temperament of my fellow anglers and fishery owners to obtain pardon for any slips that may have occurred. I can only offer an assurance that they will be put right in the next edition.

Finally, to all who have helped me in any way in compiling this book, I say a sincere 'thank you'. In that I wholeheartedly acknowledge that, in many respects, this work is as much yours as mine.

'Rosbeg',
2 Kilcarn Court,
Navan,
Ireland.

DEDICATION

This book is dedicated to my wife, Rose,
whose encouragement and support contributed
in no small way to its completion;
and to our son, Patrick,
for his guidance and enjoyment.

NORTHERN
FISHERIES REGION

Dunfanaghy

Derry

FOYLE
AREA

FISHERIES
CONSERVANCY
BOARD
FOR
NORTHERN IRELAND

Belfast

Ballyshannon

Bangor

Sligo

Ballina

Armagh

Monaghan

NORTH WESTERN
FISHERIES REGION

Castlebar

WESTERN
FISHERIES
REGION

Clifden

Mullingar

EASTERN
FISHERIES
REGION

Galway

Athlone

Dublin

SHANNON
FISHERIES REGION

Shannon

Limerick

SOUTHERN
FISHERIES
REGION

Clonmel

Killarney

Waterford

Wexford

Waterville

Macroom

Cork

SOUTH
WESTERN
FISHERIES REGION

1   *The Fishery regions of Ireland*

2   *The Foyle Fisheries Area*

1   Foyle Area

The Foyle area is unique in that it straddles the border between
Northern Ireland and the Republic of Ireland. It is administered by
the Foyle Fisheries Commission, a statutory body set up under the
1952 Foyle Fisheries Act and entrusted with the conservation,
improvement and protection of the fisheries in the Foyle catchment. It is an area rich in angling lore, with the emphasis being
chiefly on salmon. The rivers in the area were – and many still are –
famous for their prolific runs of spring and summer fish. As in all
areas where salmon predominate, the trout fishing is largely
ignored. Yet there is some good trout fishing in these parts – of
both the stocked and the wild variety. You could spend several
days walking and fishing the loughs of west Donegal and east
Tyrone, among some of the most beautiful scenery in Ireland. The
Foyle area has its own angling regulations, the chief one being that
a rod licence is required to fish for both brown trout and salmon
(this includes anglers under 18 years of age). A special Foyle Area
Extension Licence is available for the whole season provided the
applicant can produce at the time of application a current season
game-fishing rod licence issued by a Regional Board in the Irish
Republic or the Fisheries Conservancy Board of Northern Ireland.

1   *Newly painted and ready to go*

LOUGH INN   C 51 38
LOUGH FAD   C 53 38
Permission: Not usually required

These two loughs lie to the west of the T73 Quigley's Point–Moville road. To get to Lough Inn, take the mountain road up the side of Glencaw Hill; the lough is to the right after 3½ miles. It can also be approached from Carndonagh. Lough Inn holds small brown trout and you might be lucky to get an occasional sea trout from August on.

Lough Fad lies to the north-east on the northern side of Tawash Hill. It is reported to hold only char that average 6 oz. They are sometimes taken on fly in May and June, and there are reports of char up to ¾ lb having been taken here.

LOUGH DEELE   C 07 05
Permission: Not usually required

Lough Deele is the source of the Deele River which flows east towards Raphoe. It lies deep in the mountains 6 miles south-west of Letterkenny and is best approached via a small road from the east. This is a difficult walk through forest and across bog and will take at least 1½ hours to complete. The effort of getting there – and back – is generally well rewarded – the trout average nearly ¾ lb and some excellent catches have been reported. An average catch

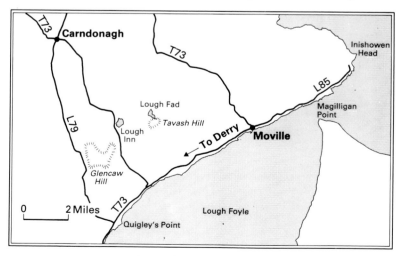

3 Inishowen – Foyle Area

should produce 6 trout. The northern side is dangerous and should be avoided, but the other banks are safe. The standard lough flies work well and you may well have a day to remember in superb surroundings.

LOUGH MOURNE   H 06 89
Permission: Not usually required

Lough Mourne is an impressive-looking stretch of water by the N15 road between Ballybofey and Donegal. You may be tempted to fish, but don't bother because the trout are very small indeed.

TRUSK LOUGH   H 12 90
Permission: Not usually required

Trusk is 3 miles south of Ballybofey. The trout there average ½ lb and you might be lucky and get one up to ¾ lb. This lough is used a lot by speedboats, which can make the fishing very uncomfortable.

LOUGH GOLAGH   H 01 74
LOUGH BARDERG   H 02 74
CROAGHADALOUGH   H 02 73
Permission: Not usually required

Access to these three loughs is either off the small mountain road to the north and in by the west side of Lough Boyle or by taking another small road from the west and coming in past Lough Keeran. Either way, it is difficult going and will take well over an hour. Golagh has a nice stock of good trout averaging ¾ lb, with some to nearly 3 lb. The banks are difficult to fish in places, but at some points it is possible to wade. One of the best areas is the long, narrow bay at the north-west. Golagh can be good on its day – sometimes very good – but at times you will be lucky if you get one or two. Small lough flies work well and it is worth trying a Buzżer pupa pattern if you notice duckfly around.

Lough Barderg is a short distance to the east. The fish here are somewhat bigger, but are difficult to rise.

Croaghadalough is a short walk to the south of Lough Golagh. It holds good-quality trout with many in the 1 lb class. Again they are slow to take, but it is worth a try and you will fish it all the way around in an hour.

LOUGH DERG   H 05 72

Permission: The Prior, Lough Derg, Pettigo, Co. Donegal.
Tel: (072) 61518

Lough Derg is a large, shallow lough of over 2,000 acres, 4 miles
north of Pettigo. This is the lough with the famous island known as
St Patrick's Purgatory, with its basilica and penitential exercises,
where pilgrims flock every year from June to August. What is less
well known is that it holds a stock of nice trout averaging just
under a pound and some much better ones too – trout to 4 lb have
been reported. The fish are pink-fleshed and their diet consists
mainly of *Gammarus* – freshwater shrimp. Other forms of fish food
and fly life are relatively scarce and consequently the trout are slow
to come to the fly. Lough Derg fishes best in May and I know of
one angler who had 13 trout on fly in one day. It has fair hatches of
chironomids and sedges and evening fishing gives best results. One
favourite area is along by the north-east shore where the river flows
out. Boats are available for hire from Mr P. Monaghan at the quay.
Private angling boats are not allowed without permission from the
Prior. It is worth sounding a note of warning: this lough can blow
up very rough and it has many rocky shoals just under the surface.

LOUGH UNAN   H 08 71

Permission: Not usually required

Lough Unan is an inaccessible little lough to the south of Lough
Derg. The trout are very small and do not repay the bother of
getting there.

LOUGH BRADAN   H 25 70

Permission: Department of Agriculture Game Fishing Permit, available from Tyrone Angling Supplies, Bridge House, Bridge Street,
Omagh, Co. Tyrone

Lough Bradan is a gin-clear mountain lough, well stocked with
brown trout which are naturally free-rising. It is situated 6 miles
north-east of Ederny and nearly 5 miles west of Drumquin. Access
is via a by-road to the north and there is a car park close to the
water. Bradan gets a hatch of chironomids, a very big hatch of
sedges, and a prolific caenis hatch. Useful wet-fly patterns are
Bibio, Blae and Black, Fiery Brown, Invicta, Silver Invicta, Green
Peter, Murrough and Daddy. The season runs from 1 March to
20 October and all legal methods are allowed, except groundbait
and maggots. Fishing is from the bank only but not from the weir
on the north side. Boats are not allowed.

LOUGH LEE   H 25 75
Permission: Department of Agriculture Game Fishing Permit, available from Tyrone Angling Supplies, Bridge House, Bridge Street, Omagh, Co. Tyrone

Lough Lee lies nearly midway between the B72 Ederny–Castlederg road and the B50 Armagh–Castlederg road. It is approached off a by-road from the north and there is a walk' of about 1 mile following the marker posts. This is a lough of just under 40 acres, gin-clear, and full of well-shaped, hard-fighting trout that look a bit like sea trout. The trout average ¾ lb and fish to 2 lb are taken every season. Small traditional lough flies work well and all legal methods except groundbait and maggots are allowed. The season runs from 1 March to 20 October. This is sheep country and anglers are advised not to bring dogs along.

LOUGH ASH   C 48 00
Permission: Department of Agriculture Game Fishing Permit, available from:
Mr Gerry Devine, 2 Aughafad Road, Dunnamanagh, Co. Tyrone;
Mr R. Cunningham, 10/12 Bridge Street, Strabane, Co. Tyrone;
Foyle Fisheries Commission, 8 Victoria Road, Derry, Co. Derry

Lough Ash lies to the north of the B48 Plumbridge–Dunnamanagh road and is entirely dependent on stocked trout. A number of quite large brown trout are stocked every season with a view to providing anglers with good catches. The season runs from 1 March to 20 October. There is a 4-fish bag limit and a 10-inch size limit. The western shore is dangerous and closed to anglers and the best fishing is from the north and south shores. The shoreline is well served with stiles and footbridges and there is a car park nearby. Boat fishing is not allowed.

MOOR LOUGH   H 44 97
Permission: Department of Agriculture Game Fishing Permit, available from:
Mr Gerry Devine, 2 Aughafad Road, Dunnamanagh;
Mr R. Cunningham, 10/12 Bridge Street, Strabane, Co. Tyrone;
Foyle Fisheries Commission, 8 Victoria Road, Derry, Co. Derry

Moor Lough is situated just over 3 miles south of Dunnamanagh in scenic hill country. It is well signposted and access to it is good, so much so that it can be recommended for disabled anglers. The season runs from 1 March to 20 October. There is a 10-inch size

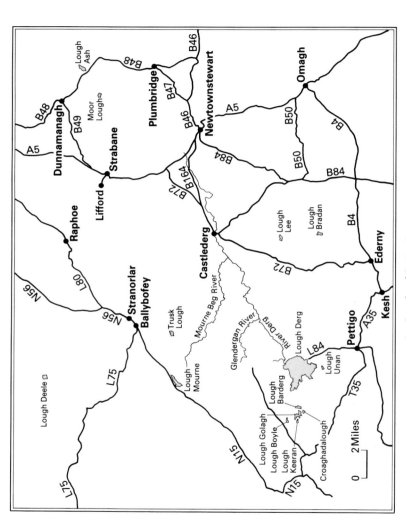

4 *Loughs of the Foyle system*

limit and a 4-fish bag limit in operation. Boats are allowed but no outboard motors, and it is fly fishing only from a boat. All legitimate methods except groundbait and maggots are allowed off the bank. Moor Lough is stocked with brown trout and their average weight is 1 lb. Standard traditional fly patterns work from a boat and lures and nymphs are favoured from the bank.

5   *Northern Ireland Fisheries Conservancy Board Area*

2 Northern Ireland Conservancy Board Area

The Northern Ireland Conservancy Board Area can offer the game fisherman – and particularly the trout fisherman – a wide variety of lough and stillwater fishing, ranging from bank fishing in urban artificial reservoirs to boat fishing, big-lough style, with all the challenges and excitement that fishing on a large, wild lough can hold. The waters have one thing in common: they all hold good-quality trout and in sufficient numbers to give the visiting angler first-class sport. One of the reasons for this happy state of affairs is the great work that is carried out by the Fisheries Division of the Department of Agriculture for Northern Ireland since it was given responsibility for the acquisition and development of fisheries. The access to many fisheries has been improved and stock density has been increased in many cases in response to angling pressure and demand. My first experience of trout fishing in Northern Ireland was on Lower Lough Erne and the numbers and quality of the trout were really excellent. A rod licence is required for each fishing rod used by anyone over 18 years of age to fish anywhere in the Conservancy Board Area (except the sea) and by anyone under 18 years fishing for salmon or sea trout. A Game Fishing Permit is required in many instances – except on 'free' fisheries – and there are permits to cover various requirements – (a) general season; (b) juvenile game; (c) 15-day; (d) daily; (e) local season. Licences and permits are available through a wide network of distributors.

ALTNAHINCH RESERVOIR   D 11 23

Permission: Department of Agriculture Game Fishing Permit, available from:

The Hatchery, Bushmills;

R. Bell, 38/40 Ann Street, Ballycastle, Co. Antrim;

Mrs N. McLernon, North Irish Horse Inn, Dervock, Ballymoney, Co. Antrim;

Messrs F. & A. Cusick, Post Office, Armoy, Ballymoney, Co. Antrim;

Smyth's Tackle, 17 Enagh Road, Ballymoney, Co. Antrim;

E. G. Cassells & Son, 43/45 Main Street, Ballymoney, Co. Antrim;
Mr A. Truss, 79 Main Street, Bushmills, Co. Antrim

This reservoir is situated at the head of the Bush River, 4½ miles
north-east of Clough Mills. It is in a very attractive location with
pine forest to the north and south. It holds a native stock of
free-rising trout and, in addition, is stocked with brown trout
averaging 1 lb. There are some quite large fish in there and test
nettings have turned up trout to 5 lb. Access to the water is good
with a car park by the west shore. The season runs from 1 March to
30 September. There is a 10-inch size limit and a 4-trout daily bag
limit.

DUNGONNELL RESERVOIR   D 18 17

Permission: Department of Agriculture Game Fishing Permit, available from Fyfe's Stores, 194/196 Glenravel Road, Cargan, Co.
Antrim

Dungonnell Reservoir is a long, narrow stretch of water covering
some 70 acres on a windswept moor to the south of Craigna-
maddy. It is approached off the A43 Ballymena–Cushendall road.
Turn off at Cargan and the rest of the way is signposted. This water
holds a stock of native trout which is supplemented with stocked
fish on a regular basis. The west and south shores are firm and well
suited to bank fishing but care should be exercised along the north
side. The trout average nearly 1 lb and there is always a nice breeze
blowing to help hide the leader. Good flies include Bibio, Black
Pennell, Blae and Black, Butcher, Hare's Ear and Greenwell's
Glory. The season runs from 1 March to 31 October.

KILLYLANE RESERVOIR   J 28 97

Permission: Department of Agriculture Game Fishing Permit, avail-
able from:
J. Matthews, 72 Ballymoney Street, Ballymena, Co. Antrim;
Foster Sports, 60 Main Street, Larne, Co. Antrim;
B. Craig, 30 Market Square, Ballyclare, Co. Antrim;
D. Martin, Ardymagh, Ballyclare, Co. Antrim;
P. McGroggan, 34 Broughshane Street, Ballymena, Co. Antrim

This reservoir is situated just south of the A36 Ballymena–Larne
road. Bank fishing is easy in normal water levels, but care should
be taken when the levels drop in late summer as patches of soft mud
can cause problems. Killylane is unusual in that it is entirely
dependent on natural recruitment and the trout are small – by

reservoir standards – but fight well. It fishes best in April and gets a small hatch of black chironomids. Useful fly patterns are Blae and Black, Mallard and Claret, Sooty Olive, Fiery Brown and Butcher. The season runs from 1 March to 31 October.

WOODBURN RESERVOIRS J 36 90
LOUGH MOURNE J 40 92

Permission: Department of Agriculture Game Fishing Permit, available from:
J. Hill, 4 West Street, Carrickfergus, Co. Antrim;

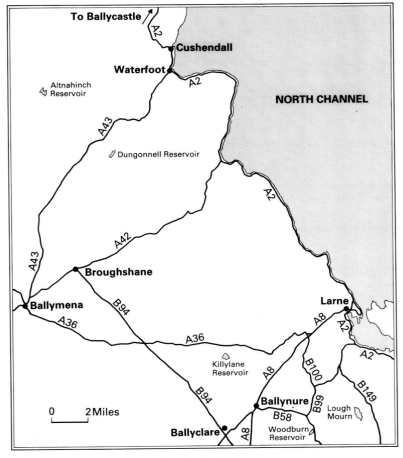

6   *North Antrim*

D.I.Y. Centre (Carrick) Ltd, 2 Market Place, Carrickfergus, Co. Antrim;

B. Craig, 3 Market Square, Ballyclare, Co. Antrim;

Sport and Leisure, 15/17 Irish Quarter West, Carrickfergus, Co. Antrim;

C. & T. Beattie, 39 Main Street, Ballycarry, Carrickfergus, Co. Antrim

These waters vary in size from 18 acres up to the 127 acres of Lough Mourne. They all lie north of Carrickfergus and the season runs from 1 March to 31 October, except for the North reservoir where the season is announced annually. Angling is not permitted before 8 a.m. or after 10 p.m. There is a 4-trout daily bag limit and an orthodox fly fishing only is allowed on the Upper and Lower South reservoirs. All legitimate methods on the others, except groundbait and maggots. North Woodburn is stocked with rainbow trout and the others with brown and rainbow trout. The size limit is 10 inches.

PORTAVOE RESERVOIR   J 55 82

Permission: Department of Agriculture Game Fishing Permit, available from:

John M. Clegg & Co. Ltd, 48 Regent Street, Newtownards, Co. Down;

Mr D. Newell, Trap and Tackle, 6 Seacliffe Road, Bangor, Co. Down

Portavoe, about 2 miles north of Donaghadee by the A2, covers some 30 acres. It holds a good stock of brown and rainbow trout and is a very attractive place to fish. The season is from 1 March to 31 October and there is a 4-trout daily bag limit. Only orthodox fly fishing is permitted and not more than twenty rods are allowed on the water at any one time. The water level tends to drop sharply during the summer and this can have adverse effects on the fishing.

STONEYFORD RESERVOIR   J 21 69
LEATHEMSTOWN RESERVOIR   J 21 72

Permission: Department of Agriculture Game Fishing Permit, available from Mr G. Mairs, Stoneyford Cash Stores, Stoneyford, Lisburn, Co. Antrim

Stoneyford, which is 160 acres, and Leathemstown, which is 28 acres, are two of the most popular trout fisheries in Northern Ireland. They are both to the north-west of Lisburn. The reservoirs

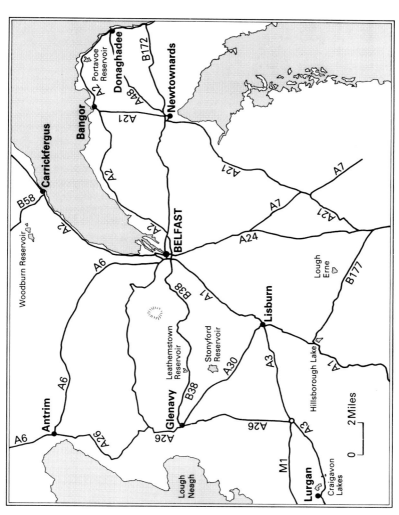

7 *Bangor, Belfast, Lurgan*

are stocked with takable brown and rainbow trout. Angling is not allowed before 8 a.m. or after 10 p.m. The season runs from 1 March to 31 October. There is a 4-trout bag limit and a 10-inch size limit. All legitimate methods are allowed but groundbait and maggots are not permitted.

CRAIGAVON CITY PARK LAKES   J 08 58
Permission: Department of Agriculture Game Fishing Permit, available from:
McCaughley Bros, Silverwood Service Station, Silverwood Road, Lurgan, Co. Armagh;
Fisheries Conservancy Board, Mahon Road, Portadown, Co. Armagh;
S. Newell, 4 Queen Street, Lurgan, Co. Armagh;
Walter Mason & Son, 71/73 Bridge Street, Portadown, Co. Armagh;
Mrs D. Ferguson, Rockeden Guest House, 22 Watson Street, Portadown, Co. Armagh

These lakes have been designed as a feature of Craigavon City Park and cover an area of 168 acres. They are stocked with rainbow trout and the opening and closing date is announced annually. There is a 4-trout daily bag limit and a 10-inch size limit. All legal methods are allowed except groundbait and maggots. Anglers may bring along their own boats or hire boats from Craigavon Borough Council Recreational Department. Fly fishing only is permitted from boats.

HILLSBOROUGH LAKE   J 24 58
Permission: Department of Agriculture Game Fishing Permit, available from:
Lisburn Sports Centre, 1–9 Southfield Square, Lisburn, Co. Antrim;
McBride's Sports Shop, Haslem's Lane, Lisburn, Co. Antrim;
D. McKeown, Fishing Tackle, 155 Moira Road, Lisburn, Co. Antrim

This lake of some 40 acres, situated in Hillsborough Forest, is stocked with brown and rainbow trout. Hillsborough Forest is a country park offering a wide variety of activities in lovely surroundings. The park is rich in wildlife and the scenic parkland is a favourite walking area. Fishing is only one of the interests catered for and anglers should be careful to observe the notices where fishing is prohibited. The season is from 1 March to 31 October. There is a 4-trout daily bag limit and a 10-inch size limit. All legal methods are allowed but groundbait and maggots are not permitted. This is a perfect place for a day out with the family where the younger members can be introduced to fishing.

BALLYKEEL LOUGH ERNE   J 32 56
Permission: Department of Agriculture Game Fishing Permit, available from:
Lisburn Sports Centre, 1–9 Smithfield Square, Lisburn, Co. Antrim;
P. E. West, West End Sports, 12 Bow Street, Lisburn, Co. Antrim;
R. McMaster, 14 Main Street, Ballynahinch, Co. Down;
McBride's Sports Shop, Haslem's Lane, Lisburn, Co. Antrim;
T. K. Carlisle, Sports Centre, High Street, Ballynahinch, Co. Down

This is a natural lough lying 4 miles north-west of Ballynahinch and 6 miles south-east of Lisburn. It is south of the A49 and anglers must use the official entrance off the Lisburn–Ballynahinch road. Fishing stands have been provided on the west side and all the other banks are safe for wading. It is stocked with brown and rainbow trout and orthodox fly fishing only is allowed. There is a 4-trout bag limit and a 10-inch size limit and the season runs from 1 April to the 31 October. There are good hatches of chironomids and early in the season the trout take especially well.

LOUGH BRICKLAND   J 10 40
Permission: Department of Agriculture Game Fishing Permit, available from:
J. C. Smith, Sports Specialist, 7/9 Kildare Street, Newry, Co. Down;
Lake View Service Station, Loughbrickland, Co. Down;
James Coburn & Sons, 32 Scarva Street, Banbridge, Co. Down;
A. Ryan, West Lodge, Bessbrook, Co. Armagh;
W. R. Trimble Ltd, 25 Downpatrick Street, Rathfriland, Co. Down;
T. Davey, 59 Hill Street, Newry, Co. Down

This lovely lough presents a splendid sight to travellers along the A1T from Newry to Banbridge. It also holds some fine trout. It is stocked annually with both brown and rainbow trout and each season produces some magnificent browns. The north and south ends should be avoided when wading but the rest is perfectly safe.

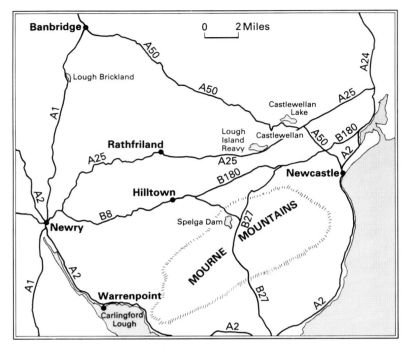

8   *County Down*

The west shore is well served with stiles, footbridges and a gravelled path. There is a bag limit of 4 trout and the lough fishes well in the evenings to the chironomid hatch early in the season. Use nymphs, standard lough wet flies or lures, and enjoy good sport in lovely surroundings.

CASTLEWELLAN LAKE   J 31 36

Permission: Department of Agriculture Game Fishing Permit, available from:
Department of Agriculture, Forest Office, Castlewellan Forest Park, Co. Down;
Department of Agriculture, Forest Office, Tollymore Forest Park, Co. Down

This is a lake of some 100 acres situated in a scenic wooded area with forest walks, picnic area and a caravan site available nearby. It is stocked with brown and rainbow trout and the season is from 1 March to 31 October. There is a 4-trout daily bag limit and a

10-inch size limit, and orthodox fly fishing only is allowed in March. Thereafter, it is all legal methods except groundbait and maggots. The lake is easily accessible with lakeside walks and is a perfect place for a family fishing expedition.

SPELGA RESERVOIR   J 26 26

Permission: Department of Agriculture Game Fishing Permit, available from:

W. R. Trimble Ltd, 25 Downpatrick Street, Rathfriland, Co. Down;

J. C. Smith, Sports Specialist, 7/9 Kildare Street, Newry, Co. Down;

T. Davey, 59 Hill Street, Newry, Co. Down;

Tollymore and Castlewellan Forest Parks, Co. Down

Spelga Dam, as it is popularly known, is set in the heart of the Mourne Mountains in some of the remotest and liveliest scenery in Northern Ireland. It is also very accessible off the B27 from Hilltown to Kilkeel. It holds brown trout, the season is from 1 March to 31 October, and all legal methods except groundbait and maggots are allowed.

BRANTRY LOUGH   H 74 52

Permission: Department of Agriculture Game Fishing Permit, available from:

Hamilton's James Street, Cookstown, Co. Tyrone;

John F. Devlin, The Deerpark Inn, 18 Main Street, Caledon, Co. Tyrone;

R. Morrow, 49 Rehaghey Road, Aughnacloy, Co. Tyrone;

R. J. Farmer, 23–29 Killyman Street, Moy, Co. Tyrone

Brantry Lough lies off the B128 Aughnacloy–Benburb road and approximately 6 miles south of Dungannon. This is a rich limestone lough holding brown trout. It is situated in a very sheltered position, which can make the fishing very difficult at times. There are hatches of chironomids, olives, even some mayfly and a good sedge hatch. A good ploy is to fish a dry Mayfly, Gnat, Buzzer or Sedge according to season if the trout start showing at the surface in the evening. This is a lough of 60 acres and boats are allowed, but no outboard motors. All legal methods go (no groundbaiting or maggots) but only orthodox fly fishing from the boat. The season runs from 1 March to 31 October and there is a 4-trout bag limit and a 10-inch size limit.

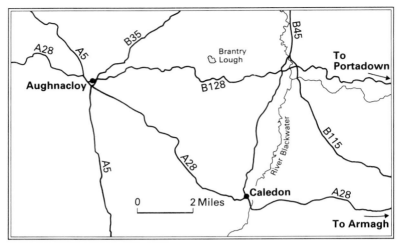

9   *Brantry Lough*

LOUGHANALBANAGH   H 53 44
Permission: Not usually required

This is a small mountain lough situated on a high windswept moorland to the east of Slieve Beagh and near the Tyrone–Monaghan border. It is a long way from the nearest road and at least a good 2-mile walk, which will probably take as many hours. It is wise to tell some one where you are going and when to expect you back. Loughanalbanagh holds a small stock of good brown trout, with some possibly to 4 lb. It fishes best with a good breeze and there can be good sport too on a summer evening with sedges and heather moths. Every fish in the lough seems to come to the surface to feed in the calm conditions at dusk and a suitable dry fly can often bring a tug, a splash and a lovely trout. The two small loughs to the east of Loughanalbanagh both hold good stocks of free-rising trout to ½ lb or even a little better. Standard wet flies work well in smaller sizes.

LOUGH CORRY   H 46 35
CORRANNY LOUGH   H 46 33
Permission: Department of Agriculture Game Fishing Permit, available from:
Erne Tackle, Main Street, Lisnaskea, Co. Fermanagh;
Carrybridge Boat Co., Lisbellaw, Co. Fermanagh;
Mrs M. E. Dillon, Maguiresbridge Post Office, Co. Fermanagh

Lough Corry is a mountain lough situated in Lisnaskea Forest. It is a developed fishery and holds a good stock of brown trout to 3 lb, many of which are wild trout. Boats, without outboards, are allowed on Lough Corry, which is about 16 acres in area. Shore fishing is also good. The lough is now in a very sheltered situation, being completely surrounded by trees. It has a good hatch of murrough and other small sedges with pale wings and green body and evening dry-fly fishing in late May and June can be great fun and rewarding too.

Corranny Lough is in the fork of the road north of Dernawilt crossroads. It has a number of fishing stands and it is possible to fish all round the shore. Corranny holds both brown and rainbow trout. The season for both loughs runs from 1 March to 30 September. There is a 4-trout bag limit and a 10-inch size limit.

ESCHLEAGH LOUGH   H 45 34
Permission: Department of Agriculture Game Fishing Permit

This is another small lough to the west of Lough Corry in Lisnaskea Forest. It holds a very good stock of brown trout up to ½ lb and usually fishes best in the evening. There are forest roads all around it and it is fishable from the bank and stands.

LOUGH LACK   H 22 73
Permission: Not usually required

Lough Lack is about 25 acres in area and is situated in Lough Bradan Forest, surrounded on three sides by young plantation. The access to it is by a forest road off the B72 Ederny–Castlederg road. It holds a good stock of ½–¾ lb trout and you may even get one of 1 lb or better. These trout take very fast and fight hard and deep. They are very free-rising but hard to hook and you will have to go down in fly size to have much success. It should be remembered that it is May before this lough fishes well. Try a Greenwell's Glory, Golden Olive, Sooty Olive, Invicta, Zulu, and possibly a Green Peter or Murrough at dusk. The bank is nearly all fishable and at certain points it is safe to wade.

LOWER LOUGH ERNE   H 10 60
Permission: Department of Agriculture Game Fishing Permit is required if fishing north and west of an imaginary line drawn from the mouth of the Ballinamallard River on the northern shore to the nearest point of the western shore opposite Castlehume on the

eastern shore. Anglers under 18 years of age do not require a permit when fishing on Lough Erne unless fishing for salmon or sea trout

Lower Lough Erne is a big lough, some 18 miles long from Enniskillen to Rosscor viaduct and 37,800 acres in size. In shape, it looks a little like a small version of Lough Corrib and the resemblance continues with its vast areas of shallow water and rocky areas. The season runs from 1 March to 30 September and there is a 6-trout bag limit and a 12-inch size limit. Trout stocks have made a remarkable recovery in this lough in recent years due mainly to improved natural recruitment from the streams, and there is a certain amount of artificial stocking done by the department as well. There is a good duckfly hatch in late March and April and useful flies at this time are Hare's Ear, March Brown, Fiery Brown, Golden Olive, Blae and Black, Bibio and Black Pennell. The mayfly season is without doubt the most important fly fishing period on the lough. The mayfly makes its appearance around 20 May and the good fishing continues well into June. First it is wet-fly fishing with a Green Drake or a Gosling and dapping the natural, and later – on suitable afternoons and evenings – there can be great spent gnat fishing. There is a big sedge hatch at the end of July and into August and the daddy is an important fly on the lough from August on into September, when wet-fly fishing over shallow water is very productive. The following areas are all good for wet-fly fishing when conditions are right: Castle Bay, Loftus Gap, Gubnagale Point, the Rough Islands – one of the best drifts on the lough – Ferny Gap, Lusty Island and all along the south shore of Boa Island, Gay Island, Creefin Island, the west side of Inishmakill, and west along the shore from Heron Island and on past Hill's Island. Boats are available for hire at a number of locations, including the following: Hotel Carlton, Belleek; Lough Erne Hotel, Kesh; Stella Marine, Castle Archdale; Lakeland Marina Ltd, Muckross, Kesh. Visitors booking a boat for the first time are advised to take a boatman until they get familiar with the lough. The water is not very clear and underwater rocks are difficult to spot. Trolling for big trout is popular on Lough Erne and the best fish recorded was just over 19 lb.

LOUGH AWADDY   H 03 64

Permission: Not usually required

This is a small lough on the Fermanagh–Donegal border. It is approached off the B136 Belleek–Pettigo road. Take the by-road to the north 2 miles west of Pettigo and 1½ miles along that road

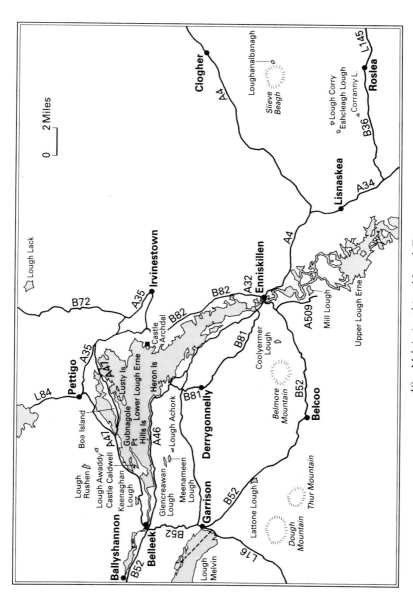

10 *Melvin (north) and Lough Erne*

there is a forest road to the lough with a car park by the shore. The trout here average ½ lb and rise freely. An average catch should produce 3–4 trout and it is possible to get fish here up to about 1¼ lb. It can be fished all round and wading is possible, but be careful. Fly hatches are poor and the trout here are not fussy about which fly they take.

LOUGH RUSHEN   H 01 66
Permission: Riparian owners

This lough is also on the Fermanagh–Donegal border. Most of it is in Co. Fermanagh, but the best access is off a by-road on the Donegal side. It has a nice stock of trout ranging in size from ½ to 1½ lb. Recent reports indicate that the fishing is not as good as it used to be and that the trout are smaller. There are good hatches of duckfly, olives, sedges and even mayfly. Lough Rushen is easy to fish from the shore and seems to fish best in the evening. An unusual feature of this lough is that it is considered not to fish well in a west wind. Flies to try include Hare's Ear, Blae and Black, March Brown, Connemara Black, Murrough and Invicta.

LOUGH KEENAGHAN   G 97 59
Permission: Department of Agriculture Game Fishing Permit, available from:
Carlton Park Information and Fishing Centre, Belleek, Co. Fermanagh;
Lough Erne Hotel, Kesh, Co. Fermanagh;
H. W. Stewart, Leggs Post Office, Co. Fermanagh

This is a lough of some 40 acres, 2 miles from Belleek on the A47 Pettigo road. It is stocked annually with brown and rainbow trout and, being a limestone lough, has a good stock of natural trout too. The season runs from 1 March to 30 September and there is a 4-trout bag limit and a 10-inch size limit. Only orthodox fly fishing is allowed. Boats may be hired from Mr John McGauran, Ballymegaghran, Leggs Post Office, or from the Carlton Hotel, Belleek. The average size of the trout here is over 1 lb and you are in with a good chance of getting a fish up to 5 lb. In fact, this must rate among the best half-dozen loughs in the country. It has good hatches of duckfly, olives, mayfly, buzzer and sedges and a fall of daddies from August. All the usual flies associated with these work well and a few to keep in mind are Blae and Black, Hare's Ear, Sooty Olive, Golden Olive, March Brown, Connemara Black,

2   Lough Melvin – fishing the shore (N. Ireland Tourist Board)

Mayfly, Spent Gnat, small Sedge patterns and a Daddy. Fishing is mainly from the north and south shores and fishing stands are provided where bankside vegetation makes fishing difficult. There is a car park at the north side.

LOUGH MELVIN   G 90 52

Part of Lough Melvin is in Northern Ireland, with a shoreline of 3½ miles from the County Bridge, past Garrison to Inniskeen. A Department of Agriculture Game Fishing Permit is required, which is valid only for the Northern Ireland area of the lough. Permits are available from Casey's Lake Hotel, Garrison. Melvin Bar, Garrison; P. F. McGovern, Melvin Villa, Garrison; Carlton Park Information and Fishing Centre, Belleek, from which boats may be hired too. See page 61 for details of the fishing.

GLENCREAWAN LOUGH   H 02 56
MEENAMEEN LOUGH   H 02 55
LOUGH ACHORK   H 04 55
Permission: Department of Agriculture Game Fishing Permit

These loughs lie in a very scenic mountain and forest area to the south of Lower Lough Erne. They are approached from Enniskillen by taking the A36 and the B81 through Derrygonnelly and following the signposts for a scenic drive. Coming from Belleek, follow the forest drive signs. These three loughs are all to the north west of the one-way (NB) scenic drive. There is a charge for using the forest drive. These are three good loughs with plenty of trout averaging 1 lb, with wild brown trout going to at least 3½ lb – not taking into account the rainbows that are sometimes stocked into Glencreawan. This is limestone terrain and the well made trout and prolific fly hatches bear witness to this fact. Chironomids, olives and sedges abound and the trout are on the feed here from March. Meenameen has even a mayfly hatch. The season is from 1 March to 30 September. The size limit is 10 inches and there is a 4-trout bag limit. Anglers may put a boat on any of these waters. Achork is 10 acres, Glencreawan is 47 acres and Meenameen, 46 acres.

COOLYERMER LOUGH   H 17 42

Permission: Department of Agriculture Game Fishing Permit, available from:
G. A. Cathcart, Bellanaleck Post Office, Co. Fermanagh;
Lakeland Tackle & Guns, Sligo Road, Enniskillen, Co. Fermanagh

This 45-acre lough which lies to the north of the A4 Belcoo– Enniskillen road is stocked with brown trout. The season runs from 1 March to 30 September, with a 4-trout bag limit and a 10-inch size limit. Fishing stands are provided and boats are available for hire from Mrs M. Brownlee, Coolyermer, Letterbreen. Privately owned boats are not allowed.

MILL LOUGH   H 23 38

Permission: Department of Agriculture Game Fishing Permit, available from:
G. A. Cathcart, Bellanaleck Post Office, Co. Fermanagh;
Lakeland Hotel, Bellanaleck, Co. Fermanagh

This is a large limestone lough 4 miles south of Enniskillen on the A509 Belturbet road, a little south of Ballanaleck village. It has been cleared of coarse fish and is stocked with brown and rainbow trout – some of which grow very big indeed. It has given some really excellent fishing in recent years. The season runs from 1 March to 30 September and there is a 4-trout bag limit and a 10-inch size limit. There are long stretches of clean shore on the south and east sides with plenty of space for bank fishing. Anglers should exercise caution when wading in certain areas due to the soft marl bottom. Orthodox fly fishing only from bank and boat, and boats may be hired from G. A. Cathcart, Ballanaleck Post Office;

J. Foster, Torreyloman; G. L. Stephenson, Tully; and R. C. Keyes, Ardtonagh. Privately owned boats are not allowed.

LATTONE LOUGH   L 99 44
Permission: Riparian owners

Lattone Lough lies along the B52 Garrison–Belcoo road, almost 6 miles from Garrison. This is a lough of over 100 acres with the mountains of north Leitrim rising up to the south and the Fermanagh hills to the north. It is almost equally divided in an east–west direction by the border with the Republic of Ireland. It holds a fair stock of brown trout averaging ½ lb and they can provide good lively fishing from May, especially in the evening. The banks are good, with a gravel shoreline. Standard wet fly patterns and a small sedge pattern should produce results.

Dunfanaghy
Buncrana
Letterkenny
Dunglow
Derry
Ardara
Donegal
Ballyshannon
Belfast
Sligo
Cavan • Cootehill
Arva
Galway
Dublin
Limerick
Waterford
Cork

11   *Northern Fisheries Region*

3 Northern Fisheries Region

The Northern Fisheries Region stretches from Malin Head, in the north of Co. Donegal, along the coast to Dunleavy's Island (off Mullaghmore Point) in Co. Sligo. In includes west Donegal, part of Co. Leitrim and Co. Sligo and extends in a south-easterly direction to Lough Gowna in Co. Cavan and Lough Egish in Co. Monaghan. The Donegal–Leitrim part of the region has much to offer the game angler, while the Cavan–Monaghan area is equally well endowed with loughs, but these are now mainly taken over by coarse fish species. Donegal is blessed with trout loughs, from small ponds in the mountains holding possibly no more than a dozen brownies to great sheets of water like Beagh and Glen, with brown trout and sea trout in abundance and even the occasional salmon here and there to increase the excitement.

There are a number of very active angling associations in that county which do much to improve the quality and accessibility of the fishing. Dunfanaghy Anglers' Association always makes the visiting angler feel welcome, while I am sure there are very few who have fished all 130 loughs of the well maintained Rosses Fishery (Iascaireacht na Rosann) spread over five river systems. Dungloe is the capital of this quiet game fishing Mecca. Further to the south, the Ardara Loughs have much to offer. Lough Melvin, set right in the middle of this region, is the jewel in its crown. Here the angler has a chance, depending on the season, of a spring salmon, a grilse or any one of four distinct strains of brown trout.

The Region is divided into two districts: Letterkenny and Ballyshannon. The Letterkenny district stretches from Rossan Point north to Malin Head and the Ballyshannon district covers the remainder of the region to the south-east. The open season for taking salmon, sea trout and brown trout on rod and line is set out below.

LOUGH FAD   C 39 43
LOUGH NAMINA   C 39 42
Permission: Not usually required

These loughs are referred to locally as the Twin Loughs and lie to either side of the Buncrana–Cardonagh road. Fad is the larger of the

LETTERKENNY DISTRICT

	Salmon	Sea trout	Brown trout
Whole district	2 February to 30 September	2 February to 12 October	1 February to 12 October
Except Grana	1 March to 30 September	1 March to 12 October	1 March to 12 October
Lackagh	1 January to 30 September	1 January to 30 September	1 February to 30 September
Owenea and Owentocker	1 March to 30 September	1 April to 30 September	1 April to 30 September
Leannan	1 January to 30 September	1 January to 30 September	15 February to 30 September

BALLYSHANNON DISTRICT

	Salmon	Sea trout	Brown trout
Whole district	1 March to 30 September	1 March to 9 October	1 March to 9 October
Except Drowes	1 January to 30 September	1 January to 30 September	15 February to 30 September
Lough Melvin	1 February to 30 September	1 February to 30 September	1 February to 30 September
Erne	1 March to 30 September	1 March to 30 September	1 March to 30 September
Duff	1 February to 30 September	1 February to 30 September	1 February to 30 September

two, with a road running along the north and east shores. It is very deep and holds only small brownies and you will do well if you get one of ½ lb. It holds a large population of small char and they can sometimes be taken on fly off the shore in May. The most popular fly patterns are Peter Ross, Mallard and Claret, Black Spider and Wickham's Fancy.

Lough Namina is to the south of the road. Again the trout are plentiful but very small. They average about 5 oz but here you may be lucky enough to get one of ¾ lb or better.

MINTIAGHS LOUGH   C 38·5 40·5
Permission: Not usually required

This lough is to the east of and adjacent to the T 73 Buncrana–Clonmany road. It is a lough on which you need a boat because of the reeds. It holds a big stock of small brown trout and is best fished on summer evenings with small flies. If you are careful you can fish in shallow water between the reedbeds and the shore. You must hold your fish tight when you hook them to prevent them escaping into the reeds. Expect to get up to a dozen, a couple of which should weigh between ½ and 1 lb. Small standard lough fly patterns will do.

INCH LEVEL LOUGH   C 34 22
Permission: Not usually required

This is a large, shallow expanse of water between Inch Island in Lough Swilly and the mainland at Burnfoot. The water is brackish and the level is maintained by means of floodgates in the dam wall. It now holds occasional salmon and sea trout but was once noted as one of the greatest sea-trout fisheries in Donegal. The trout are mainly taken on sand eels and by spinning, though you may still chance to get one on a Teal Blue and Silver or Peter Ross off the corner of the dam.

BLANKET NOOK   C 35 23·5
Permission: Mr T. Black, Blanket Nook, Newtown Cunningham, Co. Donegal.

This is another artificial sea-water lough on the shores of Lough Swilly, where the level is controlled by floodgates. It holds occasional salmon and sea trout and fishes best in July. It can be fished from the shore and July is the best month for sea trout.

LOUGH FERN   C 18 23
Permission: G. McNulty, Hon. Secretary, Letterkenny and District Anglers' Association, Hawthorn Heights, Letterkenny, Co. Donegal.

The Letterkenny and District Anglers' Association exercises rights on that part of the lough to which it has title and the rest of the lough is free fishing. This was one of the great spring salmon loughs until its stocks were hit by UDN in the 1960s, a disaster from which it never recovered. It is now fished for its brown trout and can give superb sport. The trout average ½ lb and fish up to 1 lb are encountered fairly frequently and you may even get one over 2 lb. It is a shallow lough, nearly 1½ miles long by ½ mile wide and can be fished all over early in the season and again in August and September. It gets choked with weeds from June to August in a dry season and this makes rowing a boat or using an outboard motor impossible. Bank fishing can be quite productive and the west (Portleen) shore is most favoured. When it is fishable from a boat, it rarely disappoints and it's a bad day that does not produce 3 or 4 nice trout. Favoured fly patterns are Mallard and Claret, Connemara Black, Wickham's Fancy, Black Pennell, Bibio, Butcher and Sedge patterns. There are no boats for hire but an angler may put his own boat on the lough and outboards are allowed.

COLUMBKILLE LOUGH   C 20·5 27

Permission: (for part of the lough) Mr G. Cullen, Letterkenny and Swilly Angling Club, Kirkstown, Letterkenny, Co. Donegal.

This lough lies less than one mile due east of Milford and is approached off a by-road that links the L78 Millford–Carrowkeel road with the T72 Millford–Rathmelton road. The lough is only one field away from the road and access is opposite the little pond on the roadside. The trout average about ¾ lb and in the past the lough is known to have produced trout of over 4 lb. The north and west sides are easily fished while the east side is unfishable. There is another little lough a few hundred yards to the south-east with silver pink-fleshed trout averaging around the ½ lb in weight.

SHANNAGH LOUGH   C 21 45
KINNY LOUGH   C 20 44

Permission: Not usually required

KINDRUM LOUGH   C 18 43

Permission: Portsalon Hotel, Portsalon, Co. Donegal.

These loughs are on the Fanad Peninsula near Fanad Head. Shannagh used to hold a small stock of good brown trout that were mainly taken on worms, but now holds mainly escapee rainbows. The trout in Kinny Lough are small, averaging about ½ lb, and it can be fished all round. Kindrum holds some nice trout that are mainly taken spinning. The trout in this area are large-finned, take with great force and fight strongly.

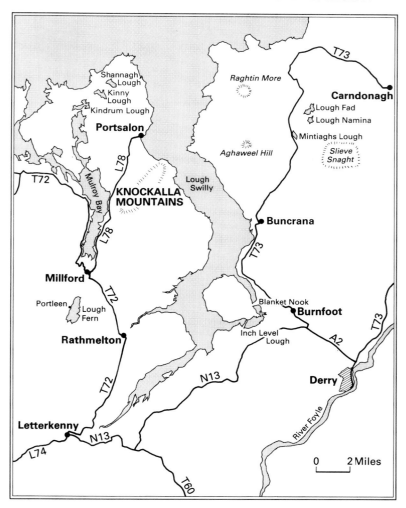

12   *The Fanad Peninsula and Inishowen*

GARTAN LOUGH   C 05 16

Permission: G. McNulty, Hon. Secretary, Letterkenny and District Anglers' Association, Hawthorn Heights, Letterkenny, Co. Donegal.

Gartan Lough is nearly 2½ miles long and lies off the L82 road near Church Hill. It holds small brown trout, averaging about 4 oz, and occasional salmon. It is in a very scenic and attractive area and, while there is no jetty, access is good and it is relatively easy to launch a boat.

LOUGH NACALLY   C 06 18
Permission: Inquire locally

This small lough lies to the north of Gartan Lough and there is good access to it from the south via secondary roads, one of which runs by the shore on the west side. The average size of the trout is ½ lb, with some to 1½ lb. It holds an excellent stock and on a summer evening trout can be seen rising all over the lough. There is no shore fishing due to the reeds and it is too deep for wading. It is well worth fishing from a boat but keep a lookout for submerged tree stumps.

LOUGH AKIBBON   C 07 19
Permission: Not usually required

This lough lies to the west of the L82 about 2 miles north of Church Hill. It is set in a very scenic location and it has a reputation for restoring the confidence of disheartened anglers. It holds a large stock of trout averaging 9 inches in length and weighing approximately 6 oz. There are two small woods, one on the east and the other on the west bank; otherwise three-quarters of the bank is fishable and a selection of small traditional flies will suffice.

LOUGH INSHAGH   C 14 19
LOUGH NAMBRADDAN   C 02 19
Permission: The Superintendent, Glenveagh National Park, Church Hill, Co. Donegal.
Tel: Church Hill 88 or (074) 37088

Fishing is not permitted on either of these loughs in order to prevent disturbance to the wildlife of the area.

GLEN LOUGH   C 10 29
Permission: Letterkenny and District Anglers' Association; Day tickets available from John Doherty, Derryscleagh, Glen Lough, Termon P.O., Co. Donegal.
Tel: (074) 38057

There are three other fishery owners on the lough, but day tickets are only let on the Letterkenny Association water. Three boats are

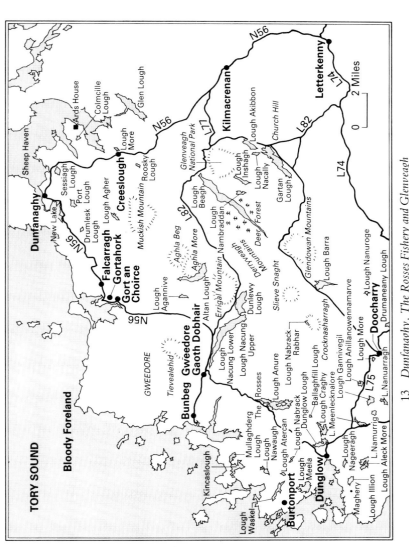

13 *Dunfanaghy, The Rosses Fishery and Glenveagh*

available for hire and outboards are allowed but not supplied so anglers are advised to bring their own. This used to be one of the great spring salmon loughs, but it never really recovered from the effects of UDN. Occasional salmon are now taken in April and May and a 28-lb fish was taken in 1985. The brown trout are small but the lough produces a few from 3 to 4 lb every season and a 9-lb fish was recorded a few years ago. It is as a sea-trout fishery that the lough is now best known and in August and September it can produce really excellent sport. The average size of the sea trout is 1½ lb and a Peter Ross is one of the favourite wet flies, together with Teal, Blue and Silver, Connemara Black, Butcher, Wickham's Fancy, etc. Dapping is very successful and brings up the bigger fish, with the average size taken on the dap running to about 2 lb. In recent times, three anglers are known to have taken 200 sea trout to their boat in seven days. Glen is an interesting lough, deep on the north-west side and shallow to the south-east. Bank fishing is not allowed.

LOUGH BEAGH   C 01 20
Permission: The Superintendent, Glenveagh National Park, Church Hill, Co. Donegal.
Tel: (074) 37088

3   *Lough Beagh and Glenveagh Castle*
(Commissioners of Public Works in Ireland)

Lough Beagh (Veagh) is a large lough of volcanic origin, nearly 4 miles long by about ½ mile wide. It can be approached from Letterkenny by taking the N56 and turning left on to the L77 Gweedore road, or by taking the L82 road from Gweedore. As well as a good stock of brown trout the lough holds occasional salmon, and the sea trout arrive in August. The brown-trout fishing can vary greatly. One day your catch will only average 6 oz, while another day the trout will run from ½ lb to 1 lb with the chance of a 2-lb or 3-lb fish, usually taken around the islands. The sea trout run late and it is definitely August before the fishing picks up. When it does, it can be really good with up to 20 trout to the boat per day and there is always the chance of a 3-lb or 4-lb fish. The south-west end is the favourite fishing area. Only fly fishing and dapping are permitted and favoured patterns are Connemara Black, Fiery Brown, Peter Ross, Teal, Blue and Silver and Alexandra. There are three boats with outboards for hire. Beware of waterspouts in rough weather. This is a very scenic lough, surrounded by mountain and deer forest. Bank fishing is not allowed.

LOUGH MORE   C 06·5 30·5
Permission: G. McNulty, Hon. Secretary, Letterkenny and District Anglers' Association, Hawthorn Heights, Letterkenny, Co. Donegal.

This is a small lough beside Creeslough village. It used to hold an excellent stock of brown trout averaging 10 oz, with fish to 2 lb, but stocks have been greatly depleted in recent years by greedy and uncaring anglers. If you do catch fish, I suggest you return them safely to the water to conserve stocks. Useful fly patterns are Golden Olive, Wickham's Fancy, Black Pennell, Butcher and Connemara Black. Bank fishing only and about 25 per cent of the shoreline is fishable.

ROOSKY LOUGH   C 04·5 29
LITTLE ROOSKY LOUGH
Permission: G. McNulty, Hon. Secretary, Letterkenny and District Anglers' Association, Hawthorn Heights, Letterkenny, Co. Donegal.

This is a small narrow lough just over a mile south-west of Creeslough village. Access is gained by the farmhouse on the north-west shore and approximately half of the bank is fishable. The average size of the trout is over 1 lb though the lough used to hold trout of 2–5 lb before stocks were reduced by gross over-fishing. The fishing is now very dour but a small stock of good trout still survives. There are hatches of duckfly in spring, mur-roughs in June, and Green Peter in late July and August. This is one of the few loughs in Donegal to get a hatch of these large sedges.

Little Roosky is a small lough up the hill to the south of Roosky Lough; access is off a small by-road. It holds a fair stock of nice silvery trout that look like sea trout and average ½ lb.

LOUGH COLMCILLE   C 07 34
Permission: Not usually required

This is a small lough on the peninsula about 3 miles due north of Creeslough. It holds a small stock of brown trout that are reported to be bottom feeders and very dour. They seldom rise to a fly.

SESSIAGH LOUGH   C 04 36
Permission: Dunfanaghy Anglers Association, c/o Arnolds Hotel, Dunfanaghy, Co. Donegal.
Tel: (074) 36208

Sessiagh is a lough of about 80 acres which holds a good stock of nice brown trout. It is developed and stocked by the local angling association. The water is alkaline and gin-clear and the trout average 1lb. It fishes best at dusk, and spring and autumn fishing is better than in midsummer. Dapping can be particularly productive in August and September. The most successful wet fly patterns are Mallard and Claret, Black Pennell, Teal and Green, Invicta, Greenwell's Glory, and Wickham's Fancy. A selection of nymphs and dry flies can also prove useful. There are four boats for hire and outboards are allowed but not supplied. Bank fishing is allowed and the banks are good all round.

KILL CAMBLE LOUGH   C 02 36
Permission: Dunfanaghy Anglers Association, c/o Arnolds Hotel, Dunfanaghy, Co. Donegal.
Tel: (074) 36208

This is a small lough of about 5 acres. It has been stocked by the local angling association to encourage local junior anglers, and visiting juniors may fish it too. Approximately a third of the bank is fishable.

NEW LAKE   C 00·5 36

Permission: Dunfanaghy Anglers Association, c/o Arnolds Hotel,
Dunfanaghy, Co. Donegal.
Tel: (074) 36208

This is a new lake, as the name suggests, having been formed in the
1920s as a result of an Atlantic storm. It is 230 acres in size and very
shallow with an average depth of 6 feet. It holds an excellent stock
of brown trout averaging 1 lb with many to 2 lb and even better. It
has good hatches of olives in May and a good sedge hatch. This
must surely be one of the best brown-trout fisheries in Donegal.
There are six boats for hire and outboards are allowed but not
available. There is a causeway up the middle of the lough with two
gaps in it to allow boats to pass from one side to the other. This was
once the avenue to the landlord's house and as one drifts on a clear
day the fields, pathways and gates on what once was farmland,
before that fateful storm, are clearly visible below the waves. It
fishes particularly well to the dap in August and September.

PORT LOUGH   C 01 35

Permission: Dunfanaghy Anglers Association, c/o Arnolds Hotel,
Dunfanaghy, Co. Donegal.
Tel: (074) 36208

This lough lies about 3 miles south of Dunfanaghy and access is
good with a road to the shore, car park and boat jetty. Two boats
are available for hire. It is about 75 acres and holds a big stock of
brown trout averaging just under ½ lb with some fish up to 1 lb.
The fish are very free-rising and there are fairly good hatches of
chironomids and sedges. Three-quarters of the bank is fishable.
Traditional fly patterns in small sizes will do.

DRUMLESK LOUGH   B 98 34

Permission: Not usually required

This is a small lough to the east of the T72 Dunfanaghy–Falcarragh
road. A by-road runs close by the south shore. Drumlesk holds a
fair stock of free-rising trout from ½ to ¾ lb, but the banks are
heavily reeded and a boat is necessary to fish it.

LOUGH AGHER   B 200 31

Permission: Not usually required

This is a small lough in the hills about 4 miles east of Falcarragh. It holds a large stock of very small free-rising brown trout and would be an excellent location for a junior competition or for teaching young anglers. Access is via a bog road and the banks are good.

LOUGH ALTAN   B 95 23
Permission: Not usually required

Altan lies between Errigal Mountain to the south and Aghla More to the north. It is a large lough, nearly 2 miles long by ½ mile wide, and is very deep – 174 feet. It holds numerous very small brown trout and the banks are not very fishable, with a cliff along the north shore.

LOUGH AGANNIVE   B 92 25
Permission: G. McNulty, Hon. Secretary, Letterkenny and District Anglers' Association, Hawthorn Heights, Letterkenny, Co. Donegal.

This is a small lough nearly 4 miles south of Gortohork with a bog road running by its north-west end. It holds numerous small brown trout and gets some good sea trout in September. There is a sandy shore on the west and south sides and the west bank usually fishes best.

4   *Dunlewy Lough*

LOUGH NACUNG LOWER	B 86 22
LOUGH NACUNG UPPER	B 89 21
DUNLEWY LOUGH	B 92 19

Permission: Fisheries Manager, ESB Power Station, Gweedore, Co. Donegal.

This is really all one piece of water nearly 5 miles long, stretching from Cung Dam to Dunlewy at the top, and about ½ mile wide. It holds a good stock of small brown trout averaging under ½ lb, and gets a run of sea trout and salmon from mid-July. The sea-trout fishing can be slow and for some the salmon fishing is the main attraction, though the run is small and depends on freshets let down by the power station to get the fish up. Favourite areas for salmon fishing are in from the power station, along by the forest on the south shore and along the east shore of Dunlewy Lough. Bank fishing is permitted and fly fishing and dapping is the rule. Anglers may use their own boats for a fee; outboards over 4 hp are not allowed. A full list of regulations is available from the fisheries manager.

LOUGH NA BREAC RABHAR 89·5 13·5
Permission: Not usually required

This is a small remote lough on the northern slope of Crocknasharragh. It is a murderous walk of well over 2 miles from the nearest road. This is a compass and map job, and only anglers accustomed to mountain walking should attempt the journey. The lough is difficult to find and you could easily walk right past it. However, the effort could pay off – trout of up to 7 lb have been taken here, though there cannot be many of them and they are rarely disturbed by humans.

THE ROSSES FISHERY

The Rosses Anglers' Association has fishing on 130 loughs on 5 river systems in west Donegal. The town of Dungloe is the centre from which the angler makes his way to the various loughs. The angler can choose between salmon, sea-trout and brown-trout fishing and all the loughs are within a 5-mile radius of Dungloe. Permits to fish and boats for hire can be arranged through Charles Boner, Bridge End, Dungloe, Co. Donegal, Tel: (075) 21004.

LOUGH ANURE   B 82 16

Permission: Rosses Anglers' Association; day tickets from C. Boner, Bridge End, Dungloe, Co. Donegal.
Tel: (075) 21004

This is a big shallow lough of 360 acres with good access. There is a car park and boat jetty near the village of Longhanure. It is very rocky and boats should proceed with caution. The brown trout average ½ lb with lots of fish to 1 lb. It gets a good run of sea trout and occasional salmon from mid-July. This is a lovely lough with free-rising trout and considered to be one of the best in the area. It can be fished all over and gets hatches of chironomids, sedges and olives. Fly fishing and dapping only. There are two boats for hire and outboards are allowed. Bank fishing is permitted. Flies to use are Black Pennell, Golden Olive, Peter Ross, Connemara Black, Invicta, Donegal Blue, Hare's Ear, Wickham's Fancy, Devil, Bog Fly, Teal and Black, Bibio, Grouse and Claret and Jacob's Ladder. Indeed, this list of flies in various sizes will be adequate for any of the Rosses loughs.

BALLAFILL LOUGH   B 82 13

Permission: Rosses Anglers' Association; day tickets from C. Boner, Bridge End, Dungloe, Co. Donegal.
Tel: (075) 21004

This small lough holds a big stock of brown trout averaging 7 inches.

MULLAGHDERG LOUGH   B 76 20
KINCASLOUGH

Permission: Rosses Anglers' Association; day tickets from C. Boner, Bridge End, Dungloe, Co. Donegal.
Tel: (075) 21004

This is a fine big shallow lough about 2 miles west of Annagary village. The best accesss is at the football field. The trout average ½ lb and there are good trout on the shore by the football field at the south-east corner, where there is about half a mile of good bank fishing. A Bog Fly works well in summer. A boat is necessary to fish this lough properly but none is available.

The little lough to the west, known as Kincaslough, holds slob trout to 6 and 7 lb weight. They are bottom feeders and hard to catch but are by far the biggest trout in all of the Rosses.

5   *The author with a fine bag of sea trout (Central Fisheries Board)*

LOUGH NAGREAGH   B 75·5 17
LOUGH NAFULLANRANY

Permission: Rosses Anglers' Association; day tickets from C. Boner, Bridge End, Dungloe, Co. Donegal.

Tel: (075) 21004

This is a small lough by the roadside about a mile south of Kincaslough. It holds brown trout to 1½ lb but the banks are high and difficult. It is a lough that could do with a bit of development.

Lough Nafullanrany, further to the south along that road, holds small but very free-rising trout.

LOUGH NAWAUGH   B 76 17

Permission: Rosses Anglers' Association; day tickets from C. Boner, Bridge End, Dungloe, Co. Donegal.
Tel: (075) 21004

Access to this lough is at the Country Inn. It is a short walk up a hill and difficult to get at and so is rarely fished. It holds few brownies worth catching but can get a nice run of sea trout from August. This is a fine lough, with nice shore fishing, and is well worth a visit.

LOUGH WASKEL   B 74 16

Permission: Rosses Anglers' Association; day tickets from C. Boner, Bridge End, Dungloe, Co. Donegal.
Tel: (075) 21004

This is a long, deep, narrow lough to the north-east of Burtonport. It holds a very limited stock of good brown trout. Fly hatches are scarce and the fish prey heavily on sticklebacks, which is probably why they are bigger than average.

LOUGH MEELA   B 74 14

Permission: Rosses Anglers' Association; day tickets from C. Boner, Bridge End, Dungloe, Co. Donegal.
Tel: (075) 21004

This is a fine lough between Dungloe and Burtonport. It holds small wild brown trout and is also stocked with brown trout, but it is best known for its sea-trout fishing. This can be superb from late July when the sea trout rise freely, and the best areas are along by the north bank, under the school and where the rivers enter and leave the lough. Bank fishing is allowed but the banks are not easy to walk. There is one boat for hire. This is a rocky, shallow lough that can blow up in a storm and care should be taken in a big wave. Many consider this a great sea-trout lough and fly fishing and dapping are the methods allowed.

LOUGH ATERCAN   B 75 15

Permission: Rosses Anglers' Association; day tickets from C. Boner, Bridge End, Dungloe, Co. Donegal.
Tel: (075) 21004

This is a small lough by the roadside over 2 miles east of Burtonport. The brown trout are scarce but average 1 lb. Fish food comprises mainly of corixids and sedges. The shoreline is rocky and easily fished. The small lough ½ mile to the south and to the west of the same road can produce the odd good trout too – to over 2 lb.

LOUGHS NABRACK   B 77 14

Permission: Rosses Anglers' Association; day tickets from C. Boner, Bridge End, Dungloe, Co. Donegal.
Tel: (075) 21004

The small lough nearer the road has only small trout and the one further east has better fish. Both loughs sometimes get a few sea trout late in the season.

DUNGLOW LOUGH   B 78 12

Permission: Rosses Anglers' Association; day tickets from C. Boner, Bridge End, Dungloe, Co. Donegal.
Tel: (075) 21004

This is a lough of some 120 acres, 1 mile east of the town of Dungloe. Access to it is excellent and there is a fine boat jetty. It holds a good stock of small wild brown trout and this stock is augmented early each season with larger stocked brown trout. The sea trout arrive in July and from then on the fishing can be really good. Some consider that the best fishing is along by the west shore and at the mouth of the river on the east side. It can fish particularly well early in the morning and in the late evening. The islands have been planted to assist the insect life. There are six boats for hire, outboards are allowed but not supplied and fishing methods are fly fishing and dapping.

LOUGH CRAGHY   B 79 12

Permission: Rosses Anglers' Association; day tickets from C. Boner, Bridge End, Dungloe, Co. Donegal.
Tel: (075) 21004

Craghy is about 1½ miles east of Dungloe and is a very lovely lough with several islands and many headlands and bays. It is best known for its sea trout in August and September. It does not fish well in July except in a very wet season. The average size of the sea trout is ¾ lb and it has produced fish to over 4 lb. They can be free-rising and tend to spend a considerable time in Craghy before moving on. Bank fishing is permitted but the banks are not very good. It is fly fishing and dapping only. There are two boats for hire and outboards are allowed but not available for hire.

LOUGH NAGEERAGH   B 76 10

Permission: Rosses Anglers' Association; day tickets from C. Boner, Bridge End, Dungloe, Co. Donegal.
Tel: (075) 21004

This lough is over a mile south of Dungloe. It holds a fair stock of brown trout averaging about ½ lb and also holds some better trout to nearly 3 lb, but they are not numerous. It is well worth fishing because the trout are of above average size for this area. The fish are free-rising and the most productive areas are along the north and east shores. This lough is sometimes referred to as the Diamond Lake. The Little Diamond is a few hundred yards to the west. It hold similar-sized small trout and the water is very clear.

LOUGH ILLION   B 75 09

Permission: Rosses Anglers' Association; day tickets from C. Boner, Bridge End, Dungloe, Co. Donegal.
Tel: (075) 21004

This lough lies south of the road between Dungloe and Maghery. Access from the road is across a field, for a distance of 200 yards. It is about 40 acres in area, shallow, and holds a fantastic stock of brown trout between ¼ lb and ½ lb. It is one of the more popular local loughs and now gets a small run of sea trout since work was carried out on the outflowing stream. Three-quarters of the bank is fishable.

LOUGH ALEK MORE   B 76 08

Permission: Rosses Anglers' Association; day tickets from C. Boner, Bridge End, Dungloe, Co. Donegal.
Tel: (075) 21004

This is a big lough, well signposted, and has a car park and boat jetty. It holds small wild brownies, is stocked annually with takable brown trout and, as a result of development work on the outflowing stream, it gets a run of sea trout from early August. Heavy falls of ants in August bring up the best fish. This is a lovely lough and the angler seldom comes away empty-handed, though it does not fish well in stormy weather. There is one boat for hire and outboards are allowed. Bank fishing is permitted but anglers should be careful of deep rock fissures that are covered by heather and are extremely dangerous for the unsuspecting bank angler.

MEENLEKNALORE LOUGH B 80 08
LOUGH SALLAGH

Permission: Rosses Anglers' Association; day tickets from C. Boner, Bridge End, Dungloe, Co. Donegal.
Tel: (075) 21004

This lough is on the Dungloe River system. It lies to the east of the T72 Dungloe–Lettermacaward road, a little over 3 miles from Dungloe. It is noted for its sea-trout fishing from August onwards. It tends to weed up a bit and rocks tend to scrape the bottom of the boat at regular intervals. There are two boats for hire on this long, narrow lough and the banks are not very good, so bank fishing is not recommended.

Lough Sallagh is a small lough a few hundred yards to the east up the inflowing stream. It can give excellent sea-trout fishing late in the season and the bigger sea trout congregate in it. It is difficult to fish from the bank and there is usually a boat available.

LOUGH NAMURRIG B 81 07
LOUGH GANNIVEGIL B 82 07

Permission: Rosses Anglers' Association; day tickets from C. Boner, Bridge End, Dungloe, Co. Donegal.
Tel: (075) 21004

Access to these two loughs is by a bog road east off the T72 Dungloe–Lettermacaward road and a walk of about 300 yards to the water's edge. They are not worth fishing for brown trout but hold occasional salmon and sea trout from late July. The sea trout appear to rest longer in Gannivegil. Bank fishing is difficult.

LOUGH ANILLANOWENNAMARVE B 84 08

Permission: Rosses Anglers' Association; day tickets from C. Boner, Bridge End, Dungloe, Co. Donegal.
Tel: (075) 21004

This lough is to the north by the L75 Dungloe–Doocharry road. There is a jetty and boats are usually available. The brown trout are very small but it gets a fair run of sea trout from late July and even a few salmon. A Teal and Black is regarded as the best fly to take a salmon. The banks are difficult enough to fish and the east side is favoured most.

LOUGH CARNBEG   B 82 05
LOUGH NANUARRAGH   B 82 06

Permission: Rosses Anglers' Association; day tickets from C. Boner, Bridge End, Dungloe, Co. Donegal.

Tel: (075) 21004

These loughs lie on a high bog to the east of the T72 Dungloe–Lettermacaward road and nearly 5 miles south of Dungloe. There are actually four loughs in this group and to get to them you park at the bridge and walk the mile or mile and a half across the bog and up the hill. The banks are reasonably good and the fishing can be too. Each holds brown trout of a very acceptable size and you might just be lucky to get one of 2 lb. These are the exception but trout over ½ lb are reported to be fairly plentiful.

LOUGH MORE   B 86 07

Permission: Not usually required

This is a small lough at a bend on the L75 road, ½ mile north of Doocharry. It has a small stock of reasonably good trout and the average weight is near ¾ lb. The fishing can be slow and dour but once in a while produces nice bags of trout – as many as 5 or 6 in a day. Lough More is reported to hold trout over 3 lb.

LOUGH BARRA   B 93 12

Permission: Not usually required

This is a fine-looking lough but it is very poor and deep. The brown trout are extremely small and only very occasional salmon ever get up this far, and by the time both they and the sea trout reach it they are out of condition and not worth fishing for.

DRUMANEANY LOUGH   B 90 06

Permission: G. McNulty, Hon. Secretary, Letterkenny and District Anglers' Association, Hawthorn Heights, Letterkenny, Co. Donegal.

This lough lies to the north of the L75 Doocharry–Fintown road. Access is gained across the bog at a farmhouse. The average size of the trout is 10 oz. They were once very free-rising but unfortunately have been heavily overfished in recent times. Drumaneany gets a hatch of murrough on summer evenings and the angler will nearly always get a trout. The banks tend to be boggy and caution should be exercised.

LOUGH NANUROGE B 92 08

Permission: G. McNulty, Hon. Secretary, Letterkenny and District Anglers' Association, Hawthorn Heights, Letterkenny, Co. Donegal.

This lough is very remote. It can be approached via a small road north off the L75 Doocharry–Fintown road. Park at the bridge and then follow the stream up the hill and across the mountain. It is a long, difficult walk. Nanuroge holds brown trout averaging ½ lb and you may get occasional sea trout late in the season. The long narrow lough a few hundred yards to the east has an excellent stock of free-rising trout approaching ½ lb.

LOUGH NACROAGHY G 83 98

Permission: John McGill, Hon. Secretary, Ardara Anglers' Association, Ardara, Co. Donegal.

This lough lies approximately 3 miles north of Glenties and there is a poor gravel road almost to the water's edge, but it is not suitable for a motor car. This is a lough of about 30 acres, nestling in a valley 700 feet above sea level. It holds beautiful trout that weigh between ½ lb and 1 lb and it is well worth a visit any time in the season. The banks are good and 75 per cent fishable.

DERKMORE LOUGH G 81 98

Permission: Not usually required

This lough lies in the hills south of the Gweebarra River estuary. There is a road up most of the way from the Gweebarra bridge. The trout average ½ lb with some to 1 lb and better. Derkmore lough lies on a limestone base and the trout appear to be quite plentiful. Expect to get a couple of dozen when conditions are right but don't be greedy – return those you don't want. It may be a small lough but it is generally worth a visit.

KILTOORIS LOUGH G 67 97

Permission: John McGill, Hon. Secretary, Ardara Anglers' Association, Ardara, Co. Donegal.

Kiltooris lough lies approximately 5 miles north-west of Ardara and is one of the best trout loughs in the area. The bottom is sandy for the most part and food for trout is plentiful – hence the average size of around ¾ lb, with trout to 1½ lb. There are boats for hire from J. McLoone and H. Johnson by the shore of the lough.

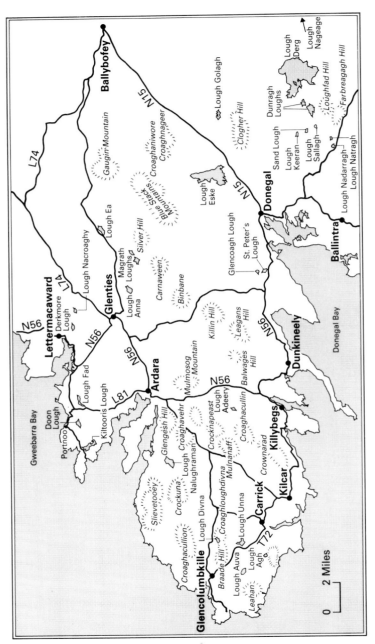

14 *South Donegal*

DOON LOUGH   G 70 98

Permission: John McGill, Hon. Secretary, Ardara Anglers' Association, Ardara, Co. Donegal.

Doon Lough is approximately a mile south of Portnoo and you can drive almost to the shore via a little road from the east. Another small road runs close by the northern shore. The lough holds a fair stock of brown trout averaging ½ lb, with some to 1 lb. There is a boat for hire from F. McHugh on the south shore and the banks are safe for fishing. It is not considered to be as good a fishery as Kiltooris Lough but it has the attraction of a very well preserved prehistoric ring fort on an island.

LOUGH FAD   G 73 97

Permission: John McGill, Hon. Secretary, Ardara Anglers' Association, Ardara, Co. Donegal.

Lough Fad is a little over 4 miles north of Ardara. It has a big stock of small brown trout averaging 3 to the pound. There is a boat for hire from Michael Boyle by the shore.

LOUGH ANANIMA   G 79 94

Permission: John McGill, Hon. Secretary, Ardara Anglers' Association, Ardara, Co. Donegal.

Ananima is over a mile west of Glenties, with a small road running to the north shore. It holds very small brown trout. However, the small lough half a mile to the north-east by the T72 road has trout to ¾ lb.

LOUGH EA   G 91 95

Permission: Not usually required

Lough Ea lies 7 miles north-east of Glenties and is the source of the Owenea River. There is a road by the west side and it is a short walk to the lough shore. The lough holds small brown trout and gets a small run of sea trout from July. The banks are good and it is said to fish best on the side along by the road.

LOUGH ANNA   G 85 92

Permission: Not usually required

This is reputed to be one of the best trout loughs in the Glenties area. It is high in the hills 2 miles south-east of Glenties and there is a very poor road up to it. Tradition has it that it was once stocked with Loch Leven trout. Anyway, the trout now average ½ lb and can be free-rising. The best fishing is along by the north shore, but the banks are steep with a cliff and it can be quite dangerous. This is a very scenic and peaceful place.

MAGRATH LOUGHS   G 88 92
Permission: Not usually required

These loughs are 1,000 feet up in the mountains to the south-east of Glenties. The little pond in the middle has trout to ½ lb.

LOUGH AGH   G 55 78
Permission: The Manager, Gael Linn, Carrick, Co. Donegal.

This remarkably beautiful lough lies high in a valley on the northern slopes of Slieve League. It is approached via a by-road off the T72A Carrick–Glencolumbkille road, but the last 1¼ miles must be covered on foot. It holds a really excellent stock of trout averaging ½ lb with fish up to 1 lb. The banks are fishable all round.

LOUGH AUVA   G 54 81
Permission: The Manager, Gael Linn, Carrick, Co. Donegal.

This lough is easily accessible, with a road running by the north shore. The brown trout are very small and stocks are poor. It gets occasional sea trout in high water after mid-August.

LOUGH UNNA   G 57 81
Permission: The Manager, Gael Linn, Carrick, Co. Donegal.

Lough Unna lies to the right of the T72A as you travel from Carrick to Glencolumbkille. It is only a short walk from the road and is the largest lough in the area. It holds a fair stock of small brown trout and from July on has a good stock of hard fighting ½-lb sea trout and occasional grilse. A good flood is needed to get them up and when they get there catches of a dozen or more are frequently made, and there will always be the odd trout of 1 lb or better among them. An angler had 3 grilse off the shore here in 1986 – in one day. The shoreline is easy to fish. Flies to try are Donegal Blue, Butcher, Jacob's Ladder, Bibio and Black Pennell.

LOUGH DIVINE   G 57 84
Permission: Inquire locally

Lough Divine is over ½ mile long by about 500 yards wide and lies between Braade Hill and Croaghloughdivina and to the south of the road from Glencolumbkille to Meenaneary. It is over half a mile from the road and not at all an easy trip for it is all uphill. The lough holds an excellent stock of brown trout averaging ½ lb. Sometimes it can be so lifeless that you would imagine there are no fish there at all and then suddenly the rise can come on and there is activity everywhere. It can go off just as quickly. There are very heavy falls of heather fly in July, when, of course, a Bibio works well – wasn't it invented to cope with such an eventuality? Otherwise, try Mallard and Claret, Black Pennell, Butcher and Connemara Black.

LOUGH NALUGHRAMAN   G 66 89
Permission: Not usually required

This is a fine big lough high in the hills of west Donegal. It is very remote and not really worth the walk for angling alone. It holds only very small brown trout and tiny char.

LOUGH ADEERY   G 71 82
Permission: Not usually required

This little lough lies high in the hills over 4 miles north of Killybegs. Access is gained to it by a bog road which runs right to the shore. Fishing is from the bank only and there is a good stock of hard-fighting brown trout averaging about 3 or 4 to the pound. From July it gets a run of sea trout. The numbers can vary greatly from year to year, but in a season with good runs quite good sport can be had from the bank. The sea trout are not big; the average is ½ lb.

GLENCOAGH LOUGH   G 87 79
Permission: Mr George Wilson, Mountcharles, Co. Donegal.

This is a small lough just over a mile north-west of the village of Mountcharles. It holds a small stock of little brown trout and is sometimes stocked with rainbow trout by the local angling club.

ST. PETER'S LOUGH   G 87 78
Permission: A Regional Fisheries Board permit

This lough lies off the T72 Mountcharles–Killybegs road outside the village of Mountcharles. It is a limestone lough and holds a fair stock of wild brown trout averaging 1 lb. In addition, it is stocked by the Northern Regional Fisheries Board with rainbow trout. There is a bag limit of 4 trout and all legitimate angling methods are allowed, but no maggots. Bank fishing only and the banks are good.

LOUGH ESKE   G 97 83

Permission: Inquiries to the Manager, Northern Regional Fisheries Board, Station Road, Ballyshannon, Co. Donegal.
Tel: (072) 51435

Lough Eske is one of the largest loughs in Donegal and lies a few miles north of Donegal town. It was once a real gem of a fishery where, in season, the angler could hope to take any one of the salmonid species on rod and line from spring salmon to char. It is still no mean fishery and can fish well, especially in September. It holds small brown trout but with the odd fish to 2 lb. The sea trout average ¾ lb and run as big as 5 lb. There is a small run of spring salmon and some summer and autumn fish. The sea-trout fishing can be good in July, August and September, but the numbers of this species entering the lough have decreased greatly in recent years. Lough Eske fishes best from a boat. In fact, bank fishing is discouraged. Trout can be caught all over, but best results are obtained in the shallows and near the banks. The north and south ends of the lough fish best for salmon and sea trout. In summer and autumn, salmon are generally taken on size 8 flies and sea trout on size 10. Favourite patterns are Donegal Blue, Silver Doctor, Golden Olive, Shrimp (a local pattern), Jacob's Ladder, Bluebottle, Black Pennell and Connemara Black. Eske is the only lough in Ireland where I know char are regularly fished for on rod and line. This happens every year during two weeks in November at certain points along the shore. Access to the lough is at a point on the south-west side; no doubt it may be opened up better in the future. Fly fishing and dapping are the most accepted angling methods, though trolling and spinning are acceptable where they do not interfere with other anglers. The late season is the best time to fish Eske and there are few more beautiful settings.

LOUGH GOLAGH   H 04 82

Permission: Not usually required

There are several loughs by this name in south Donegal. This one lies 7 miles north-east of Donegal town, high in the mountains. Access is gained to it off the N15 Donegal–Ballybofey road by a small bog road at Barnesmore. This road will take you almost as far as Lough Slug. You must walk from here, up and around the mountain. It is not too difficult and you should get there in about 25 minutes. Golagh holds a good stock of brown trout averaging ½ lb with fish to 1½ lb. It has good hatches of chironomids early in the season but it can also fish very well in July, August and September, even in flat, calm conditions. The trout are free-rising and with small flies and light tackle you can expect to get at least a dozen nice fish. The banks are good all round and it is remote, peaceful and very beautiful.

LOUGH KEERAN   H 01 74
Permission: Not normally required

This is a small mountain lough 6 miles south-east of Donegal town. Access is gained to it off the T35 Pettigo–Donegal road via a secondary road and a bog road to the west of Oughtdarnid Mountain. It holds good trout, averaging ¾ lb, with fish up to 1½ lb. It's a small lough and you will fish it in a couple of hours. If conditions are right, expect at least 3 trout for your visit. The banks are not bad and along by the reeds at the south-west end is best.

DURNESH LOUGH   G 88 69
Permission: Sand House Hotel, Rossnowlagh, Co. Donegal.
Tel: (072) 51777

Durnesh Lough is tidal and the level is controlled by floodgates. There is access to it past the caravan park on the west shore or again by a little road from the north, but the part of the shoreline by Kelly's property is private and angling is not allowed. The average size of the brown trout is ½ lb, with a few to 2½ lb. It holds a good stock of sea trout in July – when it fishes best. Boats are available from the hotel. The west shore is a favourite area for fishing from the bank and it is easy to wade.

LOUGH SALLAGH   H 02 72
SAND LOUGH   H 02 74
Permission: Not usually required

These two small loughs lie a mile apart to the north-east of Ballynakillew Mountain. It is possible to take a car part of the way up a bog road off the T35 Pettigo–Donegal road and after that it is a question of proceeding on foot. As you cross the hill, the two loughs will come into view. They hold brown trout only with an average size of ½ lb, but they are not very plentiful. The usual mountain lough flies will do.

DUNRAGH LOUGHS   H 04 73
Permission: Des Egan, Pettigo Anglers' Association, Pettigo, Co. Donegal.

These three loughs lie to the west of Lough Derg, but are not on the same river system. There is access to them via a forest road off the T35 Pettigo–Donegal road to within 200 yards of the water. There are no fish in the small lough to the north. The middle lough has the largest trout, averaging about 1 lb, but the stock is small. The big lough to the south has trout averaging ½ lb and they can be free-rising. It is a pretty lough with its islands and white sand. Both loughs fish best from June, and early morning or late evening is best.

GLEN LOUGH   G 94 69
Permission: Not usually required

This lough lies 2 miles due east of Ballintra and access is very good. It used to hold a really excellent stock of brown trout between ½ and 1 lb but it has diminished greatly in recent years. It has good hatches of olives, chironomids and caenis and also plenty of freshwater shrimp and corixids. Around 60 per cent of the bank is fishable.

LOUGH NARATH   G 94 67
Permission: Not usually required

This is another small lough south-east of Ballintra that used to hold a good stock of small trout but is now overrun with pike and perch. Only about 5 per cent of the bank is fishable.

RATH LOUGH   G 96 69
Permission: Not usually required

Rath Lough is 3 miles east of Ballintra and 60 yards from the road. It holds a good stock of brown trout of about ½ lb and fishes well on the east side, where the river flows in and you can wade. It is

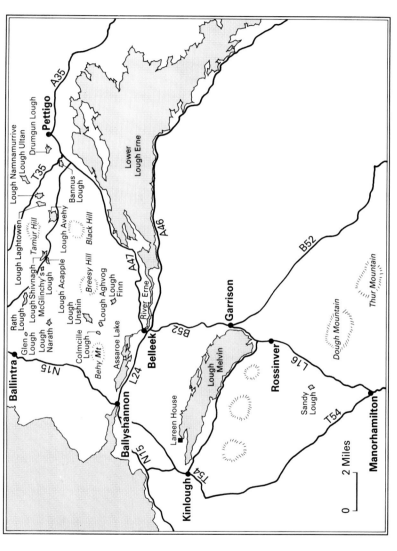

15　*Lough Melvin and North Leitrim*

very popular as a fly fishery and useful patterns are Greenwell's Glory, Black Pennell, Butcher, Fiery Brown, Golden Olive, Blue Dun and Daddy.

LOUGH NADARRAGH   H 00·5 71

Permission: Regional Fisheries Board permit, available from Gerry McMinamin, Nadarragh, Co. Donegal.

This lovely little lough lies along the T35 Pettigo–Donegal road and is developed and stocked by the Northern Regional Fisheries Board. The open season is 1 May to 9 October and fly fishing and spinning are the methods allowed. It holds wild brown trout and is stocked with brown trout and rainbows. Bank fishing only and you can wade and fish all but a small section of the north-west side. This is a good fishery that seldom fails to produce a fish or two. There is a great evening rise during the summer to white moths and spent olives, during which a Heather Moth, a Coachman or a Red Spinner nearly always takes a few fish.

LOUGH NATRAGH   H 01 71

Permission: Not usually required

This little lough holds a good stock of brown trout only, ranging in size between ½ and ¾ lb. The banks are quite good and the fishing can be lively, particularly on a dull day with a nice west wind. It is a bit off the beaten track, though. It lies north of Lough Nadarragh, off the T35 Pettigo–Donegal road, a good half hour's walk across a fairly steep hill. There is a little lough to the south-east of it which holds a fair stock of deep, pink-fleshed trout up to 1½ lb. They can be very free-rising, but the banks are bad so, while it is possible to do a little bank fishing, really you would need a small boat to fish it properly.

LOUGH SHIVNAGH   H 00·5 68

Permission: Not usually required

This lough lies just to the north of a secondary road that runs from Ballintra to Pettigo. It holds a very good stock of small trout to ½ lb and can give great sport. It is a bit difficult to fish except on the east side. Half a mile to the north-east is another lough of a similar size that is all fishable from the shore and which used to hold an excellent stock of trout. Unfortunately, pike were introduced in recent times and the trout stocks have suffered. However, it is worth a try. The banks are gravel and easy to fish and it even has a mayfly hatch.

LOUGH ACAPPLE G 99·5 67

Permission: Not usually required

This lough lies on the opposite side of the road from Lough Shivnagh (above). It holds brown trout up to ¾ lb and the bank is 75 per cent fishable. There is a mayfly hatch and the usual mountain lough flies will do – Butcher, Black Pennell, Greenwell's Glory, Connemara Black, Blue Dun and Mallard and Claret. Unfortunately, pike were introduced here too and there are fears that the trout stocks may have suffered.

McGLINCHY'S LOUGH G 99 67·5

Permission: Not usually required

This small lough lies on the same side of the road as Lough Acapple and ½ mile further west. It holds a small stock of good-quality brown trout and the fishing can be remarkably good. Don't be disappointed, though, if you don't get a response. The fish are not exactly free-rising but it is possible to get a good trout at dusk. There is a hatch of mayfly in July. Three-quarters of the bank is fishable.

LOUGH UNSHIN G 94 64
LOUGH McCALL

Permission: Not usually required

Unshin lies to the north-east of Ballyshannon on high ground between Behy Mountain and Breesy Hill. There is a road running by the south-west corner of the lough. It is a beautiful lough, set in the heather, with safe banks, several islands and a good stock of wild brownies averaging 7 oz. Useful fly patterns are Zulu, Blae and Black, Golden Olive and Blue Dun.

The small lough at the north-east corner is known as Lough McCall. There is separate access to it north from the tarred road by a forest road. It can be fished along the north-east side and holds lovely golden trout that are slightly bigger than those in Unshin.

LOUGH AGHVOG G 94 62

Permission: Not usually required

This small hill lough lies 2 miles due north of Beeleek and access is gained to it by a forest road eastwards off the Cashelard road. It is set in a hollow among the heather and can be very flat at times due to its sheltered position. It holds small brown trout, the best of which will probably reach ½ lb, but it can give great sport. The west and north banks fish best.

COLMCILLE LOUGH   G 93·5 63
Permission: Not usually required

This little lough lies by the Cashelard road opposite Lough Aghvog (above). The trout are better here and you may even get one of 1 lb. They are not very free-rising and the best chance is at dusk when a Spent Olive or Sedge pattern may just tempt a fish. It is fishable all round but the north bank is a little too high for comfort.

LOUGH FINN   G 96 61
Permission: Not usually required

Lough Finn is a remote bog lough 2 miles north-east of Belleek and close to the Northern Ireland border. There is a road in nearly all the way. The trout come about 3 to the pound and, while it fishes well at dusk, the trout in it are regarded as being more free-rising during the day than in many of the other loughs in the area. Certainly there are plenty of them and Blae & Black, Greenwell's Glory, Blue Dun and Connemara Black are all patterns that work well.

LOUGH AVEHY   H 04 67
Permission: Pettigo Anglers' Association; tickets from Des Egan, Pettigo, Co. Donegal.

This lough lies close by a road 5 miles west of Pettigo. It holds a small stock of trout averaging ¾ lb with fish up to 2 lb, and in late summer after a flood it gets a run of trout up from Lough Erne on their way to the spawning streams. It has a mayfly hatch in July. The shores are clean and easily fished and there are prospects of the trout fishing being developed further in the future.

LOUGH LAGHTOWEN   H 05 68
Permission: Pettigo Anglers' Association; tickets from Des Egan, Pettigo, Co. Donegal.

There is a small road to this lough off the Donegal road, nearly 5 miles west of Pettigo. Laghtowen holds a big stock of small trout and if you get one of ½ lb you will have got one of the best in the lough. The trout can be very free-rising and the banks are all fishable.

LOUGH NAMNAMURRIVE   H 05 68
LOUGH ULTAN   H 07 69
Permission: Pettigo Anglers' Association; tickets from Des Egan, Pettigo, Co. Donegal.

Lough Namnamurrive is nearly 4 miles west of Pettigo along the T35 Donegal road. Lough Ultan is to the north of the same road and access is gained to it by a small by-road. Both hold a fair stock of very small free-rising trout.

DRUMGUN LOUGH   H 09 67
Permission: Pettigo Anglers' Association; tickets from Des Egan, Pettigo, Co. Donegal.

This is a fair-sized lough, over ½ mile long by nearly the same width, and it lies a little over a mile west of Pettigo. It can be approached off the T35 Donegal road or by by-roads off the L84 road from Pettigo to Lough Derg. This lough used to hold a good stock of wild brown trout – and still has a fair stock – but it is heavily fished. These trout run in size from 9 oz to 2 lb. The lough is now stocked with rainbows to supplement the wild stocks. The fishing can be very good. There is a 6-trout bag limit and the banks are fishable all round.

BANUS LAKE   H 08 66
Permission: Pettigo Anglers' Association; tickets from Des Egan, Pettigo, Co. Donegal.

This is a nice little lough, nearly 2 miles west of Pettigo along the T35 Donegal road. It holds wild brownies up to 1 lb and is stocked annually by the local angling club. There are hatches of chironomids, olives, sedges, and even small mayflies in July. The banks are not good and wading is necessary. Boats are not allowed. It is fly fishing only and there is a 6-fish bag limit.

LOUGH NAGEAGE   H 17 74
Permission: Not usually required

This is the last lough in south-east Donegal that is worth fishing and it is well worth a visit, as it is widely regarded as being one of the better loughs in the area. It lies a good 6 miles up in the hills to the north-east of Pettigo and there is a by-road almost to the shore up past Lettercran Chapel. The average size of the trout is over ½ lb with several to 1 lb. They take well and a Blae and Black, Black Pennell, Mallard and Claret, Butcher, Greenwell's Glory and small Green Peter are about all the flies you will require. The bank is good and the lough is fishable all round.

ASSAROE LAKE   G 90 61

Permission: ESB Shop, Castle Street, Ballyshannon, Co. Donegal.

Assaroe Lake is an artificial water of some 1,100 acres created by the Electricity Supply Board's Cathaleen Falls Dam and is some 4 miles long by ½ mile wide. It holds a small stock of brown trout averaging 2 lb, and some sea trout and occasional salmon pass through it. Weekly and annual fishing permits are available as well as boating permits, but boating is not encouraged due to the danger of underwater tree stumps. Bank fishing is allowed only off the north bank. Trout are taken spinning and during the mayfly season. Some quite large trout are taken on Sedges and on the Daddy, the latter either dapped or fished dry. The best trout are taken by those who know the course of the old river.

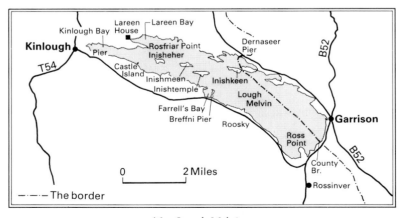

16   *Lough Melvin*

LOUGH MELVIN G 90 52

Permission:
Thomas Gallagher, Edenville, Kinlough, Co. Leitrim.
Tel: (072) 41208;
Terence Bradley, Eden Point, Rossinver, Co. Leitrim.
Tel: (072) 54029;
Northern Ireland Game Fishing Permit
(The fishing on the south-western side from Roosky Point to
Kinlough is regarded as being free.)

Lough Melvin, 8 miles long by nearly 2 miles wide, is by far the
most important salmon and trout fishery in the north-west. It
straddles the border: its north-eastern corner, from near Dernaseer
Pier to the County Bridge, is in N. Ireland, while the major portion
of the lough lies in Co. Leitrim. It can be reached from Sligo by the
N15, turning right to the T54, or by the T54 from Manorhamilton.
From Enniskillen, take the A4 to Belcoo and take the B52 to
Garrison. The angling activities around the lough are centred
mainly at Kinlough, Garrison and Rossinver.

Melvin is rightly famous for its salmon and trout fishing. The
salmon season opens on 1 February, and spring fish are taken
trolling in the Garrison area from that date and on the fly in the
Rossinver Bay area from late March and especially in April.
The grilse run begins in June and fish are taken all over the lough
from Kinlough to Rossinver, with the Rossinver Bay area being
especially good. Melvin remains today one of the few examples of
a post-glacial salmonid lough and it is still in a relatively pristine
state. The quality of the angling can be extraordinary and it is this,
together with the unique fish fauna, that draws and attracts the
anglers. The lough holds salmon, char and perch in addition to
trout, but it is the trout that are of primary interest to most anglers.
It is generally accepted by fishery scientists that there are four
genetically distinct races of trout in the lough. These are brown
trout, ferox trout, gillaroo trout and sonaghan trout – each clearly
distinguishable by coloration, size and shape. While they may share
the same spawning grounds, they don't interbreed and indeed the
ferox trout are found only in one particular river. The ferox trout
feed mainly on perch and char, while the gillaroo diet consists
chiefly of molluscs. The sonaghan feed a lot in midwater on
daphnia and also take emerging insects, while the brown trout have
more catholic tastes. For all their diversity and beauty, there is one
other factor of importance relating to Melvin trout – they are still
present in very great numbers. In 1985, 114 anglers took 759 trout
in a one-day fishing competition. The minimum trout size is

10 inches. Early season flies include Sooty Olive, Blae and Black, Peter Ross, Golden Olive, Fiery Brown, Connemara Black, March Brown and Black Pennell. From mid-May, the Gosling, Green Olive, Green and Yellow Mayflies, Green Peter and Grey Wulff are important. From July on, the Watson's Fancy, Green Peter, Mallard and Claret, Claret Bumble, Fiery Brown, Invicta and Kingsmill are important. It is worth mentioning that Kingsmill Moore invented his famous fly of the same name – Kingsmill – for Melvin. The Green Peter on the bob is by far the most successful pattern for summer salmon.

There is good public access with boat jetties at Kinlough Pier, Stracomer, Breffni Pier, Dernaseer and Garrison. Boats, and in some cases boatmen and outboards, are available for hire from Thomas Kelly, Kinlough, Tel: (072) 41497; John Fahy, Gubacreeney, Kinlough, Tel: (072) 41651; Thomas Gallagher, Edenville, Kinlough, Tel: (072) 41208; John Hill, Dernaseer, Askill, Ballyshannon, Co. Donegal; Terence Bradley, Eden Point, Rossinver, Co. Leitrim, Tel: (072) 54029; The Carlton Park, Information and Fishing Centre, Beelek, Co. Fermanagh; and Vincent Battisti, Sligo Road, Magheracar, Bundoran, Co. Donegal.

SANDY LOUGH   G 89 45
Permission: Not usually required

This is a very attractive little lough set high in the hills nearly 4 miles north of Manorhamilton. It is approached by a stone road off the L16 Manorhamilton–Rossinver road. It is not more than 15 acres but the bank is fishable all round and the trout can vary in size from ½ to ¾ lb. There are fair hatches of sedges and chironomids and the usual mountain lough fly patterns should do nicely.

ANNAGH LAKE   H 40 12
Permission: A Regional Fisheries Board Trout Angling Permit is required

Annagh is a lough of some 60 acres along the L24 Butlersbridge–Belturbet road 1 mile north-west of Butlersbridge. It is stocked annually with rainbow trout and browns are occasionally introduced too. Fly hatches consist mainly of chironomids and sedges and a big increase in the roach and perch population in recent times has led to a decrease in insect life. The angling season runs from 1 May to 30 September, with a 10-inch size limit and a bag limit of 6 trout per outing. In the busy season, the boats are let from morning until 4 p.m. and from 4.30 p.m. until dark. Artificial fly only is the rule and no bank fishing is allowed. There are six boats for hire and they should be booked in advance through Mr Vincent Bartley, Annagh House, Belturbet, Co. Cavan, Tel: (049) 22221. Traditional fly patterns work well and Connemara Black, Silver Invicta, Mallard and Claret, Sooty Olive, Green Peter and Murrough are most popular.

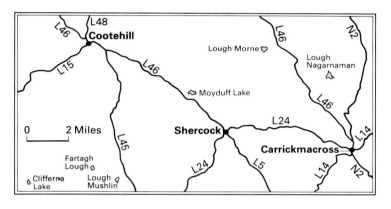

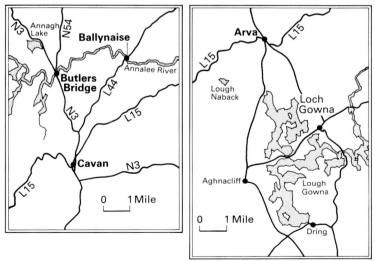

17　*North Longford, Cavan, Monaghan*

MOYDUFF LAKE   H 69 09

Permission: A Regional Fisheries Board Trout Angling Permit is required

Moyduff Lake is to the north of the L46 Cootehill–Shercock road, 3 miles from Shercock and more than 6 miles from Cootehill. The season runs from 1 May to 30 September and there is a 10-inch size limit with a bag limit of 6 trout. This lough is stocked annually with rainbow trout and holds very few wild trout, though a few to over 2 lb are taken each season. The north and south banks are easiest to fish and it is fly fishing only. Traditional patterns and chironomid pupa imitations work well and a dry fly – sedge, buzzer or olive spinner imitation – fished at dusk can sometimes take a fish when nothing else will work.

LOUGH GOWNA   N 29 89

Permission: Free

This is a large attractive lough lying almost halfway between Arvagh and Granard, with the village of Loch Gowna on the north-east shore. Public access to the lough is good at Dring, to the south, at Dernaferst Bridge and at Cloone at Loch Gowna village. Gowna once held a magnificent stock of trout, but their numbers have decreased greatly in recent times. It still holds some trout and fisheries staff report good stocks of fry in some of the streams. There is a good duckfly hatch and the mayfly hatch continues in spite of increasing eutrophication. Lough Gowna holds some fine trout and the average size must be close to 2 lb. Much larger trout are taken trolling, especially in April and May, and several good trout were reported in 1986, including one of over 8 lb. The mayfly and spent gnat fishing can still produce occasional good fish and areas worth concentrating on are at Erne Head and Woodville.

LOUGH NABACK   N 25 95

Permission: Free

Lough Naback is to the east of the L15 Arvagh–Longford road and is best approached off the Moyne–Aghnacliffe road. There is good access to the water's edge with a car park. This must be one of the most interesting loughs in the whole country. It holds a good stock of wild brown trout with an average weight of 1 lb, and 1½-lb trout are quite common. In addition to the trout, there is a char population and Lough Naback has the distinction of being one of the few Irish loughs where char can be taken on fly. It is therefore an ecologically unique environment and anything that can be done to ensure that the indigenous fish stock survives will be worth while. Roach have got into the lough in recent years and are now present in considerable numbers. There are good hatches of chironomids and sedges, and the trout feed heavily on corixids and damsel nymphs. It is still possible to take two or three nice trout for an evening's fishing and small dark flies are favoured – Connemara Black, Black Pennell, Mallard and Claret, Hare's Ear. A Wickham's Fancy is quite useful on summer evenings.

LOUGH MUSHLIN (Seeorum Lough)   H 62 01
Permission: Inquire locally

This small lough lies to the west of the L45 Bailieborough–Cootehill road about 5 miles north of Bailieborough and is approached in a southerly direction off the Tonyduff road. There is a good road to the shore and the bank is fishable halfway round. It has a good stock of hard-fighting brown trout averaging 6 oz and fish up to ½ lb are frequently taken on a dry Sedge late in the evening in July and August. Small silver-bodied flies work well and the Alexandra, Silver Invicta and Butcher are useful patterns. Another useful pattern is the Zulu and a Daddy can be relied on to take a few trout in August and September.

FARTAGH LOUGH   H 60 02
Permission: Inquire locally

This is a small lough to the west of the L45 Bailieborough–Cootehill road. It is 2 miles approximately south-west of Canningstown and the best approach is from the Mountain Lodge road. It has a big stock of trout averaging 4 to the pound. They take a fly freely but a boat is needed to fish it, as it is completely surrounded by tall reeds.

CLIFFERNA LAKE   H 54 00
Permission: Mr Brendan Cooney, Carrickacroman, Tunnyduff, Cootehill, Co. Cavan.
Tel: (042) 60187

This small lough is stocked by Laragh Angling Club and may also hold some good wild brown trout. The fishing is reserved for members of the club who live in the Laragh–Clifferna area.

LOUGH MORNE   H 76 14

Permission: Eugene McMahon, Lough Egish, Co. Monaghan.

Lough Morne is about 2 miles north of Tullynamalra Cross Road
on the L47 Shercock–Castleblayney road and midway between
Ballybay and Carrickmacross. It is managed by the Lough Egish
Rod & Gun Club and day tickets are usually available. It holds a
good stock of lovely wild brown trout and the average weight
must be close to 1½ lb. The best trout in recent years weighed
5½ lb. It is stocked by the club with takable trout. This is an ideal
trout lough, shallow and fertile with good banks and safe wading.
It has good hatches of sedges, chironomids and some olives, and
useful fly patterns are Sooty Olive, Bibio, Peter Ross and Green
Peter. Fly fishing is the most popular angling method and spinning
is allowed but not encouraged. There is a 10-inch size limit and a
6-fish bag limit.

LOUGH NAGARNAMAN   H 82 11

Permission:
Mr Gordon Sweetnam, Main Street, Carrickmacross, Co.
Monaghan.
Tel: (042) 61319;
Carrickmacross Sports Den, Main Street, Carrickmacross, Co.
Monaghan.

This lough is managed by the Carrickmacross Trout Angling
Club. It is situated nearly 5 miles north-west of Carrickmacross
and is best approached off the T2 Carrickmacross–Castleblayney
road. It is entirely dependent on artificial stocking and the trout are
regarded as being slow to take a fly. There is a bag limit of 4 trout
and fly fishing and worm fishing are the methods allowed. The
banks are fishable all round.

18   *North-Western Fisheries Region*

4 North-Western Fisheries Region

The North-Western Fisheries Region stretches from Mullaghmore Point in Co. Sligo to Pidgeon Point near Westport and includes parts of Counties Sligo, Leitrim and Roscommon and a large part of north Co. Mayo. Many anglers visiting this region spend their time fishing for salmon. Indeed, such is the preoccupation with salmon, particularly along the course of the River Moy, that one might think that no other fish swam there, so it is nice to be able to say that Lough Conn, which is the largest lough on the Moy system, and holds plenty of salmon that come to both fly and bait, is one of the country's premier trout fisheries. As well as hosting international competitions, it gets a steady stream of visitors anxious to sample its lively trout fishing. Indeed, Conn tends to dominate the brown-trout fishing and one can easily overlook jewels like the Callow Loughs and the remote hill loughs sprinkled around lovely Corslieve and Nephin Beg or high on the Ox Mountains on the Sligo–Mayo border. Who can forget Arrow, with its magnificent mayfly in May–June and Green Peter hatches in July–August, where Christmas comes twice a year for the trout – and the anglers too? Sea trout there are in plenty from Glencar Lake in the north to Keel Lough in the far south-west and you can fish them at Burrishoole and Beltra, and let the salmon be a bonus. Yes, it is hard to avoid talking about salmon in these parts. They can be taken on the fly both as springers and grilse. Three spring fish 'caught me' in one day on Beltra and Lough Feagh once gave me five grilse. The Co. Mayo loughs offer many surprises and no little sport to the angler.

The statutory salmon angling season in the Sligo district runs from 1 February to 30 September, except on Lough Gill, where the season begins on 1 January. The sea-trout season runs from 1 February to 30 September, except on Glencar, where it runs to 12 October. The brown-trout season in the district is from 15 February to 30 September, but Glencar Lough goes on to 12 October. Arrow is from 1 March to 30 September and Lough Gill is the same for brown trout.

In the Ballina district, the salmon season on the loughs runs from 1 February to 30 September and the sea-trout season is from 1 February to 10 October. The brown-trout season runs from 15 February to 10 October, except Easky Lough, which closes on 12 October.

In the Bangor district, the open season for salmon on Carrowmore Lake, Burrishoole and the Achill fisheries is from 1 February to 30 September. In practice, Burrishoole does not open until early June. The Lough Beltra season runs from 20 March to 30 September. The sea-trout season on Carrowmore Lake is from 1 February to 30 September, while Burrishoole and Achill run on to 12 October, but Beltra closes on 30 September. The brown trout season in this district is from 1 May to 30 September, except the Newport System, which opens on 20 March; the Owengarve and Glenamoy, systems which run from 1 May to 12 October; the Burrishoole, Owenduff, Ballyveeney and Achill systems, which run from 15 February to 12 October; and the Owenmore and Munhin systems, which run from 1 February to 30 September.

GLENCAR LOUGH   G 73 43

Permission:
John McDonnell, Hon. Secretary, Manorhamilton Anglers' Club, 2 Church Street, Manorhamilton, Co. Leitrim.
Tel: (072) 55217;
James McCarney, Hon. Secretary, Sligo Anglers' Association, Annelen, Cornageeha, Sligo.
Tel: (071) 62385;
Harold Sibbery, The Waterfall, Glencar, Co. Leitrim

This lovely lough lies to the south-east of Benbulbin and is approximately 2 miles long by ½ mile wide. It lies in a deep valley to the north of the N16 Manorhamilton–Sligo road, 5 miles from Sligo, and has a spectacular waterfall at its north-east corner. The open season for salmon is from 1 February to 30 September; for sea trout, from 1 February to 12 October; and for brown trout, from 15 February to 12 October.

Fishing methods are fly fishing and dapping only from the boats; spinning is allowed from the shore. The lough has a resident stock of small brown trout and gets a really good run of sea trout and a fair number of salmon. The average size of the sea trout is quite big – over 1½ lb – and local anglers claim that the lough produces the largest average size of sea trout in the west of Ireland. The best trout taken in recent years weighed 6½ lb and the best salmon was 22 lb. The fish are very free-rising, especially when fresh, and favourite fly patterns are Cahill, Green Peter, Mayfly, Teal and Yellow, Daddy, Watson's Fancy, Black Gnat and Bibio. The lough has a good mayfly hatch, as well as olives and sedges, and the sea trout take the natural flies quite freely. In fact, the sea trout take particularly well during the mayfly hatch. The southern shore is deep and the northern shore shallow and shelving. The latter shoreline and the eastern end of the lough are favourite fishing areas. This lough fishes best in a west or south-west wind. There is one boat for hire from Mr Sibbery and outboard motors are allowed. This is a lovely lough lying in the shadow of famed Benbulbin, with its wooded shoreline, waterfall and the islands at either end. Well worth a visit.

LOUGH GILL   G 71 32
Permission:
(north shore)
Mrs White, Shriff Bay, Newtownmanor, Co. Leitrim.
James McCarney, Hon. Secretary, Sligo Anglers' Association, Annelen, Cornageeha, Sligo.
Tel: (071) 62385;
Nelson & Sons, Castle Street, Sligo.
(A permit is not usually required on the south shore.)

The open season for salmon and sea trout is from 1 January to 30 September; for brown trout, from 1 March to 30 September. Gill is a large lough, nearly 6½ miles long from east to west and 2½ miles wide at its widest point. It lies about 3 miles east of Sligo and the L16 Dromahair–Sligo road runs close by the shore on the northern end and the L117 on the southern side. There is public access to the lough from a pier on the south side of the mouth of the Garavogue River, at Inishfree Pier and from the pier at Sriff Bay in the east. This lough holds brown trout and salmon. It gets a big run of spring salmon and anglers are out from opening day. Few loughs have a reputation for having salmon as the predominant angling species and this is one of them. In the four years 1981–4, the annual average salmon catch was 369. Most of the fishing is done by trolling. February and March are regarded as good months and so also is May, but after that the salmon fishing is over for the season. Gill also holds a stock of good brown trout. They tend to be dour and slow to take and anglers concentrate a lot of their trout-fishing efforts on the mayfly season from mid-May to mid-June. Some of the best trout fishing areas are on the west wide from Holywell to Church Island and around Aughamore Rock. Dapping the natural mayfly can be very productive and brings up some of the best trout. Spent gnat fishing is also available, as the female mayfly returns to the water to lay her eggs. Bank fishing is possible, with permission, at some places on the north shore. Boats and outboards are available for hire from Peter Henry, The Blue Lagoon, Sligo, Tel: (071) 2530.

COLGAGH LOUGH   G 73 36
Permission: Not usually required

This is a beautiful lough of some 100 acres, lying 3 miles east of Sligo and to the north of L16 road to Manorhamilton. Access to it is good, with a secondary road down to a car park and cemetery by the shore. It holds a good stock of magnificent brown trout averaging nearly 1½ lb and trout of 4½ lb and 7½ lb have been taken in recent times. There is every possibility that the trout stocks may increase greatly in this lough since the Fisheries Board carried out development work on the spawning river. The lough has good hatches of chironomids, olives, caenis and sedges and the best fishing months are May, June and September. There are no boats for hire and this is one lough where a boat is required to enjoy it to the full. It is quite shallow along the shore and the south-east and east banks are the areas most favoured by anglers. Useful patterns are Connemara Black, Fiery Brown, Bibio, Peter Ross, Greenwell's Glory, Invicta, Murrough and Green Peter.

LOUGH ARROW   G 78 08
Permission: Free

Arrow is one of the great Irish trout fishing loughs, where the trout average 1½ lb and fish to 6 lb and 7 lb are taken on fly annually. It is 4 miles north-west of Boyle, with Ballymote 6 miles and Ballyfarnan 3 miles away. It is a limestone lough, incredibly rich, and while it has some feeder streams it is mainly spring-fed. There is good public access at Brick Pier on the east, Ballinafad Pier to the south and Rinnbawn Pier on the west shore. There are numerous other access points as well with local permission. The duckfly hatches in late March and early April and the favoured fly patterns at that time are Blae Sooty Olive, Fiery Brown, Bibio, Red Arrow, Invicta, Connemara Black with Jungle Cock and Heckham and Red. Next come the lake olives from mid-April to mid-May and useful patterns then are Olive Bumble, Green Olive, Golden Olive, Invicta and Greenwell's Glory. May and June see not only the mayfly hatch but very good buzzer fishing at night and here red and olive pupa patterns are popular, together with dry buzzer imitations. The mayfly season generally begins about 17 May and lasts

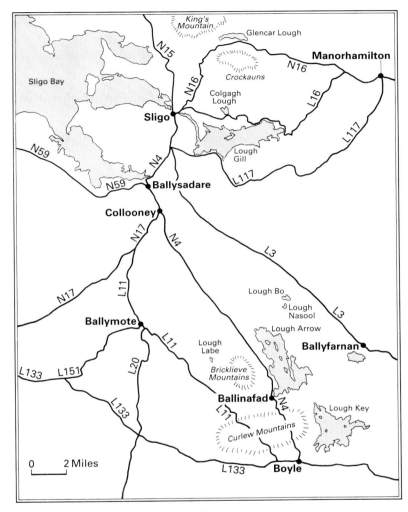

19   *Sligo area*

until the second week of June. Arrow has its own Mayfly pattern, and the Invicta, Teal and Yellow and Golden Olive work well at this time. Many prefer to dap natural mayflies, collected along the shores and on the islands. The spent gnat fishing is one of Arrow's really great attractions. At this time, murroughs hatch in large numbers after dark and this is one very exciting way of getting a big trout, but it calls for great skill and experience. This lough gets a fall of soldier beetles in July. Arrow is one of the few loughs that still gets a good hatch of Green Peter. The season for this is late July and early August, when the Peter hatches at dusk. Late August and September is a good time for drifting traditional-style with wet fly and favourite patterns at this time are Green Peter, Bibio, Invicta, and Teal and Yellow. There is a 12-inch size limit.

Arrow has such a variety of fishing that I think I should take the

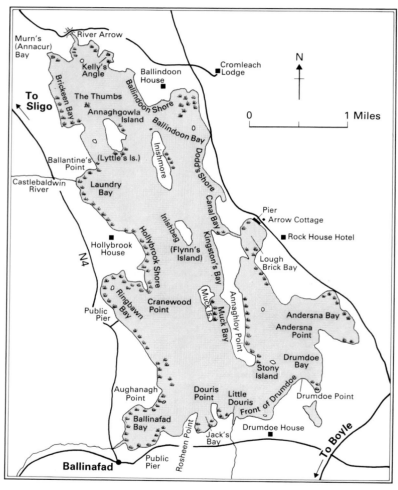

20   *Lough Arrow*

prospective visitor around the lough and explain the kind of fishing that can be expected as we go along. We will start at Brick Bay and travel in a clockwise direction. Brick Bay has a good duckfly hatch; the mayfly hatches early here; there is good Buzzer fishing at night and the murrough hatches down at the narrow neck out of the bay. Fishing can be slow along the Annaghgowan shore except for dapping in the mayfly season. McCormack's Bay is likely to produce a fish at any season. Andersna Bay has duckfly, olives, mayfly and can give good spent gnat fishing in suitable conditions. Drumdoe Bay gets a hatch of olives and, in mayfly time, this bay and across in front of Drumdoe House fishes best to the dap. The same is true of Little Douris, Big Douris and Flanagans Bay, which also has a good duckfly hatch. Jack's Bay has good duckfly and mayfly hatches and indeed fishes well right through the season. McDonald's Shore fishes well to the dap in mayfly time. Ballinafad Bay has good duckfly and mayfly hatches and can fish well late in the season. Aughanagh Point is very shallow for at least 100 yards off shore. It has good murrough fishing in May–June and Green Peter fishing in July–August. Aughanagh Shore is not much fished and fish are scarce there but Ringbawn Bay has a great hatch of duckfly and olives and fishes well late in the season. There is an excellent mayfly hatch around Cranewood Point and it offers good buzzer fishing. From Hollybrook Harbour to Laundry Bay there is a good duckfly hatch, buzzer in May–June, and a very good mayfly hatch. There is a good hatch of olives in Laundry Bay. The area from Ballantine's Point out to Lyttle's Island and up to The Thumbs gets a very good duckfly hatch, an excellent mayfly hatch and good hatches of murroughs, olives and buzzers. Lyttle's Island gets a great hatch of mayfly all around and there is a duckfly hatch in Horse Shoe Bay, which is also a noted area for spent gnat fishing. Brickeen Bay, Annacur Bay, the mouth of the river and Kelly's Bay get hatches of all the fly species found on the lough, and always hold a big stock of trout. There is a good drift along the Pumphouse shore and into Pol Na Perches in a south-east wind in mayfly time. Ballindoon Bay always fishes well and is famous for its murrough and Green Peter fishing. Dodd's Shore is mainly fished in mayfly time and there is a good shallow which runs well out into the lough (dangerous for an outboard motor when the lough is low). Ballinary Bay gets a good mayfly hatch and the Canal Bay has good duckfly and mayfly. Hardegan's Point has a dangerous shallow running offshore but is a great spot for a trout in mayfly time. Kingston's Bay has a good mayfly hatch but trout are rarely ever caught along Muck Island. Muck Bay has good mayfly and spent gnat fishing and the area from there to Stony Island has good duckfly and buzzer hatches and fishes well late in the season. Gildea's Island has a good mayfly hatch along the east shore and you can dap along the shore of Flynn's Island in mayfly time.

LOUGH BO   G 79 18

Permission: Regional Fisheries Board Permit, available from Miss N. McDonagh's shop beside the lough.
Tel: Geevagh 5

Lough Bo is a delightful little lough of about 50 acres, 4 miles to the east of Riverstown and 2½ miles north-east of Lough Arrow. It holds a natural stock of brown trout and is also stocked annually by the Fisheries Board. Trout average about 1 lb and fish up to 2 lb are caught frequently. There is one boat for hire at McDonagh's Bar. Bank fishing is also quite easy, with the road running along by the lake shore. The season is from 1 April to 30 September. There is a size limit of 9 inches, a bag limit of 6 trout, and all legitimate fishing methods are allowed.

LOUGH NASOOL   G 79 07

Permission: Free

This very attractive 15-acre lough is situated about 2 miles north-east of Bellarush Bridge at the outflow from Lough Arrow. It is stocked occasionally by the Fishery Board and because it is very rich in feeding the trout do extremely well – trout up to 10 lb have been recorded. It is very fishable, with a good shoreline, and is convenient to the road. Due to the limestone nature of the countryside, the lough can occasionally disappear overnight. The season is from 1 March to 30 September.

LOUGH LABE (Lough na Leibe)   G 73 12

Permission: Permit from Mr Edward McGettrick, O'Connell Street, Ballymote, Co. Sligo.
Tel: (071) 83305

This fishery is known locally as Lough na Leibe. It is situated up in the hills about 4½ miles south-east of Ballymote in Co. Sligo. Access is off the Ballinafad–Ballymote road. About 4 miles from Ballinafad and less than ½ mile past the junction to Castlebaldwin there is a road off to the right at a church. Follow this for a mile and a quarter and the lough is in the valley about 200 yards to your left, below the house of Patrick Milmoe, who holds the key of the boat.

The lough is stocked with rainbow trout by the North-Western Fisheries Board. The season is from 1 April to 30 September and there is a 10-inch size limit. The daily bag limit is 4 trout. All legitimate angling methods may be employed from the bank, but only artificial flies may be fished from the boat. Fly hatches are sparse. The trout average about 1 lb, but some nice trout of over 2 lb and better are taken every season.

LOUGH BREE   G 56 28
Permission: Free

This small lough of about 7 acres is 2½ miles approximately south of the N59 Sligo–Ballina road. Turn off at Dromard and take the road south to Chapel Street and proceed from there up the mountain road towards the Ladies Brae. Lough Bree holds very small brown trout. Bank fishing is possible, but the banks are very soft in places and great caution should be taken.

LOUGH ACHREE (Harte's Lake)   G 51 29
Permission: Not usually required

This small lough lies in a valley to the north of Knockachree (1,766 ft). It can be approached from the Collooney–Cloonacool road by taking the road northwards over the mountain known as the Ladies Brae, or by turning southwards off the N59 Sligo–Ballina road a mile west of Dromard and again heading for the Ladies Brae. Fishing is from the bank only and the lough holds a good stock of small brown trout, with some fish up to 1 lb – it has in the past been known to produce the odd bigger fish; a 4-lb trout was reported from it some years ago. The banks are fairly solid, except for the south-east corner, which is soft and boggy. A car may be parked, with permission, at Harte's House, off the Ladies Brae road. The season is from 15 February to 30 September.

EASKY LOUGH   G 44 22
Permission:
(western half) Not usually required;
(eastern half) Cooper Estate, Collooney, Co. Sligo.

Easky Lough lies high in the Ox Mountains in Co. Sligo and is over 100 acres in area. The open season for salmon is from 1 February to 30 September; for sea trout, from 1 February to 12 October; and for brown trout, from 15 February to 12 October.

The lough lies along the road which runs across the mountain from Dromore West on the Sligo–Ballina road to Mullany's Cross on the Cloonacool–Ballina road. There is no boat but there is plenty of shore fishing and the safest place to fish is along the road on the east side. However, many consider that the west side gives by far the better fishing, though the walking is difficult and even dangerous in places. The brown trout are small – about 3 to the pound – but free-rising, and the sea trout that get up there about August average ¾ lb with some better fish. Some anglers claim that the lough holds a stock of large ferox trout but none has ever been caught. What these anglers saw humping in the ripple were most likely salmon, which enter the lough in high water and can be taken on fly or spinner at the mouth of the river which enters at the south-east corner.

LOUGH GAL   G 43 21
Permission: Not usually required

Lough Gal is a small lough about half a mile south of Easky Lough. Access to it is across the bog off the same mountain road that leads past Lough Easky. Park by the roadside and walk due west. It is a difficult walk, because the bog is soft in places, and care is advised. This lough holds only brown trout and can fish well from April. Evening time is best and a Duckfly pattern, Golden Olive or a Brown Sedge, as well as the standard lough patterns, can get results. Gal is remote but holds some excellent trout. It does not hold a big stock of fish, but what is there is good – the average size is about 1 lb and trout to 5 lb have been recorded. This lough can be dour. You earn your fish when you get them because they don't give themselves up easily.

LOUGH RUMDUFF   G 43 21
Permission: Not usually required

Rumduff is situated about 400 yards south of Easky Lough and the same distance west of the mountain road leading to Easky Lough from Mullany's Cross. It holds a fair stock of very small brown trout. The banks are high and the fishing difficult.

LOUGH ALONE   G 36 15
Permission: Not usually required

This is a wild, lonesome lough 1,200 feet up in the Ox Mountains.

It lies about one mile due west of Lough Talt and a mile south of the L133 Lough Talt–Bunniconnellan road. It is approached through a gap in the mountains and it is a long tiring walk. Lough Alone holds a good stock of small brown trout and fish up to 3 lb have been taken. It fishes best on summer evenings, but remember to leave yourself with enough daylight to get back to the road.

LOUGH FOSSEA   G 36 14
Permission: Not usually required

Fossea is a wild, remote lough to the south-west of one of the highest peaks – 1,304 feet – in the Ox Mountains. Approach it from the L133 Bunniconnellan–Lough Talt Road. It is a long, steep climb up through a gap in the mountains and across the moor for a good 2 miles, and it feels every inch of 2 miles as well. It can also be approached from the bog road at Bunniconnellan east, but this approach probably leaves you with a longer walk. Either way, it is a stiff climb. It can be a windy place. The angler is well advised to beware of fog at times. Loch Fossea does not hold a big stock of trout but the quality is good. The average size is about 1¼ lb and trout to 4 lb have been taken. These fish appear to be of the gillaroo variety and small dark flies like the Connemara Black, Kingsmill, and Butcher seem to work best. There is a hatch of sedge in the evenings in May and June. This lough appears to fish well only in the evening. Don't go to this lough without your compass and a map.

CARROWKERIBLY LOUGH   G 26 10
Permission: Mrs Scott-Knox-Gore, c/o Liam McHale, Solicitor, Pearse Street, Ballina, Co. Mayo

This lough of about 90 acres lies to the east of the River Moy between Foxford and Ballina. It holds a small stock of trout averaging ¾ lb and can be fished from the bank in places. The road runs all along its west shore and touches it on the north and east as well.

CALLOW LOUGHS   G 30 03
Permission: Free

The Callow Loughs lie to the south of the N57 Foxford–Swinford road. They are two of the least well known trout fisheries in the west of Ireland, yet they hold excellent stocks of wild brown trout.

The northern lough is about 100 acres, and it is separated from the southern lough by a road and a bridge. Access to each is easy with the road running alongside. There is a jetty by the bridge on the south lough, where it is quite easy to launch a boat. It is not advisable to leave a boat unattended overnight. There are a lot of reeds and bushes around both loughs, and bank fishing is possible only in a few places. The loughs definitely fish best in March, April and May, and there can be some good fishing in the evenings during August. The trout average ¾ lb in the south lough, and while the average size might be slightly smaller in the northern lough it probably holds more fish. Trout up to 3½ lb have been taken on the fly, but a 2-lb trout is considered a good fish. Anglers may use an outboard motor and inquiries for boats for hire should be made to Edward Kennedy, The Modern House, Swinford, Tel: (094) 51135. Flies to use are Golden Olive, Sooty Olive, Connemara Black, Butcher, Black Pennell and Mallard and Claret.

LOUGH MUCK   G 29 02
Permission: Not usually required

This is an easily accessible lough lying 2 miles east of Foxford. Turn south off the N57 Foxford–Swinford road about 1¼ miles from Foxford or take the road that runs between the two Callow Loughs and turn off to the right 2 miles further on. The lough holds numerous small brown trout and a ½-lb fish is considered to be about the average size. The odd larger trout is taken occasionally. It is possible to wade in places, and there is a long strand at the north-eastern end where bank fishing is easy and wading safe. This lough seems to fish best in June and flies to use are Golden Olive, Sooty Olive, Black Pennell and Butcher.

LOUGH TALT   G 39 14
Permission: Free

The L133 Ballina–Tobbercurry road runs right by the shore of this lovely 200-acre lake, which lies in a beautiful valley of the Ox Mountains about 10 miles from Ballina and 8 miles from Tobbercurry. It holds a large stock of small free-taking brown trout and bank fishing can give good results. There is a boat harbour as well where a boat can be launched and boats may be hired at the Lough Talt Inn. It can be a difficult lough to fish at times, with winds coming from different directions. April is probably the month when the trout rise most freely but it can produce half a dozen trout at any time. The season runs from 15 February to 30 September.

LOUGH HOE	G 36 14
LOUGH WATTYWEE	G 36 12
LOUGH HURE	G 36 11
LOUGH ARUBBLE	G36 10

Permission: Free

These four loughs lie high in the Ox Mountains to the south-west of Lough Talt. Access to them is very bad with a long, steep walk from all roads up and across the mountains. They range in size from 2 to 5 acres. They hold fair stocks of trout from about 5 to 7 inches. The banks are very soft and dangerous in places. Hardly worth the long walk.

TULLYVELLIA LOUGHS   G 45 17
Permission: Free

These two loughs lie in a valley at about 800 feet. Take the Cloonacool road off the L133 about 2 miles east of Lough Talt and, 1½ miles south of Cloonacool, turn up a mountain road and follow it for about 1½ miles. There is nothing for it then but to walk the next 1½ miles. The best fishing is in April and May with the trout coming very freely at about 3 to the pound. The small lake to the west is the better of the two and is well worth concentrating on. It can produce some 1-lb fish and has a good clean rocky shore which is easy to fish.

GLENDARRAGH LOUGH	G 46 20
CLOONACOOL LOUGHS	G 46 20

Permission: Free

These loughs lie high in the mountains at about 1,300 feet. They can be approached by a steep climb of over a mile off the Mullany's Cross to Dromore West road, or by taking the bog road from Cloonacool village. When conditions are right, the trout can be very free-rising and come at about 3 to the pound. April and May are the best months and a Butcher is about as good a fly as any. If you get a fish of ½ lb, consider that you have done well. Both of the loughs have a good, clean, solid bank which makes bank fishing easy.

CULLENTRAGH LOUGH   M 42 82
Permission: Not usually required

This lough lies to the north of the L140 Ballyhaunis–Kiltimagh road about 5 miles from Ballyhaunis. Roads come within a short distance of the water's edge on all sides. It is a deep lake with a soft, boggy shore. There is no boat available and fishing is done from fishing stands erected by the Fisheries Board. The lough holds some good trout up to about 4 lb, but fish are not plentiful and even in perfect conditions the fishing can be dour. The best chance is at the peak of a fly hatch and there are hatches of chironomids, sedges, lake olives and even a small mayfly hatch in late May and early June. The trout fishing season is from 15 February to 10 October.

LOUGH CULLIN   G 00 21
Permission: Free

Cullin lies adjacent to the L22 from Foxford to Pontoon. It is a large shallow lough of over 2,000 acres and access to it is from the north shore only. There are three access points. The first is at Drummin off the Foxford–Pontoon road. The second is at Pontoon Bridge and is a footpath only. The third access is off the Pontoon–Castlebar road. Cullin holds an excellent stock of brown trout averaging ¾–1 lb with some fish to 4 lb. It also gets a run of salmon, both spring and summer fish. In fact, all the fish heading for Lough Conn and its inflowing rivers must pass through Cullin, and that can be an awful lot of fish. Many of them rest in Cullin on their way. The best fishing area is from Drummin on the east, northwards by Pontoon to Garrison Island on the western side. The southern half of the lough is not considered to be good fishing. The trout are free-rising and the best season is from April to mid-June. The trout feed well on lake olives in April and the mayfly hatch begins especially early on Cullin – about 15 May. Wet Mayfly patterns can be especially good at this time and it is not unusual for a boat to take maybe a dozen and a half trout in a day's fishing. A south wind is best, but fishing can be good in any wind.

Salmon are frequently taken on the fly when trout fishing – especially the fresh grilse in June – and a leader of 8 lb BS is recommended. The two hot spots for salmon are at the inflow from Lough Conn at Pontoon Bridge and again at the outflow upstream of the Railway Bridge. Access to the lough at the Railway Bridge is via Corlummin village near Foxford. Salmon are taken at each of these locations from April on fly, spinner, worm and prawn.

The fishing on the lough tapers off about mid-June. The shallows and dangerous rocky areas have all been marked with iron bars to make the lough safe for boat anglers. It is advisable to take special care in high water conditions, when large unmarked rocks may be lurking just underneath the high water. Boats and boatmen are available for hire locally and at Healy's Hotel, Pontoon, Tel: (094) 56443, and at Pontoon Bridge Hotel, Tel: (094) 56120. Seasons are from 1 February to 10 October for trout and from 1 February to 30 September for salmon. There is a 10-inch size limit for trout.

ISLANDEADY LOUGH (Bilberry Lough)   M 08 87
Permission: Free

Islandeady Lough, also known as Bilberry Lough, is situated to the north of the T39 Westport–Castlebar road. It is an attractive and interesting fishery of 1,000 acres, managed by the North-Western Regional Fisheries Board. Access to it is easy off the Castlebar–Westport road, with a car park and jetty right by the water's edge. The lough holds wild brown trout averaging over 1 lb with some up to 3½ lb. It also gets stocked annually with 2-year-old brown trout. It is a lough with a well justified reputation for good fishing and when I was responsible for compiling angling statistics for all the Inland Fisheries Trust loughs it used to come at the top of the table for the best rod-catch per day over the season in the whole country. It fishes well from April onwards and useful fly patterns are Connemara Black, Fiery Brown, Black Pennell, Green Peter, Golden Olive, Mayfly patterns, Watson's Fancy, Murrough, Bibio, Sooty Olive, Greenwell's Glory and Grasshopper. There are good hatches of chironomids, olives, mayfly and sedges. Bank fishing is allowed, but is difficult due to the soft – in places dangerous – margins. Three boats are available for hire from Austin Staunton, Islandeady, whose house is at the turn to the lough off the main road. Outboards are allowed but not supplied. Fly fishing with artificial fly only. The season for trout runs from 15 February to 10 October, and a 10-inch size limit and a 6-fish daily bag limit apply (these rules are statutory and their infringement is an offence at law). When conditions are right – a good breeze – this can be a very free-rising lough, with good fly hatches and good trout, and well worth a visit, especially for the traditional wet-fly fisherman.

TUCKER'S LOUGH   M 15 92
Permission: Not usually required

This lough lies to the east of the L134 Castlebar–Ballina road just over a mile from Castlebar. It is about 30 acres in extent and holds a stock of small brown trout to about a ¼ lb. They can be very free-rising at times. The banks are soft with high reeds in places and the best of the fishing is from the east shore.

LOUGH CONN   G 15 06
Permission: Free

Lough Conn's reputation as a fine brown-trout and salmon fishery goes back to the very beginning of angling in the west of Ireland. There is a sizeable char population present. It is a big lough – about 14,000 acres. It measures 9 miles from north to south and varies in width from 2 to 4 miles. Conn is regarded as a very free-taking lough. It is a great favourite with those who like to fish traditional-

6   *Lough Conn – mayfly time*

style in front of the boat, and because trout take the wet fly so freely very little dapping takes place there – indeed, it is almost frowned upon. Conn is the first choice in the country for international matches – a measure of its reputation for producing fish. It is managed by the North-Western Regional Fisheries Board and its devotees are quick to boast that due to the healthy state of the wild trout stocks it has never been stocked with trout or fish of any kind. It is well served by roads all round and an angler can easily launch a boat at more than half a dozen locations. There is access to the lough at Gortnorabbey Pier near Crossmolina, Errew Pier, Phiula-wakhouse Bay, Gillaroo Bay, Pontoon, Knockmore Bay, Brack-wansha, Sandy Bay and Cloghans Bay.

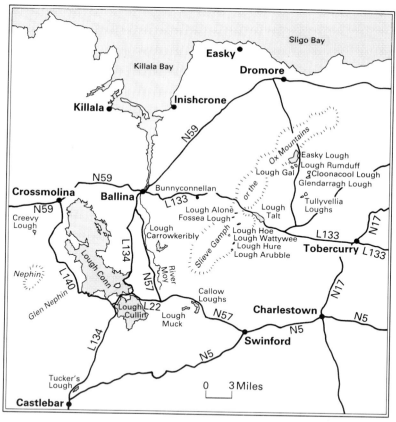

21   *East Mayo and the Ox Mountain Loughs*

Salmon are taken mainly by trolling from the end of March to July and the best areas to concentrate on are the northern end of the lough, Cornakillew, Massbrook and Castlehill Bay. Trout anglers frequently take salmon on the fly in June and July. About 600 fish are taken annually. The trout fishing begins to pick up in April and reaches its climax with the mayfly hatch in late May and June. The wet-fly fishing can be very good from late August to the end of the season. The artificial flies that work best can be divided into three groups, depending on the time of year: in the early season, Fiery Brown, March Brown, Connemara Black, Bibio, Sooty Olive (best of all), Black Pennell, Peacock Spider, Golden Olive, Green Olive, Mallard and Claret, Blae and Black; in the mayfly season, artificial Mayflies, Green Peter, Teal and Yellow, Invicta, Bumble Olive, Cock Robin, Bibio, Claret Bumble and Watson's Fancy; and, after the mayfly, all the sedge patterns (Green Peters, Murroughs, etc.), Sooty Olive, Bibio, Bumble Olive, Peacock Spider, Coch-y-bondhu, Watson's Fancy, Black Pennell, Green Olive, Invicta and Connemara Black. These can all be dressed on size 8, 10 and 12 hooks, with size 10 the most popular. The shallows are all well marked with iron bars and the best fishing areas are along the shores, in the shallow bays and on the shallows out in the middle.

There are plenty of boats and outboards for hire and even some professional boatmen. The season runs from 1 February to

7   *Lough Conn – from Pontoon Bridge*

30 September for salmon and from 15 February to 10 October for trout, with a 10-inch size limit. Conn is a well managed and exciting lough to fish, one where the visiting angler can always be sure of a welcome and good advice from the local anglers. Boats, outboards and boatmen can be arranged through the Pontoon Bridge Hotel, Foxford, Co. Mayo, Tel: (094) 56120; Healy's Hotel, Pontoon, Foxford, Tel: (094) 56443; Padraic Kelly, Newtown, Cloghans, Ballina, Tel: (096) 22250; Joseph Moffatt, Kilmurray House, Castlehill, Ballina, Tel: (096) 31227; or indeed through any of the other hotels and guest houses around the lough.

CREEVEY LOUGH   G 10 13

Permission: Not usually required

This landlocked lough of about 5 acres is situated 5 miles south-west of Crossmolina off the L137 and about a mile west of Kilmurray House. It holds a good stock of brown trout averaging 6 oz. They can be very free-rising at any time from April onwards. It can be fished from the bank in some places, but there are soft patches which are unfishable and bushes are a problem as well. The season runs from 15 February to 10 October.

LOUGH KEERAN   F 97 14

Permission: Not usually required

Take the forest road west off the L136 Castlebar–Bellacorick road at Fergus's Shop, Corcullin. Keeran is to the south of this road. After you have travelled about 2½ miles you can park on the roadside and walk 200 yards approximately to the water's edge. This is a lough of about 10 acres and holds lovely trout, but they are not as plentiful as one would wish. The average is ¾ lb and fish to 1½ lb have been taken. April is definitely the best month to fish it and the Greenwell's Spider, Iron Blue Dun and Pheasant Tail, sizes 12 and 14, are as good as any fly you could try. The north shore is probably most productive and there is a nice gravel shoreline to the north and north-east. There is no boat either on this lough or any of the others in this area, but don't worry, you will catch as many from the shore. The season is from 1 February to 30 September.

LOUGH DOO   F 97 13

Permission: Not usually required

Lough Doo lies to the south of the same forest road as Lough

Keeran (above), and the season is the same. Park on the roadside and be prepared for a half-hour's hard walking over rough ground, ploughed for planting. It is a shallow lough, holding trout averaging ½ lb but with some to ¾ lb. It can fish well from April for the fish are very free-rising. The Greenwell's Glory, Greenwell's Spider, Iron Blue Dun, Black Pennell and Sooty Olive are firm favourites and the west and south banks are the preferred fishing areas. The banks are level and easy to walk. This is one lough that is well worth the trouble it takes to get there. The trout may not be big, but they are prepared to have a go and a dull, showery day is what is required to get them in a taking mood.

LOUGH GALL   F 97 14

Permission: (west side) J. R. B. Hewat, Glenalt Syndicate, Rathmichael Lodge, Shankill, Co. Dublin.
(Permission is not required for the east side.)

Take the forest road west off the L136 Castlebar–Bellacorick road at Fergus's Shop, Corcullin. Lough Gall is to the north of this forest road and over 2½ miles from the main road. Parking space is good, and the lough is only 20 yards from the roadside. This lough holds really good-quality trout averaging 1 lb. Some are up to 2½ lb, but do not be too disappointed if you have a blank day. These fish do not give themselves up easily. The flies to take along in fairly small sizes are Sooty Olive, Golden Olive, Black Pennell, Watson's Fancy, Invicta, and Mallard and Claret. The east shore gives the best fishing, so you do not really have to go looking for permission. It has a gradual sloping shore with a good bottom and is safe for wading. Just hope that there is a soft breeze to break the surface of the water when you get there. The season is from 1 February to 30 September.

LOUGH NABROCK   F 96 13

Permission: Not usually required

Take the forest road west off the L136 Castlebar–Bellacorick road and proceed a couple of hundred yards further than for Lough Gall (above) until you come to a stream. This lough is only about a 10-minute walk south following the stream and the ground is level. Remember to bear right where the two streams meet or you might end up walking to Lough Doo. This lough holds small brown trout – about 3 to the pound – and some sea trout late in the season. A good brown trout will weigh ½ lb, but the sea trout run to 3 lb though they are very scarce. Even though there appear to be thousands of small brownies about, they are quite shy and a light leader is essential. This is a lough that can be fished at any time. April is a particularly good month but any dull day can produce a few fish. It gets a very heavy fall of reed smut in June and good sport can be enjoyed with a very small black dry fly. Otherwise, the flies to bring are Olives, Iron Blue Dun, Greenwell's Spider, Black Pennell and Butcher in sizes 12 and 14. The mouth of the outflowing stream, at the north end, is a very good taking place. The bank is easy to walk and the shoreline is gently shelving and soft for wading. The season runs from 1 February to 30 September.

LOUGH NAMBROCK   F 95 12
Permission: Not usually required

Take the forest road west off the L136 Castlebar–Bellacorick road at Fergus's Shop, Corcullin, and park by the roadside overlooking the lough. The parking space is over 4 miles from where you turn off the main road and the lough lies to the east beneath you. It is about a 10-minute walk and you must climb across the forestry fence. Keep to the high ridge where the bog is firm and in that way you can avoid the swamp that is on either side. This lough can fish well at any time from April to October, especially in the evenings. The trout are small – about 3 to the pound, with the odd fish to

8   *Lough Cullin – from Pontoon Bridge*

¾ lb. They are very silvery, unlike mountain lough trout, and jump like fresh-run sea trout when hooked. The north end of the lough appears to produce better-quality fish. Fishing here is always better on a wet day with a nice wind. This is a lough of about 20 acres. It is deep close in to the bank and the shoreline is very rocky – so be careful. The season is from 15 February to 10 October.

LOUGH BRACK   F 96 12

Permission: Not usually required

Lough Brack means 'the trout lough' and this 15-acre water is most appropriately named. It holds the best stock of good trout in this whole area. To get there, take the forest road from Fergus's Shop at Corcullin on the L136 Castlebar–Bellacorick road and proceed on past where you park for Lough Nambrock (above) right to the end of the road. You must then be prepared to walk a further ¾ mile across soft bog in a south-easterly direction. This is a lough that can produce good sport at any time from April to October (the season is from 15 February to 10 October). The average weight of trout in Brack is 1½ lb and fish of 2–3 lb are taken every season. One superb catch taken recently was 6 trout weighing 9½ lb. But they don't give themselves up easily. They can be difficult to rise at times even though you may see the odd splash in the distance. Flies to take with you are the Green Olive, Sooty Olive, Dunkeld, Iron Blue Dun, Greenwell's Glory, Green Peter and a couple of damsel nymph imitations. This water has a very notable hatch of damsel fly and the trout prey heavily on the nymphs. There is a good solid gravel bank on the north and east side but the south-west corner is the favourite fishing spot. The water is deep close in to the bank and for that reason there is no need to wade. This can be a great lough and well worth the journey.

SCARDAUN LOUGH (White Lough)   F 91 11
BLACK LOUGH   F 91 11

Permission:

Francis T. Chambers, Rock House, Ballycroy, Co. Mayo (both loughs);
J. R. B. Hewat, Glenalt Syndicate, Rathmichael Lodge, Shankill, Co. Dublin (for Black Lough)

These two loughs lie at 900 feet in the Nephin Beg range of mountains and to the north-north-west of Nephin Beg peak (2,065 feet) itself. The loughs are joined by a short stream. They can be approached from the L136 Castlebar–Bellacorick road by turning off the main road westwards at Fergus's Shop, Corcullin, and following the forest road. Alternatively, they may be approached by turning north-west up a forest road off the mountain road that runs from Srahmore to join the L136 at Keenagh. Either way, there is a 2-mile walk up the mountain from the end of the forest road. The trout in Scardaun average just under ½ lb, with some to ¾ lb. They are very free-rising and the fishing can be great fun in a north wind in April. Favourite fishing areas are on the south-east, east and north-east shores, but really the fishing can be good all round. It is a shallow lough of about 20 acres and the banks shelve off very gradually, so that deep wading is possible. The lough has a big corixa population and reed smut are abundant, particularly in June. Other flies worth having are a Greenwell's Glory, Iron Blue Dun, Connemara Black, Mallard and Claret and Butcher, all size 12 or 14. On a good breezy day – and there is always a breeze up there – you could go up to a size 10. Apart from the fishing, the views are magnificent, looking west towards Achill and the Atlantic and north-east towards Ballina and Killala Bay on a clear day.

To get to the Black Lough, follow the same directions as for Scardaun. In fact, the Black Lough is the first lough to be met on the way. It is about 10 acres and the average size of the trout bigger – 10 oz approximately – with fish to about 1½ lb. It fishes well from April onwards and has sedges, black gnat and water boatmen (corixas). The trout are free-rising, and the surface is continually broken because there is always a breeze up here. In fact, there can be far too much sometimes and it is not the place to be on a wild windy day. The shoreline is rocky and easy to walk and it is deep quite close in. The season runs from 15 February to 12 October and only the artificial fly is permitted – a statutory regulation. There are few fisheries so remote and peaceful and with such a magnificent view. Well worth the trouble it takes to get there.

CORSLIEVE LOUGH (Corranabinna Lough)   F 92 12

Permission: J. R. B. Hewat, Glenalt Syndicate, Rathmichael Lodge, Shankill, Co. Dublin.

This lough is approached by the same tortuous route as for Scardaun and the Black Lough. Then follow the stream for about a mile up the mountain from the Black Lough. It is only 4 acres, but the trout average 1½ lb and the heaviest trout recorded from it weighed 5½ lb. It has a very large corixa population and all the standard lake flies work here. Don't be disappointed if you fail to rise a fish to the flies – it is also one of those loughs worth trying a

Longford
Bay
Patrick's
Point
Crossmolina Boat
House
Pump
Houses
Gortnorabbey
Corrigeen
Longford
Island
Cloonaghmore
Point
Black
Rocks
Enniscoe
Shallow
Inishlee
Island
Shallow
Castle
Island
Juroge
Annagh
Island
Bushy Point Roe
Island
Woodford
Shallows
Bog
Bay
Cragh
Island
Annaghroe
Errew
Point
Shallow
Rinivilla
Island
Castlehill
Errew
Fir Trees
Point
Chain
Island
Sandy Bay
River
Grave
Yard
Phuilawokouse
Bay
Brackwanshagh
Lahardaun
Cuilkillew
Victoria
Bay
Cormorant
Rocks
Rinagah
Poteen Island
Knockmore
Bay
Massbrook
Point
Illannaglashy
Island
Coleman's
Shallows
School
House
Bay
Massbrook
Bay
Bilberry
Island
Six Arch
Bridge Bay
Terry
baun
Pontoon
Bridge
Gillaroo
Bay
High
Island
Drummun
Pontoon
Corlummin
Lough Cullin
Bunduvowen

Cloghans Bay
Cloghans

Castlehill Bay

Rinakilleen

0   1 Mile

22   *Lough Conn and Lough Cullin*

spinner on. The banks are extremely dangerous and the west side is the best and safest, even though the best trout are reported to be taken off the south bank. It fishes from April onwards (the season is from 15 February to 12 October). This lough lies in a valley on Corslieve Mountain 1,100 feet up. A south or south-west wind suits it best. It is one of the most fishable, scenic and remote loughs in Co. Mayo, if not in all Ireland. It is not for the faint-hearted. Those who have caught trout there can rightly boast that they have achieved an unusual and wonderful feat in remote and lovely surroundings.

LOUGH NALAGHAN   F 98 10
Permission: Not usually required

To get to this lough, look for the mountain road that runs from the L136 Castlebar–Bellacorick road at Kennagh to Srahmore and on to Lough Feeagh. Turn off this road up a forest road about a mile south of Bunaveela Lough and follow the forest road for over 3 miles. Park by the roadside and walk due east for twenty minutes, across level bog. This lough holds good trout. They are not free-rising but they average ¾ lb and some run as big as 2 lb. It can fish well at any time and the banks are good all round. All the usual traditional flies work and this lough is well worth spinning if the flies fail to produce a fish. The season is from 15 February to 10 October.

CARROWMORE LAKE   F 83 24
Permission: Seamus Henry, Bangor, Co. Mayo.
Tel: (097) 83549

Carrowmore Lake lies 2 miles north-west of Bangor in Co. Mayo. The slopes of Knocknascollop rise up along the west shore. The lake is over 4 miles long and nearly 3 miles at its widest part, though it narrows to ½ a mile at one point. It holds spring salmon from opening day (1 February) and sea trout from late June, and it has a resident stock of brown trout with some good ones among them. The predominant angling quarry – at the height of the season from July onwards – is the sea trout. Favourite fishing areas are around Herrity's Island on the south side, around Derreen's Island on the north-west side, all along the north shore and at the mouth of the Glencullin River to the east. Best conditions are a soft wind from the south-west. All the usual traditional fly patterns work, as does dapping an artificial (only the artificial fly is permitted). This

9 *A shining Spring Salmon from Lough Beltra*

lake is shallow all over and boats should take great care of rocks submerged just under the surface. There are two boats for hire from Seamus Henry, but on a lake this size the angler would be well advised to take along his own outboard. The season for trout, sea trout and salmon is from 1 February to 30 September.

LOUGH NAMACKAN   F 85 28

Permission: Not usually required

This small brown-trout lough lies to the north-west of Bangor and about halfway between the Glencullin Road and Carrowmore Lake. It is about a ¾-mile walk across the bog from the roadside. It holds a small stock of brown trout, averaging about 1 lb. There are, however, trout up to 2½ lb in it. It is a deep lough and the fish are dour, so do not be surprised if you draw a blank. It is bank fishing only and the banks are good all round. The season runs from 1 February to 30 September.

LOUGH DAHYBAUN   F 99 19

Permission: Alpine Hotel, Inniscrone, Co. Sligo.
Tel: (096) 36144

This is a large lough off the N59 Crossmolina–Bangor road about 10 miles from Crossmolina. There is a lay-by for parking and the water is 500 yards away. It has a natural stock of small brown trout with some up to 2 lb, but it is stocked with rainbow trout, some of them quite large. There are no boats available, but the banks are good and wading is possible. In fact, the east side is so shallow that it is possible to wade to the island sometimes. The best fishing appears to be along by the south-east corner of the lough. The fish are definitely big here but it can be slow and dour as well. The season is from 1 February to 30 September.

LOUGHANILLAUN   F 84 03

Permission: Francis T. Chambers, Rock House, Ballycroy P.O., Co. Mayo.
Tel: (098) 49137

This tiny lough lies 1¾ miles to the east of the N59 Mulrany–Ballycroy road. Take the forest road east from Bellaveeny Bridge and this will bring you within 200 yards of the lough. Loughanillaun has a stock of small brown trout and once produced a fish of 5 lb. It has a firm, stony shore and is reported to rise and fall with the tide some 2 miles away.

LOUGH BELLAGARVAUN   F 85 07

Permission: Francis T. Chambers, Rock House, Ballycroy P.O.,
Co. Mayo.
Tel: (098) 49137

Take the Bellagarvann road north from Bellavenny Bridge on the
N59 Mulrany–Ballycroy road. This lough is to the north of the
roadway 3 miles from the bridge. It holds small brown trout only
and fishes best in the evenings in April and May. The trout are
small and very dour. The north side is sandy; you can wade out to
the small island and fish the centre of the lake.

LOUGH GALL   F 84 08

Permission:
Francis T. Chambers, Rock House, Ballycroy P.O., Co. Mayo.
Tel: (098) 49137;
Craigie Bros, Sheean Lodge, Ballycroy, Co. Mayo.

Take the road from Ballycroy – on the N59 – to Sheean Lodge and
turn right to Pat Welsh's house. It is about a 500-yard walk from
there to the lough. This is a water of 20 acres, shallow, with a
gravel shoreline. It fishes all round but the south side is best. The
trout are scarce and average about ½ lb, but it has been known to
produce a few trout to 4 lb. If standard patterns fail, try a Muddler
Minnow or a Green Peter at dusk. The season is from 15 February
to 12 October.

LOUGH GALL   L 99 80

Permission: Francis T. Chambers, Rock House, Ballycroy P.O.,
Co. Mayo.
Tel: (098) 49137

This is a lovely lough lying to the east of the L141 Mulrany–Achill
road. You can drive all around it on the bog road. It holds trout to
about 1 lb and they can be very dour. Lough Gall is something of
an enigma, though, because a few years ago it produced 4 trout all
over 3 lb in a 20-minute spell of magic. It is just possible that sea
trout run into it as well. It fishes best on a dull day and in summer
tends to weed up. Season: 15 February to 12 October.

LOUGH GALL   L 77 98

Permission: Francis T. Chambers, Rock House, Ballycroy P.O.,
Co. Mayo.
Tel: (098) 49137

This Lough Gall lies to the east of Belfarsad on Corraun Peninsula on the way to Achill Island. It is a stiff walk of over a mile up the hill. It holds thousands of small brown trout – 4 to the pound – and an occasional sea trout. It can give tremendous sport sometimes when conditions are right. Standard wet fly patterns work well and you could try a Muddler or a Green Peter in the evening. Be careful, though; the banks are soft and boggy. The season runs from 15 February to 12 October.

LOUGHAUN   L 75 97
Permission: Not usually required

The local name for this lough is Loughauna. The bog road east from Belfarsad on Corraun will take you within 300 yards of it. Loughaun holds a big stock of small free-rising brown trout averaging 4 to the pound. It is set in a very scenic location looking out over Achill Island. Be warned: the midges bite fiercely here on a calm day. The season is from 15 February to 12 October.

LOUGH CULLYDOO   L 77 96
Permission: Not usually required

Lough Cullydoo and the lough to the north-west of it, which is nameless, are reached by the same road as Loughaun. Start from Belfarsad and there is a walk across the bog of over a mile. Both loughs hold big stocks of small but very free-rising brown trout. Cullydoo lies in a deep valley and it is sometimes difficult to get a wind on it. Season: 15 February to 12 October.

KEEL LOUGH   F 64 04
Permission: Roger Gallagher, Hon. Secretary, Achill Sporting Club, Valley House, Achill Island, Co. Mayo.
Tel: (098) 47204

Keel Lough is a big, shallow lough to the north of the L141 on Achill Island. It gets a good run of sea trout from late June, but these fish cannot get in before a big flood comes to open up the channel at the mouth of the outflowing river. This channel is blocked every winter with sand and gravel by the rollers from the Atlantic. The sea trout average ¾ lb but there are plenty of fish in the 2-lb and 3-lb class. The small trout are free-rising in a ripple, but it takes a big wave to get the big ones to move. Favourite fly patterns are Bibio, Watson's Fancy, Black Pennell, Teal and Green and Butcher. There is sometimes a boat for hire if arrangements are made in advance. The east side can be fished from the shore or by wading, but this can be difficult as you are most likely to be casting into the teeth of a stiff breeze. Spinning from the beach on the big lough down the road – the Atlantic Ocean – can often produce a few sea trout and the former Irish record sea trout was caught off a beach on Achill Island.

LOUGH NAMBRACK   F 70 08

Permission: Roger Gallagher, Hon. Secretary, Achill Sporting Club, Valley House, Achill Island, Co. Mayo.
Tel: (098) 47204

Lough Nambrack lies to the north-east on Achill Island and a small road runs close up to the eastern shore. It holds a big stock of brown trout averaging slightly under ½ lb with some fish to 1½ lb. Fly fishing only is allowed and these free-rising trout can be taken on Teal and Green, Peter Ross, Black Pennell and Butcher. The banks are soft on the east side but the north bank is good and firm.

LOUGH GALL   F 70 08

Permission: Roger Gallagher, Hon. Secretary, Achill Sporting Club, Valley House, Achill Island.
Tel: (098) 47204

Lough Gall is another small lough close to the north-east corner of Achill Island and it has a good stock of some of the finest brown trout that you would care to catch anywhere. It fishes well from April through to September and the trout take best on a dull evening. The average size is ¾ lb and fish to 4 lb have been taken in the past. It is a fairly shallow lough and the favourite fishing areas are along the south and east banks.

LOUGH DOO   F 71 09
SRUHILL LOUGH   F 71 08
LOUGH ACORRYMORE   F 57 05

Permission: Roger Gallagher, Hon. Secretary, Achill Sporting Club, Valley House, Achill Island.
Tel: (098) 47204

Lough Doo has no angling significance, while Sruhill is almost as bad. It is very brackish and only holds very occasional sea trout. Acorrymore, high up on the mountain to the west of Achill, is the

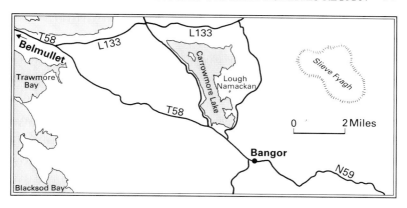

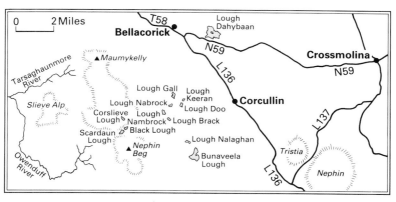

23   N.W. Mayo

water supply for the island, and holds a big stock of small trout. There is a road all the way up and the view is magnificent.

LOUGH FADDA   L 94 96

Permission: Riparian owners

This small lough lies to the north of the N59 Newport–Mulrany road. Turn off up a narrow road 1¼ miles west of Burrishoole Bridge. The lough is over a mile from the main road and difficult to reach. It holds a stock of brown trout averaging ½ lb.

CARROWBEG LOUGH   L 91 95

Permission: Not usually required

This lough lies to the south of the N59 Newport–Mulrany road. It
is about 500 yards downstream from Carrowsallagh Bridge. It has
a resident stock of brown trout which are small and it also gets a
run of sea trout and a few salmon. It fishes best in September and
has produced sea trout up to 5 lb. The south bank is overgrown
with reeds but fishing is possible off the north bank. This is a lovely

10   *Netting a salmon – Lough Furnace (Central Fisheries Board)*

little lough with good possibilities for both sea trout and salmon. Black Pennell, Bibio, Butcher, Bloody Butcher, Green Peter, Delphi and Connemara Black in sizes 8 and 10 are all worth a try. Season: 15 February to 12 October.

LOUGH FURNACE   L 96 96

Permission: The Manager, The Salmon Research Trust, Newport, Co. Mayo.
Tel: (098) 41107/41171

Lough Furnace lies about 2½ miles north-west of Newport village and is the lower lough on the famous Burrishoole salmon and sea-trout fishery. It is well signposted. The season opens on the 10 June and runs to 30 September for salmon, sea trout and brown trout. It is a tidal lough and the water can become quite brackish after a prolonged spell of dry weather. Artificial fly and dapping are the only angling methods allowed. This lough gets a good run of grilse and sea trout and the fishing can be good at any time from June to September. Salmon up to 12 lb have been taken in recent years. The average weight of the sea trout is 1 lb and the best fish in the last five years weighed 7 lb 2 oz. It was on this lough that I took my first salmon from a boat – on a Kenyaman (size 8) on the point as we drifted over the Carrigeen on a lovely September afternoon. Blacksod Bay, the Yellow River mouth and the Black Stone are good areas for sea trout, while there is always sure to be a salmon lying in Fahy's Bay, the Carrigeen, Duffy's Point, the Long Shore, the mouth of the Mill Race and the Salmon Leap. It was on this lough that the Revd Canon P. J. Gargan, the Cavan priest and well-known international fly fisherman, first popularized the Green Peter as a fly for salmon. Fly patterns worth bringing along are Green Peter, Daddy, Bibio, Black Pennell, Fiery Brown, Bumble patterns, Delphi, Camasunary Killer, Silver Doctor and Butcher – size 8 for salmon and size 10 and 12 for sea trout. There are boats and outboards for hire and it is one of the few fisheries that can provide resident boatmen if required. Bank fishing is not allowed. Furnace is a lovely lough, with shallow bays that can turn up either a sea trout or a salmon, and there is always somewhere to fish, no matter what point the wind is from.

LOUGH FEEAGH   L 96 98

Permission: The Manager, Salmon Research Trust, Newport, Co. Mayo.
Tel: (098) 41107/41171

Lough Feeagh lies about 4½ miles north-west of Newport and is the upper lough on the Borrishoole fishery. It is 2½ miles long and just over ½ mile wide and lies in a deep valley in the Nephin Beg range with Bengorm rising up to the west and Buckoogh to the east. It is noted primarily as a salmon fishery though it holds good sea trout and the brown trout run to about 1½ lb. The fishing does not really start until about 10 June when the first runs of grilse come in. (The official season is from 1 February to 30 September for salmon; from 1 February to 12 October for sea trout; and from 15 February to 12 October for brown trout. Artificial fly only. The Salmon Research Trust has a fish pass and counter and can tell exactly how many fish have passed up into the lough. Lough Feeagh is at its liveliest for salmon in June and July after a fresh run of fish. They tend to lie around the mouths of the inflowing rivers – particularly the Black River – and it is nothing to rise maybe a dozen fish in a day. Mind you, not many of them take the fly. They seem to be more interested in playing with it. It will always be one of my favourite loughs, and why not? It once turned up 5 salmon for me on an August afternoon – all on a Green Peter. The most useful fly patterns are Green Peter, Daddy, Bibio – which, incidentally, is reported to have been invented by Major Roberts for this fishery – Black Pennell, Fiery Brown, Kenyaman, Delphi, Thunder and Lightning and Watson's Fancy. There are five boats and outboards for hire and it is also possible to book a boatman whose knowledge of the drifts is really invaluable for the beginner on the lough. The best wind is a south wind, though there will always be fishing to be had by those who know the lough, no matter where the wind blows from. Maps indicating the fishing areas are provided. The best of the salmon fishing is on the east shore from Welsh's Point northwards past the mouth of the Black River and on the west shore from the Turf Banks Point past the mouth of the Glenamong River. The southern end of the lough and Schoolhouse Bay can provide lively sea-trout fishing. This is a lough that can cast a spell on you from the moment it comes into your view as you drive north along the Srahmore road.

BUNAVELLA LOUGH   F 98 09

Permission: The Manager, Salmon Research Trust, Newport, Co. Mayo.
Tel: (098) 41107/41171

Bunavella Lough lies high and remote in the Nephin Beg range and can be approached from Keenagh (4 miles) off the L136 Castlebar–

Bellacorick road or from Newport in the south (10 miles) via Srahmore village. It holds a great stock of small free-rising brown trout and a ½-lb fish would be a good one. It also has sea trout from August and the occasional salmon is taken in August and September because it is part of the headwaters of the Black River on the Burrishoole system. The best of the trout fishing is along the point on the east shore and along the north-west shore. Useful patterns are Greenwell's Glory, Greenwell's Spider, Iron Blue Dun, Connemara Black (all in sizes 12 and 14) and the standard lough patterns. This is a very scenic lough, remote and peaceful, where your fishing will be mainly for small brownies, but the setting is just beautiful on a warm spring day. Seasons as for Lough Feeagh, above.

DERRINTAGGART LOUGH L 98 95
Permission: Geoffrey Gibbons, Faraleens, Newport, Co. Mayo.

This small lough lies to the east of the Newport–Srahmore road on the way to the Salmon Research Trust. It is only a short distance from the road and holds a big stock of small brown trout – 4 or 5 to the pound. It can also hold very occasional sea trout late in the season (15 February to 12 October).

COSTELLO'S LOUGHS L 98 94
Permission: Not usually required

These small loughs lie to the north of the T71 Newport–Mulrany road about ¾ mile from Newport. The lower lough has some good brown trout to 1½ lb and fishes best in July and August. Standard lough fly patterns. Season: 15 February to 12 October.

BROAD LOUGH L 99 92
Permission: Tom Gallagher, Liss, Newport, Co. Mayo.

Broad Lough lies to the east of the N59 Newport–Westport road just over a mile from Newport. It has a good stock of small brown trout at an average weight of 3 to the pound. Everyone who has ever caught one has remarked on their large fins and great fighting qualities. Some of them run to ¾ lb. The trout are free-rising and take best in April and May. This lough has an outlet to the sea and also gets a few sea trout. Unfortunately, it is a difficult lough to fish, with soft margins and long reeds by the shore, and it is one lough that could do with some development because fishing there

11   *Drumgoney Lough or 'The Leg of Mutton Lake'*

can be great fun. The season for brown trout is from 15 February to 12 October; for sea trout, from 1 February to 12 October.

DRUMGONEY LOUGH   M 02 92

Permission: Not usually required

Drumgoney Lough is known locally as the Leg of Mutton Lake and if you stop to admire it in the valley to the south of the L138 Newport–Castlebar road it is easy to see why it got its name. It holds a big stock of small brown trout, 4 or 5 to the pound, and a ½-lb fish, not to mention a ¾-lb one, is unusual. It is at its most lively in April and May, when small standard lough fly patterns work well. The Kelly homestead, the ancestral home of the late Princess Grace of Monaco, is by its shore. Fishing opens on 20 March and closes on 30 September.

GIBSON'S LOUGH   M 07 92

Permission: Not usually required

Gibson's Lough lies to the east of the L136 Castlebar–Belmullet road about 5 miles north-west of Castlebar. Access is along the left bank of the outflowing stream, and the best fishing is around the mouth of the inflowing stream further east. Butchers and Connemara Blacks in size 12 are about all the flies one requires. The lough holds brown trout and occasionally gets sea trout in high water. A west wind is best and the brownies come 3 to the pound. It can fish from April onwards, but September is often the best month (the season is from 20 March to 30 September). The banks are very soft and dangerous, and beware of wading on the delta at the inflow. But it is a great place to fish when there is a coloured flood coming down the stream.

CASHEL LOUGH   M 07 93
Permission: Not usually required

Access to this lough is gained by a small tarred road off the L136 north of Gibson's Lough. The trout here are on the small side – about 3 to the pound – except for the occasional sea trout that makes its way up in high water. Nevertheless, it does produce the odd brownie up to 1¼ lb. The season is from 20 March to 30 September, and July is the best time to fish here. Unfortunately, the banks are very overgrown with tall reeds. In fact, the only place where it is possible to fish with any comfort and ease is off the black oak tree stumps on the east side. Standard patterns and in particular sedge patterns in small sizes work well.

LOUGH SALLAGHER   M 10 93
Permission: Not usually required

This lough lies about ¼ mile to the south of the back road (Rathbawn road) from Glenisland to Castlebar. Turn down off the road approximately 2 miles from Glenisland where a small stream flows under the road, then walk the 440 yards or so across the bog. It holds small brown trout – 4 to a pound – and a ½-lb fish is about as good as you will get. They can be free-rising sometimes and June–July is the best time to go after them. It can be fished on the north-east side or from the tree stumps on the south-east side. Season: 20 March to 30 September.

LOUGH BEN   M 10 94
Permission: Not usually required

Take the back road from Castlebar to Glenisland (Rathbawn road) and turn north for the booster station. Park at the lay-by a quarter of a mile up the road and the lough is only 20 yards away over to your right. Make sure you have some small Hare's Ears, Mallard and Clarets and Connemara Blacks in your fly box. This is the best lough in this whole area for the average size of the trout. They are a

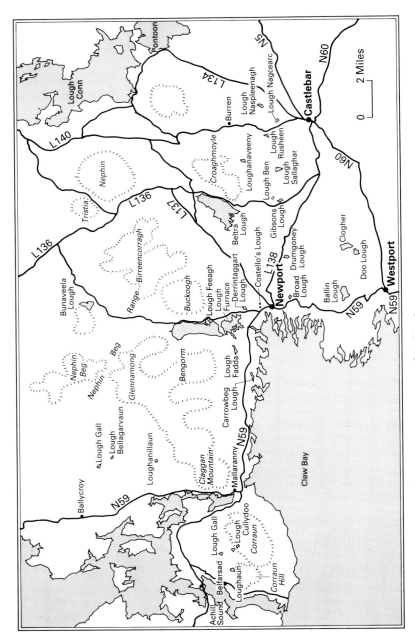

24 *North Mayo*

good ½ lb each and the best will turn the scales at 1½ lb. Mind you, for their respectable size they are also obligingly free-rising, especially if your visit is in May or June. This is a deep lake and the available food store must be good because a lot of the trout suffer from tapeworm. The banks are fairly good, but not ideal, and some anglers prefer to fish the north shore. This is a grand spot to spend an evening or even an afternoon, if you can drag yourself away from some of the more attractive 'big game' fishing that lies further to the west. The season is from 20 March to 30 September.

BALLIN LOUGH L 98 87

Permission: The Manager, Salmon Research Trust, Newport, Co. Mayo.
Tel: (098) 41107/41171

This is an unusual lough for this part of the country, in that it is stocked with rainbow trout as well as brown trout. It lies 300 yards to the east of the N59 about 2 miles north-west of Westport. The season runs from 1 May to 30 September and fly fishing only is allowed. The lough is 54 acres in area and mainly shallow but anglers are strongly advised to avoid wading. The bottom may look solid but it is only a shell of marl, and if you went through that you could be in great difficulties indeed. The trout are relatively free-rising and they are attracted to the surface by the sparse hatch of olives and sedges. May and June are probably the best months but it is worth a go at any time. Some of the trout overwinter and can weigh up to 3 lb. There are no boats available and the best areas to try are the south-west corner and all along the south shore. Once again, be careful as you walk along the bank.

LOUGHANAVEENY M 10 95

Permission: Not usually required

To get to this excellent little lough, take the back road (Rathbawn road) from Castlebar to Glenisland and turn off north for the booster station about 4 miles from Castlebar. Leave the car at the forestry gate and walk for ¾ mile east to the lough. Make sure you have a Mallard and Claret, a Green Peter and a Butcher in your fly box. You might be in for a very pleasant surprise because these are as strong-fighting brown trout as you are likely to meet anywhere and a ¾-pounder will strip line with the same dash and arrogance as a fresh-run grilse. They take well even in high summer – June, July and August – and the average size is around the ½-lb mark.

However, the ideal conditions are wet, wild and windy. There are very good hatches of sedge, some of which are quite large, which leads not a few anglers to think that they might be the real thing – Green Peters. Whatever they are, they are big and the trout love them. This is a remote and peaceful place. It is an easy lough to fish with good banks and no bankside reeds to contend with, and it can be fished all round. The walk may be a long one, and it does not get any shorter on the way back, but it can be well worth while. Season: 1 May to 30 September.

LOUGH RUSHEEN   M 13 93
Permission: Not usually required

Rusheen is a small hill lough about 2 miles north of Castlebar off the Burren road which branches left off the L134 Pontoon road outside the town. Take a small road to the left again and this takes you to the south end of the lough. It holds a small stock of brown trout that average about ½ lb. The season is from 15 February to 10 October.

LOUGH NA GCEARCH   M 14 93
Permission: Not usually required

One mile north of Castlebar, on the Burren road, take a small by-road to the right and Lough na gCearch – which, incidentally, means 'The Hen's Lough' – is about – ¼ mile further on and to the right by the roadside. The trout here are definitely of the gillaroo strain, which makes one wonder about the name of the lough. Irish folklore has it that gillaroo trout have a chicken's gizzard as the result of a saint changing a chicken into a trout one Friday back in the mists of antiquity. But back to the trout. Unfortunately, they are not very plentiful but the average size is good, being around 1 lb, and there are even some up to 3 lb in this little pond. Don't be surprised if you come away without rising a fish. Gillaroo trout are bottom feeders and can be notoriously dour. When you get one they are little jewels with big red spots and pink flesh. The banks are good and the lough can be fished from either side. Fishing opens on 15 February and closes on 10 October.

LOUGH NASPLEENAGH   M 15 94
Permission: Not usually required

Take the L134 Pontoon road from Castlebar and 2 miles from the

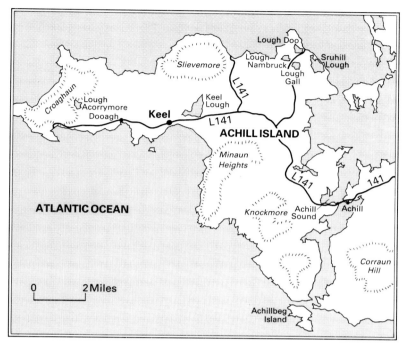

25   *Achill Island*

town take the forest road to the west up through the wood for about 1½ miles until you come to the shore of the lough. This lough has brown trout and fishes well in April, May and June. The trout are not really plentiful but the average size is good at ¾ lb. It is a deep lough and the shoreline is dangerous in places. There are only two fishable places – the north-east side by the road and the south-east corner. Useful fly patterns to try are Greenwell's Glory, Greenwell's Spider, Golden Olive, Butcher, Connemara Black and Mallard and Claret, sizes 12 and 14. Season: 15 February to 10 October.

LOUGH BELTRA   M 05 97

Permission: The Manager, Newport House, Newport, Co. Mayo.
Tel: (098) 41222, *Telex:* 33740;
The Fishery Manager, Glenisland Co-op, Castlebar, Co. Mayo.
Tel: (094) 21302

Lovely Lough Beltra! This is truly a lough for all seasons. From opening day on 20 March, with a biting black north wind blowing, until the season closes on the last day of September, with the heather turned purple and the leaves beginning to colour, few fisheries have greater potential than Beltra to quicken the pulse of the fly fisherman. It gets a run of spring salmon and they come to the fly from March until June. From June onwards, the grilse begin to appear and with them come the sea trout to keep the interest going for the rest of the season. This lough lies 5 miles north-east of Newport and 8 miles north-west of Castlebar. It is 2¼ miles long by a mile wide and an outboard motor is essential to get about. The lough is divided east and west between Glenisland Co-op and Newport House. Fly fishing is the rule and the favourite salmon patterns are Silver Badger, Silver Doctor, Black Doctor, Quack, Thunder and Lightning, Lemon and Grey, Red Shrimp and Hairy Mary – sizes 8 to 4. For sea trout, the Bibio, Bluebottle, Delphi, Green Peter, Daddy, Butcher, Connemara Black, Black Pennell and Watson's Fancy work well. The best salmon in recent years weighed 21 lb and was taken on a shrimp fly. The sea trout average about ¾ lb but fish of 4 and 5 lb are taken annually. The fish are generally free-rising and when conditions are right Beltra can produce periods of pure magic. The best of the spring salmon fishing is all along the east shore and from Clarke's Point north-wards by the mouth of the river on the west side. There are ten boats for hire, five on either side. Outboards may be booked in advance on the Glenisland side and outboards and boatmen are included in the charge for the fishing on the Newport House side. Two of the Newport House boats may also fish the east side. Early in the season, a slow-sinking or sink-tip line is preferred by some anglers and the rod should be powerful enough to control large fresh spring salmon. From June onwards, a floating line is in order and dapping can often bring up the best sea trout. There are seven islands, mostly off the south and south-west shores, and it is not really a dangerous water for the angler who is accustomed to fishing a large wild lough. Beltra is in a lovely setting, surrounded by mountains, rough pastures and small farms. It can make a lasting impression, whether your visit is on a cold spring day or a balmy summer afternoon, and there will be days when you will not have time to admire anything else but the fish.

CLOGHER LOUGH   M 03 97

Permission: Not usually required

Clogher lies approximately 3½ miles north-east of Westport. It is

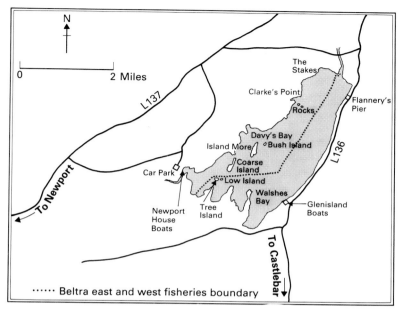

26   Lough Beltra

a fine lough, nearly a mile long and over 600 yards wide. It holds a
good stock of brown trout and the average size is a little over ½ lb
with some to 1½ lb. It is approached from the north and there is
a road so that you can bring the car down to the cemetery. It has a
good duckfly hatch in April and gets hatches of olives and sedges
later in the season. The brown trout are very free-rising and can be
fished from the shore. The bottom is soft in some places and great
care should be taken to avoid sinking in the soft marl. This is a nice
lough and the cemetery side is definitely the favourite with bank
anglers. There are a number of boats for hire and inquiries can be
made locally.

DOO LOUGH   M 02 86

Permission: Not usually required

This is a smaller lough to the south of Clogher Lough. Unfortunately, it is not possible to fish it from the bank because of high
reeds and soft margins. There is no boat for hire, but if you have a
small inflatable this is one lough where you can put it to good use.
It has plenty of nice trout around the 1-lb mark and you may even
be lucky to get one of 2 lb or better.

27　*The Western Fisheries Region*

5 Western Fisheries Region

The Western Fisheries Region extends from Pidgeon Point in Westport Bay to Hog's Head on the Co. Clare coast and stretches east to Ballyhaunis in the north and Loughrea in the south. Take a glance at a map of the region and you are immediately struck by the three great loughs of Corrib, Mask and Carra which practically divide it in two from top to bottom. These are the three magnificent free brown-trout fisheries, covering between them over 66,000 acres, that were lovingly cared for by the old Inland Fisheries Trust and are presently carefully managed by the Western Regional Fisheries Board. The angling tradition goes back into the mists of the past, but it is nice to know that the visiting angler can still enjoy fishing of a standard equal to any that has been recorded in earlier years. Indeed, last season I saw two anglers come ashore off Lough Mask with 22 trout up to 3½ lb – surely enough to satisfy the keenest angler! To the west of Corrib, Mask and Carra lies a veritable Mecca for the lough fisherman, with such a variety of brown-trout, sea-trout and salmon loughs to choose from that the prospective visitor to that area is often quite bewildered. Here we have the landscape dotted with the famous sea-trout and salmon fisheries of Connemara and south Mayo, nestling among bare mountain ridges and soft peat bogs that soak up the high rainfall and release it ever so slowly into the little spawning streams, keeping them and the loughs continually topped up. It is worth noting that T. C. Kingsmill Moore, author of that classic on Irish fishing *A Man May Fish*, spent much of his fishing holidays in this area enjoying the sea trout and salmon of Costello and Delphi and brown trout on Corrib. W. M. Thackeray was here too and in his travel log *An Irish Sketch Book* has this to say: 'O you who throw flies in English rivers and catch, at the expiation of a day's walking, casting and wading, two or three feeble little trout of two or three ounces in weight, how you would rejoice to have but one hour's sport at Derryclare or Ballynahinch, where you have but to cast and lo! a big trout springs to your fly!' The big trout still spring to the fly at Ballynahinch and a dozen may be your lot at the 'mouth of the lake' as you cast on a July evening towards the island prison of 'Humanity Dick'. Gowla, Invermore, Screeb and Costello are still passwords to good sea-trout fishing.

Angling Regulations and By-Laws
This Region is divided into three districts for administrative purposes.

The Ballinakill district covers the area from Westport to Clifden. The open season for salmon is from 1 February to 30 September, except for the Bunowen and Carrownisky systems, where the season opens on 1 April.

The open season for sea trout is 1 February to 12 October, except for the Bunowen and Carrownisky systems, where the season opens on 1 April.

The open season for brown trout is 15 February to 12 October, except for the Bunowen and Carrownisky systems, where it is from 1 February to 30 September.

The Connemara district covers the area from Clifden to, and including, the Costello sytem. The angling seasons are: salmon, 1 February to 30 September; sea trout, 1 February to 12 October; brown trout, 1 February to 12 October.

The Galway district extends from Ballynahown to Hags Head in Clare. The angling seasons are: salmon, 1 February to 12 October, except Corrib (1 February to 30 September); sea trout, 1 February to 12 October, except Corrib (1 February to 30 September); brown trout, 15 February to 12 October, except Lough Carra (1 March to 30 September), Loughs Corrib and Mask (15 February to 30 September) and Lough Rea (17 March to 15 September).

A by-law fixes the minimum size limit for salmon and trout at 12 inches for loughs Corrib, Mask and Carra. Another by-law prohibits, during the month of October, the use of any gaff or any lure other than artificial flies mounted on single hooks, in or on the banks of the River Ballynahinch and its loughs or in any boat on these waters.

MOUNTBROWN LOUGH   M 03 81

Permission: Not usually required

This delightful little lough lies approximately 2½ miles south-east of Westport and south of Mountbrown House. It can be approached off the L101 Westport–Ballinrobe road or off the N59 Westport–Leenane road via Aughagower. It holds a good stock of brown trout up to 1 lb and fishes best at dusk off the bank next to the road. Small wet flies like the Black Pennell, Mallard and Claret,

Connemara Black, Wickham's Fancy and Greenwell's Glory are all successful.

BOHEH LOUGHS   L 97 78

Permission: Mr John T. Gibbons, Hon. Secretary, Westport Anglers, Fair Green, Westport, Co. Mayo.

These two very small loughs lie to the west of the N59 Westport–Leenane road about 4 miles south of Westport. The brown trout are small and a half-pounder is a good fish. However, you may be in for a surprise from early in July, when a small run of sea trout gets through, so don't be alarmed by a much bigger swirl at your fly. Fly fishing is the more popular method and the brownies can be very free-rising. Spinning can also account for a few fish.

MOHER LOUGH   L 98 77

Permission: Mr John T. Gibbons, Hon. Secretary, Westport Anglers, Fair Green, Westport, Co. Mayo.

This lough easily catches the eye to the west of the N59 Westport–Leenane road about 5 miles from Westport. It holds a good stock of brown trout averaging ½ lb, with some up to 1½ lb. It gets a small run of sea trout from August. Fly fishing only is allowed and the two best flies are probably a Bibio and a Bloody Butcher, fished in a size to suit the conditions. The banks are soft and boggy and hard to fish. There are two row-boats for hire.

LOUGH NACORRA   L 91 77

Permission: Not usually required

This lough is known locally as the Bog Lough. It lies 1½ miles due south of Croagh Patrick and west of the N59 Westport–Leenane road. Take the by-road on the Leenane side of Knappagh and then a forest road. Follow this road westwards until you see the lough on your left down in the valley. It holds a huge stock of brown trout averaging ½ lb with the odd fish up to 1 lb. When they are in the mood, they can be very free-rising and it is one of those places where the beginner can get hooked on fishing. Nacorra has produced one of the biggest catches I have ever heard of – 112 trout to two rods in a day. The banks are fairly good, but take care just the same.

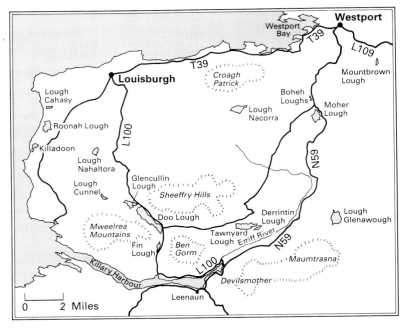

28   *S.W. Mayo, Delphi, Erriff*

LOUGH CAHASY   L 75 78

Permission: Not usually required

This small lough lies about a mile west of the Louisburgh–
Killadoon road. Turn off the main road 4 miles from Louisburgh at
the sign for Doughmakeon Beach and you will see the lough to
your right close to the beach. It holds plenty of small brown trout
with the odd one up to ¾ lb. The best fishing months are April,
May, June and September. The trout take a fly freely. It is bank
fishing only and this is best done from the south bank, as the rest of
the shoreline is very weedy.

ROONAH LOUGH   L 75 77

Permission: The Manager, Western Regional Fisheries Board, Weir
Lodge, Earl's Island, Galway.
Tel: (091) 65548

This tidal lough lies to the west of the Louisburgh–Killadoon road
about 4½ miles from Louisburgh. It gets a good run of salmon

from late June. In fact, it can hold a lot of salmon and has plenty of sea trout as well from mid-July. It is very shallow and fishes best after a flood has flushed out the salt water. Fly fishing and spinning can both be equally productive and useful fly patterns are Delphi, Silver Doctor, Bibio, Butcher, Black Pennell, Daddy and Camusunary Killer. Open season for salmon and sea trout is from 1 April to 30 September.

LOUGH NAHALTORA   L 79 74
Permission: (for part of the lough): The Manager, Western Regional Fisheries Board, Weir Lodge, Earl's Island, Galway.
Tel: (091) 65548

Turn west off the L100 Louisburgh–Delphi road 4½ miles south of Louisburgh and the lough is one mile along this by-road and to the south of it. Access is easy with the road running close to the waterside. Nahaltora holds brown trout and a few salmon, but it is for its sea trout that it is worth fishing. It holds a fair stock from late July and is well worth a try. It is by no means uncommon to take half a dozen nice fish for a day off the bank. This is a shallow lough with underwater bog deal and tree stumps everywhere. The banks are quite good. Try a Bibio, a Green Peter, a Delphi, a Daddy or a Watson's Fancy. The open season for both salmon and sea trout is from 1 April to 30 September.

12   *Finlough*

FINLOUGH   L 84 66

Permission: The Manager, Delphi Fishery, Leenane, Co. Galway.
Tel: (095) 42245

This small lough lies just west of the L100 Louisburgh–Leenane
road about 7 miles north-west of Leenane. It is the first lough on
the famous Delphi Fishery sytem of loughs and is quite small – only
about 800 yards by 400 yards. It is quite shallow and can get weedy
in summer. There are two boats available. This lough gets a run of
spring salmon and once produced 8 in one day to a single road. It
gets a small grilse run and a great run of good big sea trout from
early July. It can be fished all over and where the river runs in is a
favourite spot for a salmon – but you really need a boatman to hold
the boat in position to fish it properly. When the lough is calm in
summer, a Daddy or a Murrough fished dry can often pull up a
good trout. Otherwise, try big flies in spring for the salmon –
Silver Wilkinson, Silver Doctor, Black Doctor or Thunder and
Lightning. For the sea trout in summer it is hard to beat a fly named
after this fishery, the Delphi; also useful are Bibio, Watson's Fancy,
Daddy, Green Peter and Kingsmill. The Kingsmill fished small –
12 or even 14 – can make some fine catches.

DOO LOUGH   L 83 68

Permission: The Manager, Delphi Fishery, Leenane, Co. Galway.
Tel: (095) 42245

13   *Doo Lough*

This lough lies immediately north of Finlough to the west of the L101. It lies at the foot of the Sheeffry Hills to the east and the Mweelrea Mountains to the west. In fact, Mweelrea rises so steeply that it casts a shadow across the lough from early afternoon – something I found doesn't do the fishing any harm at all. The lough gets a run of spring salmon, some grilse and a good run of sea trout. Like Finlough, it was one of the fisheries on Kingsmill Moore's itinerary and he talks of sea trout of up to 10 lb being taken. It can still produce a memorable day's fishing and the 1985 season saw one bag of 40 sea trout to 5½ lb and a 12-lb salmon. The lough fishes best for spring salmon in March and April – the east shore along by the boat quay and up to Fisherman's Point is a favourite drift. The sea-trout fishing begins in earnest in July, though some really big fish come in from April. The whole southern part of the lough can yield a fish, even well out from the shore, and also the west shore from the 'Split Rock' right to the top as well as around the islands towards the road side. All the usual sea-trout flies work well, but I have a particular preference for the Delphi, the Daddy, Jacob's Ladder, Black Doctor and the Kingsmill. One day they want them small, the next day big – even on a size 6 hook! Because of its location deep among the mountains, Doo Lough can be treacherous in windy weather and it is well to get off it before the storm blows up to lift sheets of water and anything else in its way up into the grey sky.

GLENCULLIN L 82 69

Permission: The Manager, Delphi Fishery, Leenane, Co. Galway.
Tel: (095) 42245

This lough lies just north-west of Doo Lough and access is by a short walk across the bog to the south-east corner just above where the river flows out. It is here that the boats are kept. It is primarily a sea-trout fishery and on its day it can have few equals, but it also turns up the odd salmon every season. It doesn't really fish well until after the July floods and it is September when it comes into its best form. Fly fishing and dapping are equally effective and the trout can be taken all over, while the north-west corner is best for a salmon. It is a lough for a big sea trout and they have been taken up to 7 lb in recent years. The locals claim that it does not fish well in squally weather.

LOUGH CUNNELL L 80 70

Permission: The Manager, Delphi Fishery, Leenane, Co. Galway.
Tel: (095) 42245

This is the top lough on the Delphi system. It is best approached off the L100 Louisburgh–Delphi road; turn off at Cregganbaun as for Lough Nahaltora and take the forest road south. It holds a good stock of brown trout at about 3 to the pound, with the odd fish reaching ¾ lb.

TAWNYARD LOUGH   L 91 67

Permission: The Manager, Erriff Fishery, Aasleagh Lodge, Leenane, Co. Galway.
Tel: (095) 42252

This lough lies in a beautiful valley between the Sheeffry Hills to the north and Ben Gorm to the south. It is approached from the L100 Leenane–Westport road by taking the scenic road east at Doo Lough. Four and a quarter miles along that road you will see the lough on your right far below in the valley. Turn off at Joyce's farmhouse at the edge of the forest. Alternatively, it can be approached from the T71 Leenane–Westport road by turning off at the sign for Beat 5 on the Erriff River. There are three boats with outboards for hire and, due to its location, the lough fishes best in a west or east wind. It holds sea trout from early July and a few salmon. It can be a great lough on its day and has produced trout in

14   *Tawnyard Lough*

the past up to 9 lb. Sea trout can be caught all along the west end where the river flows in, but keep well out from the shore after first fishing close in. The north shore is also good down as far as the islands, then around the islands and the Captain's Bay on the south shore, which runs approximately halfway from the top of the lough down to the islands. The narrow part at the bottom can also produce a fish. The salmon lie close to the mouth of the inflowing river and along the north-west shore to the boat quay. Other lies are by the north shore at the big rock near the islands and on the opposite shore by the rocky ledges near the bottom of the Captain's Bay. All the usual sea-trout flies do well early in the season and it is well worth trying the dap in August and September. On a day when the trout are dour, relax and enjoy the magnificent view to the west as the clouds from the Atlantic roll in and the light changes continually.

DERRINTIN LOUGH   L 92 67
Permission: The Manager, Erriff Fishery, Aasleagh Lodge, Leenane, Co. Galway.
Tel: (095) 42252

This lovely secluded lough is approached off the N59 Leenane–Westport road. Turn west about 4 miles from Leenane at the sign for Beat 5 on the River Erriff. Cross the 'Broken Bridge', follow the forest road for a few hundred yards and you will see the lough on your left. There is one row-boat for hire. Bank fishing is permitted and the banks are reasonably good and easy to walk. The lough holds wild brown trout to about ¾ lb and it is stocked with rainbows and browns as an alternative fishery for the anglers on the Erriff when that river is out of condition. Rainbows that overwinter can reach 4 lb and a Greenwell's Glory fished wet or a dry sedge at dusk may tempt one of them. Local anglers swear by a Hare's Ear as the pattern most likely to take a good bag of wild brownies.

GLENAWOUGH LOUGH   L 99 68
Permission: The Manager, Erriff Fishery Aasleagh Lodge, Leenane, Co. Galway.
Tel: (095) 42252

This remote mountain lough lies between the Partry and Maumtrasna mountain ranges and is surrounded by steep slopes on three sides. It is best approached by turning off the N59 Leenane–Westport road at Srahlea Bridge and turning off that road again to the south heading in the direction of Erriff Wood. Ask permission to leave the car at McDonnell's farm, and then it is about a 20-minute walk up the hill. The lough holds small brown trout and char and is a pleasant and quiet place to spend a summer's evening, provided you go prepared for the midges.

LOUGH MUCK   L 77 63
LOUGH FEE   L 80 61
Permission:
Mr R. Willoughby, Salruck, Renvyle, Co. Galway;
Mr Owen King, Lettergesh PO, Renvyle, Co. Galway.
Tel: (095) 43414

These two loughs lie to the west of the N59 Leenane–Kylemore road. Turn off at the sign for Tullycross and the by-road runs along the side of both loughs. Muck is not really a big lough – about ¾ mile long and a few hundred yards wide – but Fee is nearly 4½ miles long and ½ mile wide. Together with the outflowing river, they make up the Culfin Fishery. They are set in a delightful valley running west almost to Little Killary Bay on the Atlantic. The loughs hold small brown trout and occasional salmon and, in recent seasons, have enjoyed a good run of sea trout. They fish from June and there is one boat available on each. Fly fishing is the usual method of fishing and while spinning is allowed it is not encouraged. There are two cottages convenient to the loughs and the fishing is let with the cottages. They are much in demand in July and August, but September and early October can often provide the best of the fishing.

LOC NA BRACK COACH   L 82 60
Permission: Not usually required

This is a small lough south of the T71 Leenane–Clifden road. It holds a good stock of brown trout of ½–¾ lb and fishes well from early April and right through the season. Local tradition has it that it was stocked with a strain of Scottish trout when the Clifden–Galway Railway line was being built. Fortunately, they are not blind – as the word 'coach' suggests. In fact it refers to the fact that they make poor eating because of the quality of the peat water. But they provide excellent sport.

LOUGH NACARRIGEEN   L 80 59
Permission: Not usually required

This little lough, which is about half a mile long, lies to the south of the N59 and directly opposite Creeragh Church. It is only a short walk as there is a bog road most of the way. It is on the headwaters of the Culfin system, but only holds brown trout. It is a peaty lough and the trout average about 10 oz, but fish to over 2 lb have been taken. Fishing is from the banks only and it can be fished almost all the way round, depending on the wind. Flies to use include a Butcher, Greenwell's Glory, Wickham's Fancy, Black Pennell, Mallard and Claret and a small Green Peter. This is a good little fishery and when the trout are on the take it can be remarkably lively and always turn up a good fish or two.

TULLY LOUGH   L 69 61
Permission: Inquire locally

This is quite a large lough with several islands and it lies between Tullycross and Renvyle, with roads on every side. It is a noted brown-trout fishery with the trout averaging ¾ lb and some up to 2½ lb recorded every season. Bank fishing can be arranged and there are two boats for hire. Best flies include Greenwell's Glory, Black Pennell, the Butchers, Mallard and Claret, Green Peter and Murrough. Fish rise all along the shores and by the islands and it is a very pleasant fishery with a good chance of a lively day's fishing when the trout are in the mood.

RENVYLE LOUGH   L 65 63
Permission: Renvyle Hotel, Renvyle, Co. Galway.

This lough is situated in the hotel grounds and holds a fair stock of free-rising brown trout averaging ½ lb. Fishing is available on a day ticket – free to hotel residents. There is a boat for hire. The lough gets a stocking of rainbow trout every season. Best flies include Black Pennell, Bibio, Silver Invicta, Butchers, Zulu and Dunkeld.

THE ABBEY LOUGH   L 75 58
Permission: Mrs W. Aspell, Kylemore, Co. Galway.
Tel: (095) 41145

This is a small lough off the N59 and overlooked by the magnificent Kylemore Abbey, with Doughruagh rising steeply to over 1,700 feet behind it. It is the first lough on the system and gets a run of spring salmon from April and a good run of salmon and sea trout from June. There is one boat for hire and day tickets are available.

POLLACAPPUL LOUGH   L 75 68

Permission:
Mrs W. Aspell, Kylemore, Co. Galway.
Tel: (095) 41145;
Mr John Naughton, Kylemore House, Co. Galway.
Tel: (095) 41143

This lough is to the south of the N59 Kylemore–Clifden road.
Most of it is owned by Kylemore Abbey and let by Mrs Aspell. It
gets a run of spring salmon, grilse and plenty of sea trout and fishes
best in a west or south-west wind. All the usual sea-trout flies work
well, and dapping is effective when conditions are right in August,
September and October. There is a boat for hire and a boatman can
sometimes be arranged if notice is given.

KYLEMORE LOUGH   L 77 68

Permission:
Mr John Naughton, Kylemore House, Kylemore, Co. Galway.
Tel: (095) 41143;
Mrs W. Aspell, Kylemore, Co. Galway.
Tel: (095) 41145

This is the largest of the Kylemore loughs and lies just south of
and parallel to the N59. With Benbaun Mountain to the south and
Doughruagh to the north, it only fishes well to the fly in a west or
east wind. It gets a fair run of spring salmon in March and April.
These fish tend to lie fairly close to the shore under Kylemore
House and all along the sandy beach in about 6 feet of water at the
east end. The sea trout and grilse run early in June and provide
splendid fishing when conditions permit, right through to the end
of the season. The grilse have much the same lies as the salmon but
in addition they tend to lie on a sand bar that runs up the middle of
the lough from the outflowing river at the west end for nearly half a
mile. The sea trout can be taken all along the shores and well out in
the middle on the Kylemore House (east) end. Kylemore Lough
gets a particularly good run of large trout with some to over 5 lb.
The grilse average 6 lb and salmon to 20 lb have been taken. The
fishery is fly only, but on occasions, in difficult weather conditions,
spinning is allowed. However, one of the greatest thrills on this
fishery is to hook a good-sized sea trout after dark on the fly in
August and September. Recommended salmon flies in sizes 4, 6
and 8 are Black Doctor, Silver Doctor, Silver Rat, Silver Badger,
Blue Charm and Hairy Mary. Trout flies in sizes 8 and 10 are
Green Peter, Murrough, Daddy, Watson's Fancy, Jacob's Ladder,
Butcher, Bibio and Connemara Black.

CLIFDEN ANGLERS' ASSOCIATION WATERS

Clifden Anglers' Association has fishing rights on many fisheries in the area. The majority of the loughs hold brown trout, but some have sea trout and occasional salmon. It is possible to get day tickets on all of them and boats may be hired on some at very reasonable rates. The Honorary Secretary is Mr Hugh Griffin, Dooneen, Clifden, Co. Galway, Tel: (095) 21342.

GARRAUNBAUN LOUGH   L 66 57

Permission: Inquire locally

Turn west off the T71 Clifden–Letterfrack road at Moyard and you will find the lough on the north side of this road and close by the roadside. It holds a good stock of brown trout averaging ½ lb, with some reaching the 1-lb mark. Bank fishing only is permitted, for which only the north shore is really suitable. An average catch is about 6 trout, but up to 12 have been taken at times. A small Butcher on the bob and a Black Pennell on the point should do nicely.

LOUGH TANNY   L 64 55

Permission: Mr Hugh Griffin, Hon. Secretary, Clifden Anglers' Association, Dooneen, Clifden, Co. Galway.
Tel: (095) 21342

This small lough lies to the east of the T71 Clifden–Letterfrack road just under 4 miles from Clifden. It holds a small stock of good trout up to 2½ lb but they are very hard to tempt and Tanny has a reputation for being dour. Try a Black Pennell and a Butcher – or even spinning – and be prepared for a long wait for a rise.

BALLYNAKILL LOUGH   L 64 58

Permission: Inquire of Mr Patrick O'Toole, Ballynakill, Co. Galway.

This lough lies to the south of the Letterfrack–Cleggan road and is nearly 1½ miles long by ½ mile wide. It holds brown trout only and has the reputation of being one of the best fisheries in the area. The trout average 1 lb, which is good by any standards, and some up to 3 lb have been reported. Bank fishing is possible from the south shore and there are boats for hire from Mr P. O'Toole, Ballynakill; Mr Graham Tullough, Moyard, and Mrs Cully, Moyard. Fly fishing and dapping are preferred and useful patterns

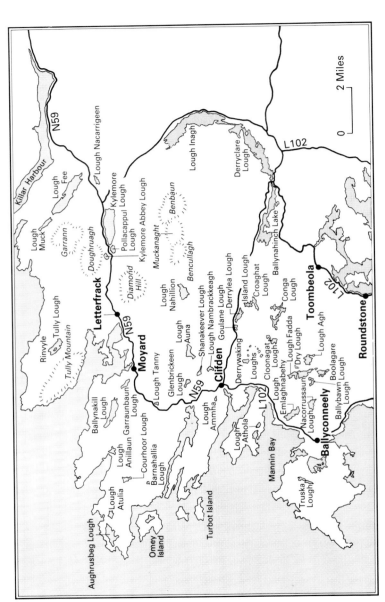

29   *The Clifden Loughs and North Connemara*

are Black Pennell, Watson's Fancy, Connemara Black, Invicta, Green Peter and Daddy.

LOUGH ANILLAUN   L 61 58

Permission: Mr Hugh Musgrave, Cleggan Farm, Cleggan, Co. Galway.

This small irregular-shaped lough with its bays and points and islands holds a fair stock of sea trout. It lies to the south of the Cleggan–Letterfrack road about a mile from Cleggan. Use standard lough fly patterns.

COURHOOR LOUGH   L 59 57

Permission: Mr Hugh Griffin, Hon. Secretary, Clifden Anglers' Association, Dooneen, Clifden, Co. Galway.
Tel: (095) 21342

This is a lovely little lough lying about 2 miles south of Cleggan. It holds a huge stock of small trout with quite a few up to ½ lb, though some have been taken up to 2 lb, and it holds some big sea trout too. Fishing is from the bank only and the north and east sides are easiest to fish. Favourite fly patterns are Invicta, Duckfly, Butcher, Daddy and Watson's Fancy.

LOUGH ATALIA   L 57 58

Permission: Mr Hubert Delap, Aughras, Claddaghduff, Co. Galway.

This small lough lies 2 miles west of Cleggan and is only a couple of hundred yards from the sea. It gets a fair run of sea trout and the usual sea trout patterns are all worth a try.

AUGHRASBEG LOUGH   L 56 58

Permission: Not usually required

Aughrasbeg is one of the most westerly loughs in Connemara, lying 3 miles west of Cleggan, and it is also one of the finest brown-trout loughs in that whole area. It fishes well from early April and can produce a fish at any time through the season, with May, August and September being the best months. It is never short of a breeze and a westerly or south-westerly is best. The fishing can be slow at times but these trout are always worth waiting for, as they average over 1 lb, 3-pounders are not uncommon and it has produced trout to 7 lb. There are boats for hire – inquire locally. Best flies are Duckfly, Black Pennell, Invicta, Connemara Black, Watson's Fancy, Dyson, Green Peter, Murrough and Daddy. Light spinning tackle with a small Mepps or Devon can often produce a fish when the fishing is slow. But don't be put off. This is a good trout fishery.

BARNAHILLIA LOUGH   L 59 55

Permission: Mr Hugh Griffin, Hon. Secretary, Clifden Anglers' Association, Dooneen, Clifden, Co. Galway.
Tel: (095) 21342

This small hill lough lies to the east of the Clifden–Cleggan coast road about 6 miles north-west of Clifden. It is almost completely surrounded by reeds but can be fished on the north side. It may not be quite so dour as some think and holds brown trout up to 1 lb. Bigger fish can be caught too and it is worth trying for a few hours.

GLENBRICKEEN LOUGH   L 66 53

Permission: Not usually required

This small lough lies nearly 3 miles by road due north of Clifden. The trout are small and it is not really worth the journey.

SHANAKEEVER LOUGH   L 66 52

Permission: Not usually required

This small, narrow lough lies to the north of Clifden – about 2 miles by road – and holds very small brown trout. It should not be confused with Lough Auna, below.

LOUGH AUNA   L 67 53

Permission: Mr Hugh Griffin, Hon. Secretary, Clifden Anglers' Association, Dooneen, Clifden, Co. Galway.
Tel: (095) 21342

Take the N59 Letterfrack road out of Clifden and turn right past the little lough on the right over a mile from the town. Follow the by-road for 1½ miles, past Shanakeever Lough on your right, and Lough Auna is at the end of the road. It is a fine lough – about ¾ mile long – and three-quarters of the bank is fishable. The trout are a nice size, many ranging from ½ to ¾ lb, and some say the average size is getting bigger. It is a good lough for both beginner and the more experienced and you will seldom come away without a few trout. The association sometimes has a boat for hire on this lough.

LOUGH ANIMMA   L 64 51
Permission: Mr Hugh Griffin, Hon. Secretary, Clifden Anglers' Association, Dooneen, Clifden, Co. Galway.
Tel: (095) 21342

This is a great little lough situated on a high plateau about one mile north-west of Clifden. The best way to approach it is up past St Anne's Home and the steep climb seldom goes unrewarded. It has a good stock of brown trout that average almost 1 lb. It fishes well from early in the season and, if you want a challenge and the chance of a few nice pink-fleshed brownies, head for Animma. Try a Butcher, Black Pennell, Invicta, Connemara Black or Fiery Brown.

LOUGH NAMBRACKKEAGH   L 67 51
Permission: Mr Hugh Griffin, Hon. Secretary, Clifden Anglers' Association, Dooneen, Clifden, Co. Galway.
Tel: (095) 21342

Take the road for the 'Dump' about a mile east of Clifden on the N59. There are some excellent trout in Nambrackkeagh, and they are not all blind, as its name suggests. Trout to over 2 lb have been caught. The average weight is under 1 lb. It is bank fishing only. The banks are good and it is a lough that is well worth a visit.

LOUGH NAHILLION   L 72 53
Permission: Mr Hugh Griffin, Hon. Secretary, Clifden Anglers' Association, Dooneen, Clifden, Co. Galway.
Tel: (095) 21342

Access to this lough is by taking the road for the TV booster station off the T71 Clifden–Letterfrack road. It is a relatively big lough nestling away to the west of the Twelve Pins. It has several islands and is fairly shallow all over. It holds a huge stock of small brown trout averaging 3 to the pound. The banks are fishable all round.

DERRYWAKING LOUGH   L 67 49
Permission: Mr Hugh Griffin, Hon. Secretary, Clifden Anglers' Association, Dooneen, Clifden, Co. Galway.
Tel: (095) 21342

This is an excellent little sea-trout lake about a mile upstream from the Salt Lake. It has an adequate stock by early July and can fish well from then until October, depending on weather conditions. There is a boat for hire. The average weight of the trout is just under 1 lb but fish to 4 lb have been recorded and there is the chance of taking a salmon as well. Flies to try are Bibio, Blue Zulu, Butcher, Black Pennell and Invicta.

CROAGHAT   L 71 48

Permission: Mr Hugh Griffin, Hon. Secretary, Clifden Anglers' Association, Dooneen, Clifden, Co. Galway.
Tel: (095) 21342

This is one of the best sea-trout loughs in this area. There is a boat for hire but don't try fishing it before July, as the brown trout are very small indeed. It is a nice lough and well worth a visit.

LOUGH FADDA   L 70 49

Permission: Not usually required

This is a narrow little lough to the west of Island Lough (below). It holds a stock of small brown trout and the banks are good, so it is worth a few casts as you pass by.

ISLAND LOUGH   L 71 49

Permission: Mr Hugh Griffin, Hon. Secretary, Clifden Anglers' Association, Dooneen, Clifden, Co. Galway.
Tel: (095) 21342

This lough lies to the south of the N59 Clifden–Galway road and holds a good stock of brown trout averaging ½ lb. It is sometimes stocked with larger fish, in which case trout up to 2½ lb are a possibility. There is one boat for hire. It fishes best in a west or south-west wind from May onwards and recommended flies are Connemara Black, Golden Olive, March Brown, Greenwell's Glory, Mallard and Claret, Zulu, Butcher, Watson's Fancy, a small Green Peter and the Daddy.

DERRYLEA LOUGH   L 70 49

Permission: Mr Hugh Griffin, Hon. Secretary, Clifden Anglers' Association, Dooneen, Clifden, Co. Galway.
Tel: (095) 21342

This lough lies to the south of the N59 Clifden–Galway road, about 3 miles from Clifden. It is nearly a mile long and there is a boat available and sometimes two. It holds an excellent stock of brown trout ranging from ½ to 1 lb, sometimes supplemented with much bigger stocked fish. It is a lively lough and fishes well right through the season. Useful fly patterns are Zulu, Blue Zulu, Mallard and Claret, Connemara Black, Sooty Olive, Wickham's Fancy and Watson's Fancy. Spinning is sometimes permitted but not encouraged.

GOULANE LOUGH   L 70 49
Permission: Mr Hugh Griffin, Hon. Secretary, Clifden Anglers' Association, Dooneen, Clifden, Co. Galway.
Tel: (095) 21342

Goulane is the small lough to the west of Derrylea Lough. It holds brown trout up to 1 lb and there is usually a boat available. It is sometimes stocked. The native fish are very free-rising and fight hard. Useful fly patterns to tempt them are small Bibio, Golden Olive, Butcher, and Black Pennell.

BALLINABOY LAKE   L 66 47
Permission: Col. A. J. Morris, Ballinaboy, Clifden, Co. Galway.

This excellent little sea-trout lough lies just short of 2 miles south of Clifden, alongside the L102 Clifden–Ballyconneely road. There is a boat available and it is fly fishing only. The lake gets its first good run of sea trout in late June and it can then fish well until October. It also gets occasional salmon. Useful fly patterns are small Silver Doctor, Bibio, Black Pennell, Butcher, Teal and Silver and Connemara Black.

LOUGH ATHOLA   L 62 48
Permission: Col. A. J. Morris, Ballinaboy, Clifden, Co. Galway.

Take the second turn to the right on the L102 Clifden–Ballyconneely road after you pass Ballinaboy and Lough Athola is on the left 2 miles down that road. It is mainly a sea-trout lough that also gets some salmon. It is tidal. There is a boat available. It can fish from late June and a small Silver Doctor, Camusunary Killer, Teal Blue and Silver and a Bibio all work well.

LOUGH FADDA
L 66 45

Permission: Mr Hugh Griffin, Hon. Secretary, Clifden Anglers' Association, Dooneen, Clifden, Co. Galway.
Tel: (095) 21342;
Col. A. J. Morris, Ballinaboy, Clifden, Co. Galway.

This lough lies just over 2 miles due south of Clifden and 3 miles by road. Approach it via a bog road which is the first turn on the right on the road from Ballinaboy to Toombeola. Fadda, as the name indicates, is a long shallow lough with lots of islands and points and little bays. It holds a superb stock of brown trout ranging from just under 1 lb to over 3 lb. It fishes best in a south wind and there is a boat available. It can be fished from the bank, which is good all round.

BOOLAGARE LOUGH
L 66 44

Permission:
Mr Hugh Griffin, Clifden Anglers' Association, Dooneen, Clifden, Co. Galway.
Tel: (095) 21342;
Col. A. J. Morris, Ballinaboy, Clifden, Co. Galway.

Boolagare lies due south of Lough Fadda and holds a good stock of brown trout. The average weight is ½ lb and a good afternoon may bring you 4 trout with the best of them nearly 1 lb.

THE DRY LOUGH
L 67 45

Permission: Mr Hugh Griffin, Hon. Secretary, Clifden Anglers' Association, Dooneen, Clifden, Co. Galway.
Tel: (095) 21342

This is a small lough to the east of Lough Fadda directly opposite the narrow part of that lough. It does not look worth fishing, but don't pass it by without giving it a try. It holds a small stock of good-sized brown trout, with some up to 4 lb. It may be your day to get one of them.

BALLYBAWN LOUGH
L 66 44

Permission: Mr Hugh Griffin, Hon. Secretary, Clifden Anglers' Association, Dooneen, Clifden, Co. Galway.
Tel: (095) 21342

Ballybawn Lough – more appropriately, loughs – lies to the south-west of Lough Fadda and is approached by the same route.

The loughs hold a good stock of brown trout averaging ½ lb, with some bigger ones. The more westerly lough is the better one and can produce trout up to 1½ lb. The banks are good and can be fished all round. Try some of the following patterns: Connemara Black, Watson's Fancy, Fiery Brown, Golden Olive, Butcher, Greenwell's Glory and Black Pennell.

LOUGH BEAGHCAUNEEN   L 67 47
Permission: Mr Hugh Griffin, Hon. Secretary, Clifden Anglers' Association, Dooneen, Clifden, Co. Galway.
Tel: (095) 21342

This lough lies to the south of the Ballinaboy–Toombeola road about one mile east of Ballinaboy. It gets a good run of sea trout from early July and holds occasional salmon as well. There is one boat for hire. It fishes best after a good flood has brought the fish up and useful fly patterns are Green Peter, Daddy, Connemara Black, Butcher, Watson's Fancy, and Teal, Blue and Silver.

CLOONAGAT LOUGH   L 69 47
Permission: Mr Hugh Griffin, Hon. Secretary, Clifden Anglers' Association, Dooneen, Clifden, Co. Galway.
Tel: (095) 21342

Cloonagat Lough lies to the north of the Ballinaboy–Toombeola road, 2 miles east of Ballinaboy, and gets a small run of sea trout late in the season. The banks are quite good but if you find it hard to stir a fish don't spend too much time on it.

CONGA LOUGH   L 70 47
Permission: Mr Hugh Griffin, Hon. Secretary, Clifden Anglers' Association, Dooneen, Clifden, Co. Galway.
Tel: (095) 21342

This is a large irregular-shaped lough to the east of Cloonagat. It holds small brownies and a few sea trout late in the season. It is not a lough that merits much attention.

LOUGH SCANNIVE   L 70 44
Permission: Mr Joe Creane, Hon. Secretary, Roundstone Anglers' Association, Roundstone, Co. Galway.
Tel: Roundstone 72

This is not a very accessible lough no matter how you try to approach it. The best route is the bog road off the L102 just north of Letterdiff House and just over a mile north of Roundstone. It is a long walk and it is advisable to seek directions locally because it is very easy to get lost. A compass and map would come in handy. This is a really good fishery holding brown trout and sea trout late in the season. The trout average 1 lb but fish to 5 lb are reported to have been taken, and when they are on the take they rise very freely indeed, with baskets of two dozen trout reported quite often. It fishes well early in the season and is a good evening lough with a big hatch of olives. The Mallard and Claret is the favourite fly. It is fishable all round but the banks are difficult in places. This lough has a large cormorant colony but the birds don't seem to make any difference to the trout stocks. The locals say that if you lose your way at Scannive you need only follow the cormorants' flight path to find the direction of Roundstone.

LOUGH NAWEELAUN   L 71 43

Permission: Mr Joe Creane, Hon. Secretary, Roundstone Anglers' Association, Roundstone, Co. Galway.
Tel: Roundstone 72

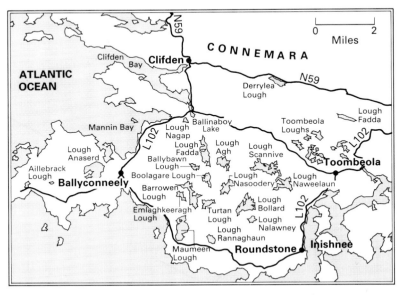

30   *S.W. Connemara and the Roundstone Loughs*

This lough is best approached by taking the bog road west 200 yards south of the Inishnee junction on the L102 Toombeola–Roundstone road. It fishes best in April, May and June for brown trout and they average ½ lb with some up to 2 lb. This is a unique fishery, accessible yet away from it all. Bank fishing only and the banks are safe. The fish are free-rising. The locals maintain that the fish used to be much bigger before the cormorant colony decreased in size.

LOUGH NASOODERY   L 67 43

Permission: Mr Joe Creane, Hon. Secretary, Roundstone Anglers' Association, Roundstone, Co. Galway.
Tel: Roundstone 72

Take the road west off the L102 Toombeola–Roundstone road about 200 yards south of the junction for Inishnee. Nasoodery holds a very good stock of brown trout that rise freely to the fly and standard fly patterns will do. This is really a virgin fishery, rarely fished and untouched by the influences that the twentieth century has had on many waters. The size of the trout varies between ½ and ¾ lb and they take freely. Expect to get at least half a dozen.

LOUGH NAGAP   L 65 47

Permission:
Col. A. J. Morris, Ballinaboy, Clifden, Co. Galway;
Mr Hugh Griffin, Hon. Secretary, Clifden Anglers' Association, Dooneen, Clifden, Co. Galway.
Tel: (095) 21342

This small lough lies 2 miles south of Clifden off the Ballyconneely road. It is to the right of the road leading to the landing site of Alcock and Brown, who made the first transatlantic flight. It holds a small stock of brown trout up to ¾ lb and the banks are easily fished. Useful patterns are Butcher, Connemara Black and Mallard and Claret.

LOUGH EMLAGHNABEHY   L 63 48

Permission: Mr Hugh Griffin, Hon. Secretary, Clifden Anglers' Association, Dooneen, Clifden, Co. Galway.
Tel: (095) 21342

This lough, which is of quite a good size, lies to the east of the Clifden–Ballyconneely road, about 4 miles from Clifden. It holds a small stock of good brown trout up to 3 lb but they tend to feed very much on the bottom and can best be tempted to take a fly on a windy day. It is thought that the lough has a big stickleback population and the trout prey heavily on them. Try spinning a Lane Minnow. Useful fly patterns are Dunkeld, Silver Invicta, Alexandra, Butcher, Bloody Butcher, Bibio and Black Pennell.

LOUGH NACORRUSAUN   L 64 44

Permission:
Mr Hugh Griffin, Hon. Secretary, Clifden Anglers' Association, Dooneen, Clifden, Co. Galway.
Tel: (095) 21342;
Col. A. J. Morris, Ballinaboy, Clifden, Co. Galway.

This lough is known locally as The Crussauns. Take the first turn north off the L102 Ballyconneely–Roundstone road, ½ mile from Ballyconneely, and follow it for nearly 2 miles until you arrive at the lough. This is a reasonably big lough and fairly shallow. It holds a good stock of brown trout averaging ¾ lb with some to 1½ lb. The banks are fishable all the way round. It fishes best in a west or south wind and useful fly patterns are Connemara Black, Butcher, Mallard and Claret, Black Pennell and Golden Olive.

LOUGH ANASERD   L 60 43

Permission:
Mr Hugh Griffin, Hon. Secretary, Clifden Anglers' Association, Dooneen, Clifden, Co. Galway.
Tel. (095) 21342;
Col. A. J. Morris, Ballinaboy, Clifden, Co. Galway.

Anaserd is one mile west of Ballyconneely and is one of the largest brown trout loughs in Connemara – over a mile long and nearly a mile wide. It is mainly spring-fed and the south and west sides are quite shallow. It holds an excellent stock of trout averaging ¾ lb with many up to 1½ lb. It can be fished all along the south shore and can be relied on to produce a few fish at any time throughout the season. Among the more popular fly patterns are Hare's Ear, Butcher, Black Pennell, Watson's Fancy, Connemara Black, Daddy, Green Peter and Heather Moth.

DOON LOUGH   L 59 43
DERREEN LOUGH

Permission: Private – inquire locally

These loughs, which lie one on either side of the road on the way to the golf links, hold a fair stock of good-sized brown trout up to 1½ lb.

TRUSKA LOUGH   L 59 44

Permission:
Mr Hugh Griffin, Hon. Secretary, Clifden Anglers' Association, Dooneen, Clifden, Co. Galway.
Tel: (095) 21342;
Col. A. J. Morris, Ballinaboy, Clifden, Co. Galway.

This lough lies about a mile west of Lough Anaserd and is the last lough in the area worth fishing. It can best be fished off the east bank. It holds some good brown trout up to 3 lb and the average size is about 1 lb. Useful fly patterns are Jacob's Ladder, Sooty Olive, Mallard and Claret, Fiery Brown, Wickham's Fancy and Butcher.

DOOHULLA FISHERY

BARROWEN LOUGH   L 66 43
EMLAGHKEERAGH LOUGH   L 65 43
MAUMEEN LOUGH   L 65 40

Permission: Mr Tinney, Ballyconneely, Co. Galway.
Tel: (095) 23529

These loughs all drain into Ballyconneely Bay via the tidal pool at Callow Bridge which is known locally as the Fool's Pool because of the number of mullet that show there in summer time. It is primarily a good sea-trout fishery and it gets a few salmon as well. It gets some large sea trout in April–May and the main run arrives at the end of June. There are two boats for hire and fly fishing only is the rule. Useful fly patterns are Peter Ross, Butcher, Black Pennell, Connemara Black, Bibio, Blue Zulu, small Silver Doctor, Green Peter and Daddy.

TURTAN LOUGH   L 66 42

Permission: Inquire locally – a permit is not usually required

This little lough lies well over a mile north of the L102 Ballyconneely–Roundstone road. The best route to it is up past Mr Stephen Diamond's house. It is one of the best brown-trout loughs in the whole area and fishes well all season. The trout average 1 lb, with some to over 2½ lb. It is quite shallow and the banks are good. The fish can be obliging too and you could expect to take up to 4 good trout for an evening's fishing. All the standard fly patterns will take fish.

LOUGH NAMANAWAUN   L 66 39

Permission: Mr Joe Creane, Hon. Secretary, Roundstone Anglers' Association, Roundstone, Co. Galway.
Tel: Roundstone 72

This nice little lough lies to the south of the L102 Roundstone–Ballyconneely road, about 4 miles from Roundstone. It fishes best in April, May, June and September and even then it can be hard enough to tempt a fish. The average size is small but it can produce the odd fish to 4 lb. The banks are very weedy and the angler will have to search out a clear spot. Some of the most useful flies are a Claret Pennell, Bibio, Claret Bumble and a Butcher. If the fish are not in the mood, you can admire the wide variety of bird life that the lough also supports.

LOUGH RANNAGHAUN   L 67 40

Permission: Mr Joe Creane, Hon. Secretary, Roundstone Anglers' Association, Roundstone, Co. Galway.
Tel: Roundstone 72

The access to this lough is up a little bog road off the L102 Roundstone–Ballyconneely road about 4 miles from Roundstone. It holds brown trout only and they come at about 3 to the pound with the odd fish to ¾ lb. It is a very lively spot, fishing well at all times. It is often described as a real tourists' lough for the trout will take a wet fly, a dry fly or a spinner very freely. The north-east shore fishes best but all the banks are safe. There is a little lough to the east of Rannaghaun that is a bit of a mystery for it can produce trout to over 1 lb.

LOUGH BOLLARD   L 69 42

Permission: Mr Joe Creane, Hon. Secretary, Roundstone Anglers' Association, Roundstone, Co. Galway.
Tel: Roundstone 72

You can approach Bollard off the L102 road, branching west up a bog road on the south side of the junction with Insihnee and then walking the last 400 yards. Another way in is past Errisbeg Hill on the west with a walk of 600 yards. The lough fishes from April onwards but the trout are small – about 3 to the pound. The banks are reasonably good and you can expect to come away with at least half a dozen nice trout. While you are at Bollard you might like to try the other loughs to the west because they all hold trout of an equal size to Bollard. Standard lough fly patterns work well.

LOUGH NALOWNEY (Rusheen na Roige)   L 69 41

Permission: Mr Joe Creane, Hon. Secretary, Roundstone Anglers' Association, Roundstone, Co. Galway.
Tel: Roundstone 72

This lough is known locally as Rusheen na Roige and it is approached up the same bog road as for Lough Bollard, above. Turn north off the L102 Roundstone–Ballyconneely road about 3 miles from Roundstone and follow this road to the west of Errisbeg Hill. The lough holds nice brown trout averaging ½ lb with some up to 1¼ lb. The water is very clear and the fish are hard fighters as well as being of an unusual humped shape. It can be fished all round and the south-east end is reputed to be best. Beware of wading, as this can be a dangerous lough. Spinning can be productive early in the season. Otherwise, the flies worth having are Claret Pennell, Mallard and Claret, Zulu, Bibio, Claret Bumble, Butcher, Watson's Fancy and Sedge patterns.

THE TOOMBEOLA LOUGHS   L 72 44

Permission: Mrs Hill, Anglers' Return, Ballinafad, Co. Galway.
Tel: (079) 66006

These loughs – about twelve in all – lie due west of Toombeola Bridge and drain into the bottom of the Ballynahinch River. They are best approached off the bog road from Toombeola to Ballinaboy. This is mainly a brown-trout fishery with sea trout in some of the lower loughs late in the season. The trout average ½ lb with some up to 2 lb. There are no boats and fly fishing tends to give better results than spinning. Recommended flies include Blue Zulu, Black Pennell, Peter Ross, Butcher, Teal, Blue and Silver, Watson's Fancy and Sooty Olive.

BALLYNAHINCH LAKE (LOWER)   L 76 47

Permission: The Fishery Manager, Ballynahinch Castle Hotel, Ballinafad, Co. Galway.
Tel: (095) 21269

Ballynahinch Lake (Lower) lies immediately north of the hotel of the same name and south of the T71 Recess–Clifden road. It is ¾ mile long and varies in width from ½ mile to a few hundred yards. It is noted mainly for its salmon and sea-trout fishing. Spring salmon are taken from the shore at Sna Beg early in the season and this is a good lie for a grilse right to the end of the season, especially in high water. The outflow can be fished from both banks and this area is noted for the quality of its sea-trout fishing and has produced sea trout to over 7 lb in recent years. A dozen can easily be taken by an angler in a day and the night fishing off the stands above the bridge is sheer magic in July, August and early September. There are two boats available and the north shore along by the road and around the Castle Island provides the best drifts. There is a particularly productive area along by the little island where the little stream flows in past the youth hostel. The lake fishes best in a west or south-west wind. It is in a lovely setting, with the woods to the south and Ben Lettery towering over it to the north. It is a good fishery, too, for through it must pass all the fish that run the entire Ballynahinch River system. Flies to use to tempt the trout are Delphi, Bibio, Butcher, Duckfly, Black Pennell, Peter Ross, Bloody Butcher, Silver Doctor and Daddy.

15   *A grilse comes safely aboard*

BALLYNAHINCH LAKE (UPPER) L 78 47

Permission: Miss Reid, Lisnabrucka House, Ballinafad, Co. Galway.

This fishery stretches from the mouth of the river known as The Canal downstream to Sna Beg. It holds a big head of sea trout, especially in July and August, and they lie along both shores. Dapping and wet fly are equally effective and a west wind is most suitable. The fishing is let with the lodge and there are two boats available. This is another excellent sea-trout fishery and there is always the chance of a salmon as well. Flies as for Ballynahinch Lower.

DERRYCLARE LOUGH L 81 47
LOUGH INAGH L 82 51

Permission: Miss Della MacAuley, Inagh Valley Inn, Recess, Co. Galway.
Tel: Recess 8

These two loughs lie in the lovely Inagh valley with The Twelve Pins (mountains) of Connemara rising steeply to the west and the Maumturk Mountain range to the east. In all, there is 5 miles of lough and river fishing – mainly lough, with two short connecting rivers. This fishery has everything – spring salmon, grilse and a wonderful run of sea trout. The springers are mainly fished in April and May, the grilse come in June and the sea trout in late June. There are three sets of 'butts', or long fishing piers, built out into Derryclare Lough for the anglers' convenience. The famous Derryclare Butts are at the top of Derryclare Lough where the river flows in. This is a good lie for a spring salmon and a wonderful stand for a night's sea-trout fishing – it can be good in the daytime too. Access to it is in by the forest road off the Inagh road. To get to the Glendollagh Butts, take the pathway down along the old railway from the Weir Bridge at Recess old railway station. Greenpoint Butts are a short walk up from the Canal Bridge at the junction of the Roundstone and Clifden roads. Strangely, there are no boats available on Derryclare Lough and all the fishing is done from the butts and the bank.

Lough Inagh has eight boats and the fishing starts here early in July, when it gets its first run of sea trout, with plenty of 3-pounders among them. It has been known for up to 50 trout to be taken here by a single boat in one day. The west shore fishes best and all along the islands. There are several good drifts for both trout and salmon at the top of the lough near the inflowing river. Favourite trout patterns in July are Watson's Fancy, Bibio (with

31   *The Ballynahinch system and the Carna Loughs*

a red centre), Butcher and Peter Ross. Later in the season add a
Jacob's Ladder, Green Peter, Daddy, Claret and Mallard, Camusunary Killer and Dunkeld. Dapping can bring up the best of the
sea trout in August and September. There is no need to fish special
flies for salmon at this time, as they will take the sea–trout flies. Just
remember to keep the strike slow. The boat jetty and boathouse are
located halfway along the east shore of Inagh. This is one lough on
which an outboard is essential, as it is too big for rowing. There are
a couple of submerged rocks so caution should be taken when using
the motor. This lough will take more than one day to explore

adequately, for it can be one of the best. It can have its dour periods and some think it fishes best midweek when it is less disturbed by a full complement of anglers.

LOUGH NABRUCKA   L 80 46

This is a fine sea-trout lough. It is a private fishery and rods . are not let.

ATHRY LOUGH   L 81 46

Permission: The Fishery Manager, Zetland Hotel, Cashel, Co. Galway.
Tel: (095) 21010

This lough is known locally as Big Athry and lies south of the T71 road. It holds sea trout from mid-June and is at its best from July. It gets a few salmon too. The fishing can be patchy. It can be dour for long periods, but it pays to persevere for after a long quiet period you are liable to get six successive rises and six good trout. The trout average 1 lb with some 4 lb, and the best fishing wind is from the south-west, with a north-westerly the second preference. Athry fishes particularly well in a wet season. The best drifts are along the road shore, the west shore and the bay where the river flows out. There is a 10-inch size limit. One boat is available, and is kept about 60 yards from the road at the Clifden end.

LOUGH NACOOGARROW   L 82 46

Permission: The Fishery Manager, Zetland Hotel, Cashel, Co. Galway.
Tel: (095) 21010

This lough is known as the Athry Crossroads Lough and it is situated at the junction of the Clifden–Carna road and divided by the road to Carna. The boat is kept on the east side, but the lough to the west is the best fishery. It holds mainly sea trout and the best period is from mid-July until early October. This lough is well sheltered and fishes best in a west-north-west or south-east wind. The best drifts on the west lough are along the road shore and in the south-west corner where the river flows in; the east lough fishes best at the lower end along by the house. It can be hard at times to rise a fish on this lough. The heaviest in recent times weighed just over 5 lb.

LOUGHYVANGAN   L 82 46

Permission: Cashel Anglers' Association – inquire locally

This small lough lies to the south-east of the junction of the Carna–Clifden road. There is a small road east from the L102, about 300 yards down from the junction, which brings you halfway to the water. This is a trout fishery only, with the fish running from about ½ lb to 2 lb. The water is very clear and obviously this is a limestone lough. It is very deep on the east side and the banks are good all round. It holds a lot of fish and can fish well from March. Best flies include Greenwell's Glory, Sooty Olive, Butcher, Black Pennell, Claret and Mallard, Green Peter and Daddy.

LOUGHAUNEMLAGHEASK (Emlough West) L 82 44

Permission: The Fishery Manager, Zetland Hotel, Cashel, Co. Galway.
Tel: (095) 21010

This lough lies about 200 yards to the east of the L102 Recess–Carna road, and there is a footpath to the jetty. It holds brown trout and sea trout and there is a 10-inch size limit. This is the top lough on this branch of the Ballynahinch system and it fishes best from August after a good flood. It can fish well in any wind but a south wind and broken weather is preferred. You can drift the shores or right up the middle and expect a good sea trout anywhere. This lough is noted for its big trout and produces several to over 5 lb every season. Two of the most popular flies on it are the Heather Moth and the Green Peter. Dapping is favoured by many regulars too.

LOUGH EMLAGH (Small Emlough)   L 81 44

Permission: The Fishery Manager, Zetland Hotel, Cashel, Co. Galway.
Tel: (095) 21010

This small lough lies to the west of the L102 Recess–Carna road. It holds small brown trout but in a very wet season it gets a small run of big sea trout in the month of September. It gets very weedy but there is plenty of space to fish from the south shore.

LOUGH NAMBRACKAGH   L 82 43

Permission: Not usually required

This little lough lies to the west of the L102 north of the Cashel junction. It holds a big stock of brown trout up to 10 oz and they have a very bright silvery appearance. It can be fished all round and is a good lough for beginners. Useful fly patterns are small Greenwell's Glory, Butcher, Black Pennell and Watson's Fancy.

CAPPAHOOSH LOUGH L 87 46

Permission: Mr Leslie Lyons, Tullaboy, Maam Cross, Recess, Co. Galway.
Tel: (091) 82462

This lough lies south of the N59 east of Recess. It is about half a mile long and narrow as well. It is part of the Ballynahinch system, as are all the other Lyons loughs upstream. Access is by a small gate off the main road near the east end. This is mainly a sea-trout fishery but it also gets a small run of salmon. The trout come up on the first good flood in late June or early July and each succeeding flood brings more. The average size of the Cappahoosh sea trout is about 1 lb, but much larger fish are taken from time to time and the best in recent years was just over 4 lb. There is a boat available. Fish can be taken all over the lough and it is important not to disturb the water too much. Certainly an outboard motor should never be used.

DERRYNEEN LOUGH L 88 46

Permission: Mr Leslie Lyons, Tullaboy, Maam Cross, Recess, Co. Galway.
Tel: (091) 82462

This is another small lough that lies to the east of Recess village and north of the N59 Galway–Clifden road. It holds a good head of sea trout from the early July floods and fishes well right into October. It gets a few salmon as well and of all the Lyons loughs it is the one where you are most likely to hook one. Like Cappahoosh, it fishes best in a west wind. This lough fishes well in September and early October. A boat is available and there is really no need for an outboard. The rules are fly fishing and dapping only, and useful patterns to take along are Bibio, Green Peter, Daddy, Watson's Fancy, Connemara Black and a small Thunder and Lightning.

SHANNAGHCLOONTIPPEN LOUGH L 90 45
(Shanakeela Lough)

Permission: Mr Leslie Lyons, Tullaboy, Maam Cross, Recess, Co.

Galway.
Tel: (091) 82462

This lough is always referred to as Shanakeela Lough. It lies to the south of the N59 and 4 miles west of Maam Cross. Parking space is along the main road and it is only a short walk across the field to where the boat is kept. Fish present include brown trout, salmon and sea trout. The sea trout are the most plentiful and Shanakeela produces some good ones. The bulrushes are beginning to encroach on this lough but there is still plenty of space. The best drifts appear to be along the south side where the shallows extend well out. Pay particular attention to the little bay to the south-west where the little stream flows in. Again it is fly fishing and dapping only, and, in the interest of good fishing, don't disturb the water with an outboard. Useful flies are Heather Moth, Daddy, Green Peter, Bibio, Sooty Olive, Watson's Fancy and Peter Ross.

LOCHADHEAS   L 91 45

Permission: Mr Leslie Lyons, Tullaboy, Maam Cross, Recess, Co. Galway.
Tel: (091) 82462

This small lough lies to the south-west of Oorid Lough (below). It holds a fair stock of brown trout with some almost reaching the 1-lb mark. Fish it from the bank and use small lough patterns such as a Butcher, a Black Pennell, etc.

OORID LOUGH   L 92 45

Permission: Mr Leslie Lyons, Tullaboy, Maam Cross, Recess, Co. Galaway.
Tel: (091) 82462

Oorid is the big, impressive lough that lies to the south of the N59 Galway–Clifden road and just over 2 miles west of Maam Cross. It is the top lough on the system and anglers are often surprised to learn that it too gets its fish from Ballynahinch. It is a long way from here to Toombeola Bridge at the bottom. It is mainly a sea-trout fishery but holds small brownies too. The first fish get up in late July and this is really an August, September and October lough. Again, fly fishing and dapping is the rule and there are two boats for hire. Outboards are allowed. It is a safe lough for the most part but there is a rocky reef that is sometimes submerged on the east side and anglers should exercise caution in this area. Like the other loughs in the area, it fishes best in a west wind. On account of

Oorid's size, it is sometimes difficult to locate the trout, so the angler must continue to drift until he rises a fish and then quietly fish around that area for some time. There is a long bay running south and there is a good drift across the mouth. This is a lough with a reputation for producing big trout and a favourite spot to pick one up is on the outside of the small island. The fish seem to congregate here, attracted by the insects that may be blown from the trees. Flies to bring along include Claret Bumble, Bumble Invicta, Green Peter, Daddy, Bibio, Watson's Fancy, Kingsmill and Bloody Butcher.

ILLION LOUGH L 89 47

Permission: Mr Leslie Lyons, Tullaboy, Maam Cross, Recess, Co. Galway.
Tel: (091) 82462

This little lough lies to the north of Derryneen old school off the old road. It holds a small stock of brown trout but tends to get very weedy and difficult to fish.

LOUGH APHEEBERA L 81 37

Permission: Not usually required

Apheebera lies to the east of the L102 Recess–Carna road and is the first lough on the Gowlabeg system. Access to it is north of Glinsk and it is a long journey by foot. The lough is over half a mile long but quite narrow and most of the banks are fishable. It holds a good stock of small brown trout and it can get quite a good run of sea trout from early August. The average weight is ¾ lb but fish up to 1½ lb are common. They rise well to the fly, particularly on a dark day with a nice breeze from the west. All the usual fly patterns work well, particularly Butcher, Black Pennell, Connemara Black, Peter Ross, Green Peter and Daddy.

MAUMEENMANRAGH L 82 36

Permission: Not usually required

This small, shallow lough lies half a mile south-east of Lough Apheebera. It holds a fair stock of brown trout averaging 3 to the pound. The banks are difficult to fish. Greenwell's Glory, Butcher, Black Pennell and Peter Ross in small sizes all work well.

LOUGH AWEE   L 84 37

Permission: Not usually required

Awee is the top lough on the Gowlabeg system. It is a fine lough nearly ½ mile long by about 500 yards wide and it has a remarkable sandy shore. It can fish well all round and holds good brown trout up to 1½ lb, though the average weight is about ¾ lb. Standard lough fly patterns all produce good results and Awee can give good sport.

CULLAHERICK LOUGH   L 80 38

This lough is on the west of the L102 north of Glinsk. It is very weedy and not worth fishing.

LOUGH NANEEVE   L 80 38

Permission: Not usually required

Naneeve is a small lough that lies about 1½ miles north-east of Glinsk and ½ mile in from the road. It holds a big stock of small brown trout, but few of them weigh more than 6 oz.

LOUGH NAGRAIGUE (Glinsk School Lough)   L 79 37

Permission: Not usually required

This lough lies due east of Glinsk, behind the school. It is approached by a small bog road and is only a 15-minute walk along it. It holds a good stock of brown trout averaging ½ lb. They rise freely to the fly and fight well. As many as 12 or 15 are frequently caught in a visit. The usual fly patterns all produce good results. The shoreline is solid and easily walked and the lough can be fished all round.

LOUGH BOLA   L 76 34

Permission: Part of this lough is strictly private and inquiries about access should be made locally.

Lough Bola lies between the Glinsk–Carna road and the coast road. It is best approached off the coast road at Moyrus – a good mile's walk to the water's edge. Bola holds brown trout only and there is a big stock of fish averaging ½–¾ lb. The fish are beautifully marked, deep, and fight well. Larger trout are caught as well and every season fish to over 2 lb are recorded. This lough can fish well from April, and August and September give good sport too.

Fishing is from the bank only and the banks are good. An average catch should consist of 8–10 trout, but much larger bags are recorded. This is quite a large lough and it will take most of a day to fish all round it. Useful fly patterns are Butcher, Black Pennell, Greenwell's Glory, Hare's Ear, Peter Ross, Dunkeld and Red Tag.

LOUGH NAGEERON L 75 31
LOUGH BUNNACLIFFA L 74 32

Permission: These loughs are regarded as private. It is possible to obtain permission to fish them and inquiries should be made locally.

Both of these loughs are situated off the coast road south-west of Moyrus. They hold good stocks of free-rising brown trout, ranging in size from 6 oz to ¾ lb. These are good loughs for beginners and the experienced small-lough angler will enjoy them too. The season extends from 1 March to 30 September. All legitimate methods are allowed and fly fishing, spinning and worm fishing are practised.

LOUGH KEAMNACALLY L 79 32

Permission: (for part of the lough) Mr D. E. Brown, Carna Anglers' Association, Carna, Co. Galway.

This small lough lies to the east of the L102, about ½ mile north of Carna. It is possible to park by the roadside and get to the water in 5 minutes. It holds a fair stock of small brown trout and they come about 3 to the pound. From July onwards, it gets a small run of sea trout. The average size of these fish is ¾ lb, with a few up to 2 lb. Bank fishing only – which is quite difficult because the banks are very overgrown.

DOOLETTER LOUGH L 78 34

You might be tempted to have a try here. Give it a miss. The banks are swampy and dangerous and there are no fish in it anyway.

LOUGH ALIVEE L 79 33

Permission: Not usually required

Park the car along the Glinsk–Carna road and take the old road in to this lough, which lies to the east of it. Alivee is a small lough, conveniently situated, and holds a good stock of brown trout. The average size is about ¾ lb but fish to 1½ lb are taken frequently. The banks are pretty good and the fishing begins to pick up here in April. You are always in with a chance of a few nice trout on this deep little lough. All the usual fly patterns work well, but try a Butcher, small Black Pennell, Black and Peacock Spider, Watson's Fancy, Dunkeld or Hare's Ear.

LOUGH KEERAUN   L 78 31

Permission: (for part of the lough) Mr D. E. Brown, Carna Anglers' Association, Carna, Co. Galway.

This little lough lies south of Carna alongside the road on the way to Mweenish Beach. It holds a small stock of brown trout averaging 6 oz but there seems not to be many in it.

LOUGH TRUSKAN   L 80 30

Permission: (for part of the lough) Mr D. E. Brown, Carna Anglers' Association, Carna, Co. Galway.

Truskan lies to the north of the Carna–Kilkieran road and the season here runs from 1 March to 30 September. You can park alongside the road. It holds a good stock of brown trout, most of them are around ½ lb but with some up to 1 lb. They make up for their lack of weight by their willingness to take. It is a shallow lough and the banks are fairly good.

LOUGH SHEEDAGH   L 80 31

Permission: Mr D. E. Brown, Carna Anglers' Association, Carna, Co. Galway.

This lough lies to the north of the L102 Carna–Kilkieran road. The brown trout here can weigh up to 1 lb. It drains into Mweenish Bay and gets a run of sea trout and occasional salmon from mid-June and the fishing can be good from then until the end of September, depending on the weather conditions. Best flies are Connemara Black, Black Pennell, Blue Zulu, Teal, Blue and Silver and Butcher.

LOUGH SKANNIVE   L 80 31

Permission: (for part of the lough) Mr D. E. Brown, Carna Anglers' Association, Carna, Co. Galway.

Skannive is to the north of the L102 Carna–Kilkieran road. It can be approached by a number of routes. There are two access roads at Carna and Ardmore up past Lough Truskan and a road in from Kilkieran as well. This is a fine lough holding sea trout and occasional salmon from mid-June. The size limit is 10 inches and fly fishing and dapping are the methods allowed. It can fish well right through the season and the fish are free-rising. The average weight is about ¾ lb with some up to 3 lb and over. Bank fishing is not really possible, but there are a number of boats for hire. These are kept on both east and west shores. This is a big lough and if the wind is more than force 4 you will need an outboard. This is allowed but not supplied locally. It is an attractive lough with islands and several bays and even an ancient stone fort. Flies worth trying are Green Peter, Claret Bumble, Delphi, Butcher, Mallard and Claret, Connemara Black, Daddy, Blue Zulu and Camusunary Killer.

LOUGH PIBRUM	L 81 33
GLENNAUN LOUGH	L 80 34

Permission: Inquire locally

Both of these loughs lie to the north-east of Carna in very remote and peaceful country. There are two access roads off the L102 Carna–Kilkieran road. One is at Ardmore and runs north past Lough Skannive and the other comes in from the east at Kilkieran. Then there are a number of bog roads in the hills and lay-bys have been made along some of these for parking. Pibrum holds good brown trout and gets a small run of sea trout in September. Glennaun is a long lough running from east to west and the sea-trout fishing can be quite good from the bank, especially in September. All that is needed is a big flood and high water to get the fish up. There is another small lough to the south-west of Pibrum that is well worth a try too because all the fish that end up in these two must first pass through it.

LOUGH IERIN	L 81 31
LOUGHAUNORE	L 82 32

Permission:
For Ierin, inquire locally;
For Loughaunore, Mr D. E. Brown, Carna Anglers' Association, Carna, Co. Galway.

These two small loughs lie due west of Kilkieran. Access to them may be gained west from Kilkieran or north from Ardmore on the

Carna road. Loughaunore holds small brown trout and no sea trout because of a dam placed there to hold back the water for a local water supply. Lough Ierin holds mostly brown trout and gets a late run of sea trout in September. Both are very exposed and rarely without a ripple. Bank fishing is possible on both of these and fly fishing is preferred. All the usual brown-trout and sea-trout flies work well. Well worth a try, particularly late in the season.

GLENARUIDMORE LOUGH   L 84 34
Permission: Not usually required

Glenaruidmore and three smaller loughs all lie in a valley to the west of the L102. Access to them is by a bog road about a mile north of Kilkieran. They are almost totally surrounded by forest and hard to fish. Most of the time they are mirror-calm. The larger lough holds fairly good brown trout, averaging 6 oz, and there are small trout in the other three loughs. The best chance of getting a few fish is in March and April.

LOUGH ACONEERA   L 87 36
Permission: Not usually required

This is a fine-looking lough to the west of the L102 Invermore–Kilkieran road. It holds small brown trout and occasional sea trout. It is tidal and mullet often make their way into it. The shoreline is uneven and it is difficult enough to fish. All legitimate angling methods are allowed.

LOUGHANILLAUN (Gowla Lake)   L 84 41
Permission: The Fishery Manager, Zetland Hotel, Cashel, Co. Galway.
Tel: (095) 21010.

This is the largest and probably the most important lough on the whole Gowla system, and comprises about a dozen interconnected loughs holding brown trout, some salmon and a big stock of sea trout. It is for the sea trout that the fishery is best known. Gowla Lake lies to the north of Cashel–Screeb road about 3 miles east of the Zetland Hotel. There is a short sand road to the boat jetty where there is a car park and lunch hut. The sea trout come in late June and the fishing gets into full swing in July. The trout average 1 lb but this lough has produced sea trout to 6½ lb and salmon to 10 lb. Gowla is an attractive lough, dotted with islands, and has a

32 *Gowla, Invermore, Inverbeg, Screeb, Lettermucka, Furnace and the Lettermore Fisheries*

multitude of small bays and hidden inlets. Fly fishing and dapping only. Three boats are available and boatmen can be arranged. The first two weeks of July usually produce a small number of big sea trout. This lough fishes well in stormy weather with plenty of rain about. Some of the best drifts are along the north shore from the outflowing river to the mouth of the inflowing river and around Rabbit Island. The whole bay at the mouth of the outflowing river can be particularly good when the fish come in fresh. There is a good drift on your left after you go through the narrow gap into the east lake. In a west wind drift towards all the islands in the centre of the lough. Some would say that for best results on Gowla it is imperative to stay close to the shoreline and along by the islands. This is further borne out by the fact that if it gets too rough and windy to fish from the boats very good baskets can be taken from the shore. Look out for a big sea trout on this lough in September. All the usual fly patterns work, but make sure and have a Claret Bumble, Camusunary Killer, Daddy, Black Pennell and Green Peter.

LOUGH CONG L 85 42

Permission: The Fishery Manager, Zetland Hotel, Cashel, Co. Galway.
Tel: (095) 21010

This is a small brown-trout lough to the north-east of Gowla Lake. It is a long walk from any road and the shortest journey is by boat across Gowla Lake. It holds small brown trout to ½ lb and the banks are good when the water is low, but there is a sluice at the outlet to create an artificial spate on Gowla and this can leave the banks very swampy. It is not often fished and the brownies take freely.

MANNIONS LAKE L 82 41

Permission: The Fishery Manager, Zetland Hotel, Cashel, Co. Galway.
Tel: (095) 21010

Access to this lough is off the Cashel–Screeb road before you come to Upper Gowla Bridge. Park in the quarry to the west of the bridge and walk across the hill. It is only about 100 yards. This is a shallow lough that holds good sea trout from about mid-July and fishes well right into October. It fishes particularly well in high water with a good wind blowing. There is sometimes a boat available but even without it this lough is worth fishing from the bank, especially with a good wind blowing from the south or west. Black Pennell, Fiery Brown, Mallard and Claret, Bibio, Murrough and Daddy should produce 2–3 fish, but expect more on a good day.

GLENTURKAN LOUGHS L 82 42

Permission: The Fishery Manager, Zetland Hotel, Cashel, Co. Galway.
Tel: (095) 21010

These loughs lie to the east of the Recess–Carna road. They hold small brown trout and occasional sea trout but are very weedy and difficult to fish. In an area with so much fishing readily available, they are scarcely worth the trouble of getting there.

LURGAN LOUGH   L 81 41

Permission: The Fishery Manager, Zetland Hotel, Cashel, Co. Galway.
Tel: (095) 21010

This little lough lies to the east of the L102 Recess–Carna road, only 15 yards opposite the junction with the Cashel road. It holds wild brown trout up to ¾ lb, but the big rainbows stocked by the hotel are the main attraction. The banks are good and it can be fished all round. You are unlikely to come away without a trout and the most productive fly patterns are Dunkeld and Mallard and Claret.

KILLAUNCROM LOUGH   L 80 43

Permission: Not usually required

Killauncrom involves a walk of well over a mile. There is an unused bog road that you take west off the L102 Recess–Carna road about a mile north of the Cashel junction and then you follow the outflowing stream to the lough. There is a 10-inch size limit. Killauncrom holds a big stock of small brown trout and because the place is not often fished they take freely. The banks are boggy but are fishable about halfway round. An average day's fishing should produce 6–8 fish and on a good day you will get many more. Try a Butcher, Black Pennell, Peter Ross, Watson's Fancy, Sooty Olive and a Red Tag.

FEAGHROE LOUGH   L 84 42

Permission: The Fishery Manager, Zetland Hotel, Cashel, Co. Galway.
Tel: (095) 21010

Feaghroe lies to the north of Gowla Lake, but is best approached off the L102 Recess–Carna road. Take the small tarred road east to Lettershinna village. Park the car and you will see this lough about 500 yards further on to the south-east. It holds brown trout, sea trout and occasional salmon. There is a 10-inch size limit. This lough can fish well from early July and fishes particularly well in high water. There is a boat available. Useful fly patterns are Black Pennell, Green Peter, Bibio, Claret Bumble, Camusunary Killer and Murrough.

WHITE'S LOUGH   L 85 43

Permission: The Fishery Manager, Zetland Hotel, Cashel, Co. Galway.
Tel: (095) 21010

This small lough lies to the north-east of Feaghroe Lough on the inflowing river. It should not be confused with the small lough to the south. White's Lough is fished from the shore. It is rarely without a salmon and is famous for producing big sea trout. This is a really great little lough when conditions are right and it is always worth fishing.

CAHEREESHAL LOUGH   L 83 43

Permission: The Fishery Manager, Zetland Hotel, Cashel, Co. Galway.
Tel: (095) 21010

Cahereeshal is approached by the same route as Feaghroe Lough, above. Leave the car at Lettershinna village and walk the last 300 yards in a northerly direction. It is a small lough, full of lively, hard-fighting little brown trout. They average under ½ lb and you are likely to get 10 or 12.

LOUGHAWILLAUN   L 84 44

Permission: The Fishery Manager, Zetland Hotel, Cashel, Co. Galway.
Tel: (095) 21010

To get to Loughawillaun, take the small road almost to Lettershinna village but, before you quite arrive at the village, start walking across the bog in a north-easterly direction, keeping the two small loughs on your right. This is going to be a long walk – a good 1½ miles – and it will take a minimum of 30 minutes to get there. The lough holds brown trout and sea trout after the August floods. It is one of the better loughs on the whole system. The sea trout average ¾–1 lb, but it gets some good ones too and they have been caught up to 5½ lb. This lough is shallow and dotted with islands, as the name denotes. There is one boat, but some people prefer to fish it from the shore. This is a very isolated place. There are no set drifts and you are likely to pick up a fish anywhere. It is really a September–October fishery and the flies to bring are Green Peter, Murrough, Daddy, Bibio, Black Pennell and Watson's Fancy.

KANE'S LOUGH   L 85 44
Permission: Not usually required

This is a small lough lying to the south-east of Loughawillaun and a few hundred yards beyond it. The walk is a long one but could well be rewarded because the lough holds lovely, deep, hard-fighting brown trout. It fishes well from March and can be particularly good in April. The average weight of the trout in Kane's is 1 lb and fish to 2 lb are taken every season. The banks are fishable, but the southern bank is a bit high. There are islands along the east side and it is possible to wade out to them and fish all round. If you want a challenge, then head for Kane's Lough – you are unlikely to come back empty-handed. Favoured patterns are Mallard and Claret, Sooty Olive, Invicta, Murrough and Daddy.

THE BADGER'S LOUGH   L 85 44
Permission: Not usually required

Take the same route as for Kane's Lough (above); this small lough lies to the south of it. It is a long walk – take good care that you can find your way back again – but it is usually well worth the effort. This is a small lough that is very remote indeed but holds brown trout to over 3 lb and the average size is remarkably large – nearly 2 lb. These are well-shaped, hard-fighting trout. You will do well to get 2 in a day, but you can be sure that one of them will be a good one. Try and get there in April and try them with a Sooty Olive, Duckfly, Peter Ross, Black Pennell, Butcher, Watson's Fancy and Bibio.

LOUGH NAMBRACKMORE   L 86 43
Permission: Not usually required

Take the tarred road east off the L102 Recess–Carna road, park the car at Lettershinna and prepare for a long walk. This lough is a good 1½ miles from Lettershinna. You are about halfway when you reach White's Lough, which you should keep on your right. Nambrackmore is the largest lough in the area and it has three islands. The banks are good and can be fished all round. It holds a good stock of brown trout up to 2½ lb. It is essential to have a wind on it, so don't set out unless there is a nice breeze blowing. Fly fishing is the most popular fishing method, but some prefer to spin for the big ones. This is a lough for anglers who like a challenge and very often they are rewarded for their efforts. Again, try it early in the season and bring a Sooty Olive, Butcher, Black Pennell, Watson's Fancy and Bibio.

INVERMORE LOUGH

Permission:
Mr Tom Ryan, Auctioneer, Cong, Co. Mayo.
Tel: Cong 35;
The Fishery Manager, Zetland Hotel, Cashel, Co. Galway.
Tel: (095) 21010

This lough is approached by taking the sand road north off the L102 Screeb–Carna road at Invermore Bridge. The lough is close by this road and the boat is at the nearest point. This lough holds sea trout and salmon and can fish well from early June until October. The trout are free-rising for the most part and vary in size between ¾ lb and 6 lb. However, it is generally regarded as producing better than average sea trout and there are days when the majority of the catch will weigh 2 lb or over. It can be fished all over for trout and the bay where the river drains (known as the 'salmon pool') out is a favourite lie for a salmon. An average catch should consist of 6–8 trout and bigger catches are frequently recorded. The lough is very shallow and it is a bit like a minefield with rocks lurking everywhere under the surface in the dark peat-stained water. Don't be put off. It is well worth while putting up with them for surely this is one of the best sea-trout fisheries in the west of Ireland. The usual sea-trout flies all work, but don't be without a Green Peter and a Peter Ross.

LOUGH AVALLY   L 89 39

Permission:
Mr Tom Ryan, Auctioneer, Cong, Co. Mayo.
Tel: (092) 46035;
The Fishery Manager, Zetland Hotel, Cashel, Co. Galway.
Tel: (095) 21010;
Paddy Nee, Hon. Secretary, Rosmuck Anglers' Association, Turloch, Rosmuck, Co. Galway

This lough lies on the opposite side of the sand road to Invermore Lough (above) but, unlike it, this is mainly a brown-trout fishery. The brown trout average 1 lb and sea trout up to 4 lb have been taken. It is a deep lough and fishes best in a west or east wind. Some of the best fishing may be had in the area of the sandy bay along the west shore. Avally can be a slow lough to get fish out of because the sea trout seem to wander in and out, but it has good potential and ought not to be overlooked, especially in the month of July.

LOUGH ALIGGAN (Luggeen Lough)   L 88 40
LITTLE LUGGEEN

Permission:
Mr Tom Ryan, Auctioneer, Cong, Co. Mayo.
Tel: (092) 46035;
The Fishery Manager, Zetland Hotel, Cashel, Co. Galway.
Tel: (095) 21010

Luggeen is a long narrow lough and is approached via the same sand road from Invermore Bridge on the L102 as the previous lough. This is another of the great sea-trout loughs in this area. There is a 10-inch size limit and it is fly fishing and dapping only. Three boats are available and there is a small car park and lunch hut. When conditions are right, this can be a free-taking fishery and has produced sea trout up to 6¾ lb and salmon to 10 lb. The fishing starts here as early as mid-June. Luggeen can be fished all along the south shore, both close in and well out. Both ends are good as well, but the middle section of the north shore is regarded as too dour and is rarely fished. The lough fishes best in a west or an east wind; if the wind blows from the south, tie up the boat and fish from the shore. This can be a great lake and it certainly is a favourite with sea-trout fishermen. It once produced 69 sea trout to three rods on a very bright day. Don't be without a Claret Bumble and a Kingsmill late in the season.

To the east – under the bridge – is a small lough known as Little Luggeen. It can be fished by anglers fishing Big Luggeen. It is well worth a try, especially if there is a nice west wind blowing. There is a good salmon lie in the farthest south-east corner.

LOUGH CURREEL   L 87 42

Permission:
Mr Tom Ryan, Auctioneer, Cong, Co. Mayo.
Tel: (092) 46035;
The Fishery Manager, Zetland Hotel, Cashel, Co. Galway.
Tel: (095) 21010

Take the same sand road as for Luggeen, above, and continue past the lunch hut, across the bridge and up the new forest road to the end. From here a walk of about 20 minutes on along a well defined path will bring you to Curreel. Again it is fly fishing and dapping and no outboards, for obvious reasons – this lough has just about as many hidden underwater rocks and reefs as you will meet anywhere. But don't be put off. This is one of the most peaceful, beautiful and productive fisheries in the whole of Connemara. It is also one of the most consistent loughs for big sea trout. The trout get up there about mid-July in a wet season and, from mid-September until closing day in October, it can be magic. The trout average nearly 1½ lb and fish to 6¾ lb have been taken. A notable feature of the lough is the lovely cut-stone bungalow on the island where you can pull in and have your lunch. It is unlikely that you will fish for sea trout in these parts for very long before someone says to you, 'Have you been to Curreel?' All the usual sea-trout flies work well. A Camusunary Killer is worth trying and a Connemara Black is probably the best fly of all. There are those, too, who favour a Claret Murrough, and others who like to dap. In September-October, never be without a Daddy. You can pick up a trout anywhere on this lough. Favourite drifts are along by the north shore from the inflowing river, and from the islands west of the bungalow to the mouth of the outflowing river.

STUCKIE LOUGH   L 88 42

Permission: Not usually required

This small lough lies about half a mile due north of Curreel (above) and access to it is by the same route. This is an unusual lough in that it is located in the middle of a bog with no apparent spawning stream, and yet it holds a good stock of lovely brown trout. These fish can be quite free-rising and some are over 3 lb. Most of the banks are fishable – there are some reeds – and the best time to pay a visit is either April or September. Fly fishing is the usual way of fishing it and favourite patterns are Mallard and Claret, Sooty Olive and Daddy.

OWENGARVE LOUGH (Shanaket Lough)   L 87 43

Permission:
Mr Tom Ryan, Auctioneer, Cong, Co. Mayo.
Tel: (092) 46035;
The Fishery Manager, Zetland Hotel, Cashel, Co. Galway.
Tel: (095) 21010

To get to Shanaket is an adventure in itself, so heed the directions carefully – including which side of the river to follow. Turn off the N59 Galway–Clifden road 20 yards west of Caher Guest House near Recess. Cross the bridge and bring the car about half a mile to a small lay-by overlooking Cappahoosh Lough. Then walk due south up the hill, following the white marker posts, down the other side and across the forest fence, and then across the bog until you reach Emlough East (described below). Take the boat and row to the south of that lough and tie the boat securely. Walk along the left bank of the river until you reach Cushmeg Lough. Take the boat that is tied at the river mouth and row south and into Shanaket through the narrow neck. Shanaket holds brown trout and sea trout up to 5 lb and fishes particularly well in August, September and October. Make no mistake, this can be a lively fishery, especially after a September flood. It can be fished all over, but the best area is probably the bay on the north side, where the outflow enters from Cushmeg. All the usual fly patterns work, but put your faith in a Daddy, a Green Peter, a Murrough, a Delphi and a Kingsmill.

CUSKEAMATINNY LOUGH   L 86 44
(Cushmeg Lough)
Permission:
Mr Tom Ryan, Auctioneer, Cong, Co. Mayo.
Tel: (092) 46035;
The Fishery Manager, Zetland Hotel, Cashel, Co. Galway.
Tel: (095) 21010

Access to Cushmeg is gained by following the same long adventurous route as to Shanaket. Once again, it can be well worth all the effort. This is another of these remote loughs on the Invermore system where you could have a day to remember. It is a great lake for big sea trout and for a good catch too, especially in September. The quality of the trout is excellent and catches of 8 or 10 are not unusual. In 1985, two anglers had 19 sea trout for 37 lb in 2½ hours and the best fish was 4¾ lb. A couple of years previously, one angler had 7 for 19 lb in just 2 hours in flood conditions. The Daddy is definitely the favourite on Cushmeg and dapping can get good results too. The best fish ever was 6½ lb. There are two islands and there is a lunch hut on one of them. The best fishing areas are around the islands and along by the north shore. This is one lough where it pays to fish close to the shore. A truly great sea-trout lough!

LOUGHANNEMLAGH (Emlough East)   L 87 45
Permission:
Mr Tom Ryan, Auctioneer, Cong, Co. Mayo.
Tel: (095) 46035;
The Fishery Manager, Zetland Hotel, Cashel, Co. Galway.
Tel: (095) 21010

Emlough East is reached by the same route as described for Cushmeg (it should not be confused with Emlough on the Gowla Fishery). It is one of the top loughs on the Invermore Fishery and doesn't fish well until late in the season – from August at the earliest on into October. It is predominantly a sea-trout lough and has produced some good ones in the past. Trout considered well over 10 lb have been seen spawning in the inflowing stream. It is a shallow lough with many islands which may be fished all over, though favoured areas are along by the east shore and around the mouths of the inflowing and outflowing streams. There is one boat, but if the wind does not suit drifting try bank fishing. Two of the better flies on Emlough East are a Daddy and a Green Peter.

LOUGH AGAY   L 88 44
LOUGH MONGAUN   L 88 44
Permission: Not usually required

To reach these two loughs take the forest road off the N59 Maam Cross–Recess road opposite Derryneen Lough and the old school. The loughs lie on either side of this forest road about one mile from the main road. Each of them holds brown trout with an average weight of ½ lb and, in a wet season, they get a run of small sea trout up to 1 lb. Both can be fished all round the bank and they are certainly worth a try late in the season, especially if there has been a lot of rain.

LOUGH BUNNAHASK   L 89 41
Permission:
Mr Tom Ryan, Auctioneer, Cong, Co. Mayo.
Tel: (095) 46035;
The Fishery Manager, Zetland Hotel, Cashel, Co. Galway.
Tel: (095) 21010

Take the sand road north from the L102 Screeb–Carna road at Invermore Bridge and continue past Luggeen Lough. Then take the car up to the end of the new forest road about ½ mile past the lunch hut and park by the roadside. Then walk east for 400 yards across the bog. It can be a very lively sea-trout lough from early July and it holds occasional salmon too. Don't be put off by its size. The trout here are free-rising and average 1 lb, with some to 5 lb. There is one boat and, if it drifts too fast, tie it to a stone and keep fishing.

LOUGH DUFF   L 88 41

Permission: Not usually required

Lough Duff lies about a ¼ mile due east of Curreel, above, and is approached by the same route. It holds small brown trout only and, as may be expected in an area with such good fishing, Duff is rarely fished.

LOUGH ARUSHEEN (Rusheen)   L 90 42

Permission:
Mr Tom Ryan, Auctioneer, Cong, Co. Mayo.
Tel: (095) 46035;
The Fishery Manager, Zetland Hotel, Cashel, Co. Galway.
Tel: (095) 21010

Take the sand road north off the L102 Screeb–Carna road ½ mile east of Invermore Bridge. Bring the car 1¼ miles approximately and walk the remaining 1½ miles north along the path to the boat pier. This is a good 40-minute walk. Rusheen involves the longest walk of all the Invermore sea-trout loughs and the angler should remember to allow plenty of time for the return journey on a September or an even darker October evening. This lough comes into great demand around mid-September. Little wonder! It can hold very big sea trout and can be fished all over. All it needs is a ripple for the sea trout to start taking. It once produced 13 sea trout weighing 29 lb with the best trout 5¼ lb, and in another memorable day's fishing two rods took 35 sea trout. All the usual sea-trout flies work well, but the Daddy and the Green Peter are favourites. Keep a Sooty Olive on the middle dropper – it is the fly that accounted for most of the big catch mentioned above.

Barnahask is a small, narrow lough running south from Rusheen. It can hold sea trout, too, in high-water conditions and is well worth a few casts either on the way to or from Rusheen.

SRUFFNACONNEELAGH LOUGH   L 91 43

Permission:
Mr Tom Ryan, Auctioneer, Cong, Co. Mayo.
Tel: (095) 46035;
The Fishery Manager, Zetland Hotel, Cashel, Co. Galway.
Tel: (095) 21010

This lough is a further ¾ mile to the north-east of Rusheen. It gets a run of sea trout in September and holds fair-sized brown trout. It is so far off the beaten track that it is rarely fished.

INVERBEG LOUGH   L 90 39
Permission: This is a private fishery and rods are not usually let

Inverbeg Lough lies to the north of the L102 Screeb–Carna road. It gets a good run of sea trout from late June and occasional salmon.

LOUGH INVERNAGLERAGH   L 91 39
LOUGH NAGAVNYGARRIVA   L 92 40
SHANNAVARA LOUGH   L 92 42
Permission: These loughs are not usually let

The former is known as the Home Lough and the latter as Owengarie. They both get a good run of sea trout from July.

LOUGH AROOLAGH   L 92 38
Permission:
Paddy Nee, Hon. Secretary, Rosmuck Anglers' Association, Turloch, Rosmuck, Co. Galway;
Mr T. J. Clarke, Ti Clark, Rosmuck, Co. Galway.

This is a fine brown trout lough situated at the junction where the Rosmuck road joins the Screeb road about 2½ miles west of Screeb. It holds a very big stock of brown trout averaging about ½ lb. Hardly a season passes without some big catches being made, but in spite of its proximity to the sea it does not hold salmon or sea trout. There is a boat available and fly fishing and dapping are the favoured methods. Useful fly patterns are Wickham's Fancy, Mallard and Claret, Connemara Black, Invicta, Black and Peacock and Dunkeld. A note of historical interest: Pearse's Cottage overlooks this lough.

LOUGH ADAV   L 93 40
Permission: The Manager, Screeb Fishery, Screeb, Camus P.O., Co. Galway.
Tel: (091) 74110

Adav involves a long walk, but for many it has proved well worth it. It lies far to the north of Screeb powerhouse. Take the narrow tarred road that runs north 400 yards west of the powerhouse and continue for about 1 mile to the end of Glencoh village. Park the car and walk a further 1½ miles due north. The season opens here on 1 February and fly fishing is preferred. The lough holds good stocks of brown trout with the unusually good average size of ¾ lb and fish to 2 lb are reported to have been taken. They can be very free-rising, especially in March, April and September. The shore-line is good with a sandy beach on the north side and the lough is fishable all round. By anyone's reckoning, this is a good little fishery in spite of the trouble it takes to get there. If you like an adventure and a challenge, then head for Adav and take along a Black Pennell, Invicta, Mallard and Claret, Watson's Fancy and Connemara Black.

LOUGH AHALIA   L 95 39
Permission: The Manager, Screeb Fishery, Screeb, Camus P.O., Co. Galway.
Tel: (091) 74110

Ahila is situated north of the junction of the L100 and L102 at Screeb. It is really three interlinked loughs: the lower one is Glencoh Lough, the one in the middle is Derrywonniff, while the top one is known as Screeb Lake and is sometimes referred to by anglers and locals as the Lunch-Hut Lake. Ahalia is the bottom lough on the Screeb system and is a famous salmon and sea-trout fishery. It is also at present the site of extensive hatchery opera-tions, with the purpose of increasing the stocks. This lough holds equally good stocks of salmon and sea trout and the season runs from May until October. Only the top part of the lough is fished – the Lunch-Hut Lake – and it is divided into three beats with boats and boatmen available by prior arrangement. It can fish well in any wind, but a northwesterly is preferred. The lough is shallow and produces sea trout up to 6 lb and salmon to about 14 lb. The pool where the river flows in is a separate beat and can hold a lot of salmon – it once produced 35 salmon for Lord Davis in 3 days. A fishing lodge and accommodation are available with the fishery. While only the top lough is fished at present, it is possible that Derrywonniff could also be developed into a fishery. Fishery protection staff have reported seeing salmon lying in the narrow neck of water and, anyway, all the fish that enter the system must pass through. Bring a few salmon flies in sizes 6, 8 and 10 – Silver Doctor, Black Doctor, Thunder and Lightning, Blue Charm, Hairy Mary, Silver Badger and Stoat's Tail. For the sea trout, try Claret Bumble, Daddy, Peter Ross, Kingsmill, Watson's Fancy, Bibio, and Teal, Blue and Silver.

LOUGH KNOCKAUNAWADDY   L 97 39
GLENTRASNA EAST LOUGH   L 98 39
Permission: The Manager, Screeb Fishery, Screeb, Camus P.O.,

Co. Galway.
Tel: (091) 74110

These two loughs lie to the east of L100 Maam Cross–Screeb road, about a mile north of Screeb Lodge. Access to Knockaunawaddy is off the main road opposite Screeb Lake and Glentrasna East is approached via the tarred road to Glentrasna village. Just to confuse things further, Knockaunawaddy Lough is frequently referred to locally as Glentrasna West Lough. Both are situated on a sidestream of the Screeb system and a good flood is needed to get the fish up to them. Indeed, it is not until late August that they hold adequate stocks, and then of sea trout only. Though both loughs are shallow and tend to get a bit weedy, fish tend to take fairly freely. The average size is ¾ lb and a favourite taking place is at the mouth of the inflowing stream on each lough. Information about boats can be obtained at Screeb Lodge. Fly fishing and dapping are the recognized fishing methods and there is a 10-inch size limit. Both loughs are particularly lively for a couple of days after a big flood and favoured fly patterns include Claret Bumble, Delphi, Camusunary Killer, Connemara Black, Murrough, Green Peter and Daddy.

LOUGH AUGHAWOOLIA   L 97 41
(Cornageeragh Lough)

Permission: The Manager, Screeb Fishery, Screeb, Camus P.O., Co. Galway.
Tel: (091) 74110

Cornageeragh lies along the Maam Cross–Screeb road and there is parking space by the side of the road. This is not a big lough; there is one boat and an outboard motor is not allowed. Angling methods are fly fishing and dapping and there is a 10-inch size limit. It can be equally good both as a sea-trout and a salmon fishery and the fish often get held up here until a flood comes to take them over the waterfall on the inflowing river. It can fish well in any wind and has produced sea trout to over 6 lb. It is shallow and fishes all over and can produce fantastic results when the conditions are right. A favourite fishing spot is at the mouth of the inflowing stream when there is a good current pushing into the lough. It is one of those places where one is almost certain to pick up a salmon. Useful fly patterns are Claret Bumble, Invicta, Bumble, Bibio, Watson's Fancy, Thunder and Lightning, Silver Doctor, Black Pennell and Connemara Black.

LOUGH NAHILLION (Lough Illonie)   L 99 42

Permission: The Manager, Screeb Fishery, Screeb, Camus P.O.,
Co. Galway.
Tel: (091) 74110

Park the car by the side of the road at Cornageeragh Lough (Lough
Aughawoolia) and take the pathway on the opposite side of the
road and follow it for over a mile. Illonie holds brown trout with
an average weight of ½ lb and late in the season it can produce a
few sea trout. It is not highly regarded as a fishery compared with
some of the other superb loughs around.

LOUGH DOWN   L 97 42

Permission: The Manager, Screeb Fishery, Screeb, Camus P.O.,
Co. Galway.
Tel: (091) 74110

Park on the side of the L100 Maam Cross–Screeb road and follow
the stream from above the waterfall at Cornageeragh Lough for
about ¾ mile. Lough Down is a small lough that can be fished
from the bank. It holds good brown trout up to ¾ lb and
occasional sea trout late in the season. It can fish reasonably well in
either April or September and standard lough fly patterns will do.

LOUGHAUNFREE (Cornaree Lough)   L 96 42

Permission: The Manager, Screeb Fishery, Screeb, Camus P.O.,
Co. Galway.
Tel: (091) 74110

Cornaree Lough lies to the west of the L100 Maam Cross–Screeb
road, and is another of the interlinked loughs on the Screeb system.
Park at the old quarry by the roadside. This is another of those
loughs that needs a good flood or two to bring up the salmon and
sea trout. It is therefore usually July before it starts fishing well and
it can then be good to the end of the season. For some reason
Cornaree holds particularly good sea trout, well above the average
for the rest of the fishery. Every year, 4-lb and 5-lb sea trout are
taken. It is a shallow lough that can be fished all over. One boat is
available, but outboards are not allowed. Try all the usual fly
patterns – especially Bibio, Watson's Fancy and Green Peter.

LOUGH NAHASLEAM (Lough Asleam)   L 96 43

Permission: The Manager, Screeb Fishery, Screeb, Camus P.O., Co. Galway.
Tel: (091) 74110

This lough is bisected by the L100 Maam Cross–Screeb road. It is another of the loughs on the main system and furthermore has a fairly sizeable spawning catchment of its own, particularly on its western side. Parking space is along the road. There are two boats available and outboards are not allowed. This lough fishes from July and holds sea trout and salmon. In fact it holds a lot of salmon, and a good way of tempting one is to stand on the shore at the south-east corner of the west lough and cast across the current in that particular spot. It is important to stand well back. Otherwise, hope for broken weather and north-west wind. This is a shallow lough that fishes all over. It will also give you a chance of taking a better than average sea trout – up to 6 lb. Many come to the dap and this method can be very productive and particularly worth a try on one of the brighter days with even a light wind.

LOUGH SHINDILLA (LOWER)   L 96 45

Permission:
Mr Michael Keogh, Peacock's, Maam Cross, Co. Galway.
The Manager, Screeb Fishery, Screeb, Camus P.O., Co. Galway.
Tel: (091) 74110

Lower Shindilla lies to the south-west of the junction of the N59 and L100 at Maam Cross. It holds brown trout – of small average size – and can get a good run of sea trout and an equally good run of salmon in a wet season. Otherwise salmon and sea trout will be scarce until a few floods have passed down. There is a boat available.

LOUGH SHINDILLA (UPPER)   L 94 45

Permission:
Mr Harry Hodgson, Currarevagh House, Oughterard, Co. Galway.
Tel: (091) 82313;
The Manager, Screeb Fishery, Screeb, Camus P.O., Co. Galway.
Tel: (091) 74110

This is the top lough on the Screeb system and the first big lough to the north of the Maam Cross–Clifden road, about ½ mile west of Maam Cross. It is about 1½ miles long and has a number of islands. It can fish in any wind and holds brown trout and, late in the season, it gets a run of salmon and sea trout. In fact it offers a good chance of a salmon, and the best drifts are along the shore, especially towards the western end of the lough. It needs plenty of water to get the fish up and the most suitable fishing conditions are a strong west or south-west wind and cloud overhead. There are boats available and these are kept at the Clifden end of the lough along by the wooded island.

ARDDERRY LOUGH   L 97 45
Permission: Mr Jim Symes, Maam Cross, Co. Galway.

This is the big, long lough to the south of the N59 at Maam Cross. It is a shallow lough, holding brown trout, and – in a wet season – a relatively small head of sea trout and occasional salmon. It has the name of being a dour fishery, which one can easily understand since it is right at the top of the system.

LOUGHAUNULTERA (The Camus Lakes)   L 96 34
Permission: The Manager, Screeb Fishery, Screeb, Camus P.O., Co. Mayo.
Tel: (091) 74110

This is a series of interconnected loughs running in a north–south direction and lying between Camus Hill to the west and the L100 Screeb–Costello road to the east. They can be approached off the L100 across the bog, but the going can be very soft. A better approach is to take the old bog road south off the Screeb–Camus road, leaving the car along the roadside. These loughs hold brown trout and have a reputation for producing them in large quantities. The average size is ½–¾ lb and the fish rise well to the fly and catches of 10 and 15 trout are made regularly. They are certainly very free-rising and it is one fishery that can be recommended as giving good, lively fishing. The northern lough – which has no name – seems to hold the largest trout. One remarkable catch of 75 trout to ¾ lb was taken by an angler in a single day in recent times. The season runs from 1 March to 12 October and fly fishing is probably the most effective method of all. Successful fly patterns are Greenwell's Glory, Butcher, Black Pennell, Watson's Fancy, Peter Ross and various nymphs, pupae and small dry midge and sedge patterns.

LOUGH FURNACE   L 97 36

Permission: Mr P. Berridge, Furnace Lodge, Camus P.O., Co. Galway.

This lough is situated to the east of the L100 Screeb–Costello road, about one mile south of Screeb Lodge. It gets a run of sea trout and occasional salmon from July and is best from then until fishing ends on 12 October. There are two boats available and these are moored at the northern point of the lough beside the lodge. Furnace provides good sea-trout fishing and can be particularly lively after a July flood, situated as it is very close to the sea. The fishing is generally let on a weekly basis along with the fishing lodge. Flies to use are Butcher, Bibio, Kingsmill and Watson's Fancy early in the season and Daddy, Green Peter and Murrough in September–October. No doubt other flies are effective too and I have seen a lovely bag of trout up to 4 lb taken on a Yellow Mayfly in early October.

LOUGHNAGARRIVHAN (Garrivan Lake)   L 99 35

Permission: Mr P. Berridge, Furnace Lodge, Camus P.O., Co. Galway.

Garrivan Lake – as it is called locally – lies on a plateau about a mile to the south of Furnace Lough and is on the same river system. Access is gained to it via the sand road from Camus School to Lettermore-Nacoillew village, passing by the cemetery. There is one boat on the lough. It fishes well after a flood has brought up the sea trout and it gets some good ones. It is usually let in conjunction with Furnace Lodge.

LOUGH CARRAFINLA (Lettermucka Fishery) L 96 28

Permission: Mr P. Berridge, Furnace Lodge, Camus P.O., Co. Galway.

Lough Carrafinla is by the roadside to the west of the L100 Screeb–Costello road. It holds sea trout from July onwards until the end of the season. It is tidal and shallow and the trout have a reputation for being hard to catch and are reputed to feed on the bottom. Late in the season it gets a very big run of small sea trout – finnock – that are referred to by the local anglers as harvesters. This lough is let to the Rosmuck Anglers' Association late in the season and inquiries about permission to fish should be made at Furnace Lodge. There is a boat available.

LOUGH HAWNAGHANEEKYNE	L 96 28
LOUGH VAURATRUFFAUN	L 97 28
LOUGHAUNWEENY	L 97 28
LOUGH NAMROUGHANIA	L 98 30

Permission: These loughs are all part of the Lettermucka Fishery. They are let to the Rosmuck Anglers' Association and the fishing is reserved for members of that association (Paddy Nee, Hon. Secretary, Rosmuck Anglers' Association, Turloch, Rosmuck, Co. Galway).

LOUGH ILLAUNTRASNA   L 88 25

Permission: An tUasal Pol O'Foighil, Tir an Fhia, Leitir Mhor (Lettermore), Contae Na Gaillimhe (Co. Galway).

This lough is by the roadside to the north of Gorumna Island. It holds a stock of small brown trout and is difficult to fish because of bank conditions.

LOUGH NAGOWAN	L 87 23
LOUGH AWALLIA	L 87 23
LOUGH HIBBERT	L 87 22

Permission: An tUasal Pol O'Foighil, Tir an Fhia, Leitir Mhor (Lettermore), Contae Na Gaillimhe (Co. Galway).

These loughs are by the roadside on Gorumna Island. They hold small brown trout and some larger ones up to 1 lb. Lough Nagowan also holds occasional sea trout. The open season is from 15 February to 30 September.

BALLYNAKILL LOUGH   L 86 22

Permission: An tUasal Pol O'Foighil, Tir an Fhia, Leitir Mhor (Lettermore), Contae Na Gaillimhe (Co. Galway).

This lough is about ½ mile long by 400 yards wide at its widest point and has several small bays and promontories. It lies to the south-west of Gorumna Island. There is a road on two sides of it and even though it is one of the most remote island loughs in Connemara it is amongst those most worth a visit. It holds brown trout averaging 1 lb, but you are more than likely to get one of 1½ lb and trout to 4 lb have been taken every season. The shoreline is difficult enough to fish, but you will find the south and south-east shores easy enough. The trout here do not rise as freely as in other loughs with much smaller fish. Nonetheless, it is worth a try and I have not met anyone who has fished it who has not expressed a wish to go back again. Useful fly patterns are Duckfly, Peter Ross, Sooty Olive, Invicta, Greenwell's Glory, Fiery Brown, Black Pennell, Bibio, Watson's Fancy, Green Peter and Daddy.

LOUGHAUNWILLIN (Carraroe Lough)   L 93 25

Permission: Mr Frank Barrett, Hon. Secretary, Carraroe Angling Club, Co. Galway.
Tel: (091) 95228

This is a fair-sized lough lying north of Carraroe with roads on two sides. It holds a big stock of brown trout averaging 6 oz, but can also produce quite a few fish up to ¾ lb. This lake has recently been stocked with brown trout. It fishes well from the bank and the stocked fish average 1½ lb. There is a bag limit of 3 trout per day. All the usual lough fly patterns are worth a try.

GLENICMURRIN LOUGH (Costello Lake)   L 99 30

Permission: The Manager, Costello & Formoyle Fisheries Co., Bridge Cottage, Costello, Co. Galway.
Tel: (091) 72196

This is the largest lough on the system and is sometimes referred to as Costello Lake. The reason for this is that, together with the outflowing Cashla River, it forms the separate fishery of Costello. The rest of the loughs upstream on the system go to make up the Formoyle Fishery and, to add to the confusion for the uniniated, one of these loughs is known as Lough Formoyle. Glenicmurrin lies to the west of the Oughterard–Costello road and is linked to the sea by a short river. There are no steep falls and the sea trout can run all the time. It is without doubt one of the best-known fisheries in the west of Ireland for the quality of its sea-trout fishing and it can get a fair run of salmon too. It is a large, shallow lough that can be fished in any wind. There are three and sometimes four boats available and outboard motors are not allowed. There are two approach routes to the lough: the first is via a short sand road to the boat quay at the southern end of the lough and the other is via a bog road off the Screeb–Costello road at Carrafinla Lough. The lough is usually divided into four beats, and each boat has a beat for the day. The first good runs of sea trout come in June and the fishing continues through to 12 October. The average size of the trout is 1 lb, but there are quite a few in the 3–4 lb size range and even up to 6 lb. It was one of the loughs, together with the others on the system, that Kingsmill Moore fished for nearly twenty seasons and on which he developed his famous Bumble patterns. No doubt they still work, together with the fly – Kingsmill – called after him and the usual sea trout patterns as well.

LOUGH CLOONADOON M 00 31

Permission: The Manager, Costello & Formoyle Fisheries Co., Bridge Cottage, Costello, Co. Galway.
Tel: (091) 72196

This is a poor-sized lough lying to the north-east of Glenicmurrin. It is approached off the Oughterard–Costello road via a sand road that runs parallel with the east shore of Glenicmurrin. It holds brown trout and sea trout but the stock of sea trout is not big because it has only very limited spawning facilities of its own. They tend to rest here waiting for water to take them higher up the system. It fishes best a couple of days after a big flood when it has got a fresh complement of fish.

MUCKANAGH LOUGH L 99 33

Permission: The Manager, Costello & Formoyle Fisheries Co., Bridge Cottage, Costello, Co. Galway.
Tel: (091) 72196;
Mr Peter Walsh, Glenicmurrin, Costello P.O., Co. Galway.

This lough also belongs to the Formoyle system and is approached off the L100 Screeb–Costello road via sand roads above or below Kinvarra school. Like Cloonadoon, it holds large stocks of small brown trout and some sea trout. It has the reputation of being a dour enough fishery where the fish are slow to rise to the fly, but like many others can have its good days, particularly in July.

LOUGH RUSHEEN M 01 32

Permission: The Manager, Costello & Formoyle Fisheries Co., Bridge Cottage, Costello, Co. Galway.
Tel: (091) 72196

Rusheen is one of the good fisheries on this system. It is really only a big pool and is difficult to reach. It is usually approached from the Costello–Oughterard road by Formoyle Lodge. Follow the footpath to Lough Formoyle and take a boat to the mouth of the outflowing river. Then walk down the right bank to where the Rusheen boat is tied up. Rusheen holds both salmon and sea trout and can fish well from July, with fish up to 5 lb and a lot of trout in the 2½–3 lb bracket. It fishes particularly well after a fresh.

LOUGH FORMOYLE   M 02 32

Permission: The Manager, Costello & Formoyle Fisheries Co., Bridge Cottage, Costello, Co. Galway.
Tel: (091) 72196

This fishery is located to the west of the Costello–Oughterard road about 8 miles from Costello. Park at Formoyle Lodge and take the footpath to the water's edge. The lough is very shallow on the western side and around the big island, and these areas hold a lot of sea trout after a flood but in low water they are mostly too shallow to fish comfortably. Salmon lie on the points along the south shore and the bays hold the sea trout, as does the area eastwards towards the mouth of the inflowing river, which is one of the favourite drifts. There is one boat available and the lough fishes well in any wind, except a northerly. It is one of the great loughs for many dedicated sea-trout anglers.

DERREEN LOUGH   M 02 32

Permission: The Manager, Costello & Formoyle Fisheries Co., Bridge Cottage, Costello, Co. Galway.
Tel: (091) 72196

Derreen is little more than a big pool of about 5 acres lying in a sheltered, boggy position. It may look insignificant and uninviting, but few loughs can match it for the density of its sea-trout and salmon stocks. It lies above a high waterfall and consequently it takes a high summer flood to get the fish up. Sea trout can be taken all over and, while the same is practically true for salmon, the area to the south-east of the inflowing river is especially good. It has produced up to 30 sea trout to a rod in a day, can fish well at night and is always a good bet for a salmon.

SCHOOL HOUSE LOUGHS
LOUGH NAVREAGHLY   M 02 30
BOVROUGHAUN LOUGH   M 03 29

Permission: The Manager, Costello & Formoyle Fisheries Co., Bridge Cottage, Costello, Co. Galway.
Tel: (091) 72196

These loughs lie to the east of the Costello–Oughterard road and there is usually a boat available on each of them. They hold fair stocks of sea trout from August and the fishing can be very good, especially in a wet season with lots of water to get the fish up.

LOUGH CARRICKILLAWALLIA   M 02 34
(Carrick Lough)

Permission: The Manager, Costello & Formoyle Fisheries Co., Bridge Cottage, Costello, Co. Galway.
Tel: (091) 72196

Park in the lay-by on the roadside about 10 miles from Costello on the road to Oughterard. Carrick is to the west – a fishing sign marks the spot – across the footstick (footbridge) and along by the footpath for ¾ mile. This is another of those loughs that must have a summer flood to bring up the sea trout and salmon. It can fish well in any wind. The centre is deep, but it fishes well along by the shores and the mouth of the inflowing stream is rightly famous. It is a lough that must be fished carefully, without causing too much disturbance to the water, because it can all be covered in a day and you may have to go back on drifts that you fished earlier.

LOUGH SEANACEARCH   M 01 36
LOUGH ENEOR   M 01 36

Permission: The Manager, Costello & Formoyle Fisheries Co., Bridge Cottage, Costello, Co. Galway.
Tel: (091) 72196

Take the Lettermorenacallaigh road east off the L100 Screeb–Costello road at Camus school and park the car before you come to the cemetery. Then take the path up the hill and you will see these two small loughs in the valley. They are both good brown-trout fisheries with trout averaging ¾ lb. The banks are quite good. Useful fly patterns are Greenwell's Glory, Butcher, Black Pennell, Mallard and Claret, Bibio and Watson's Fancy.

LOUGH ACLOGHER (Clogher Lough)   M 03 36

Permission: The Manager, Costello & Formoyle Fisheries Co., Bridge Cottage, Costello, Co. Galway.
Tel: (091) 72196

Clogher Lough lies to the west of the Costello–Oughterard road, about 6 miles from Oughterard. It is approached by a forest road. Park at the lay-by and walk the last half mile. Once the sea trout get up, Clogher, when in one of its good moods, can be one of the finest fisheries in Connemara. It holds sea trout and salmon and it is generally accepted that the average size of the trout is bigger than on any other lough on this system. There are days when they can average nearly 2 lb. This lough is divided by a long island and the navigation route is by the northern point, except in very high water. To the west of the island, the trout are bigger, but hard to rise. To the east, there is a smaller average size of trout and they rise more freely. You are likely to rise a salmon almost anywhere on the east side and especially near the inflow from the rivers. Unfortunately, the forest was planted too close on the east and north shores and this lake now fishes best in a north-west, west or south-west wind. In light wind conditions try small flies, such as Heather Moth, Claret Bumble, Kingsmill, Bibio, Watson's Fancy and Daddy.

LOUGHAUNERIN   M 01 38

Permission: The Manager, Costello & Formoyle Fisheries Co., Bridge Cottage, Costello, Co. Galway.
Tel: (091) 72196

Loughaunerin lies to the north-west of Clogher. It is best approached off the L100 Screeb–Costello road. Take the road for Lettermorenacallaigh village just south of Camus school and park before you come to the cemetery. Then walk up the hill in a north-easterly direction. This lough holds brown trout only. They are very plentiful and take freely. The average size is about ½ lb but there are a fair number up to ¾ lb as well. There is no boat but the banks are reasonably good.

SHANNAWONA LOUGH   M 03 39

Permission: The Manager, Costello & Formoyle Fisheries Co., Bridge Cottage, Costello, Co. Galway.
Tel: (091) 72196

Shannawona Lough is perched high on the shoulder of a mountain of the same name. It is remote and difficult to reach across a rough bog and up the mountain. It is the uppermost sea-trout lough on the system and requires lots of water to get the fish up. It can, however, be well worth a visit in September or early October, as it holds good trout and, if there is no boat available, it can be fished from the bank. Indeed, bank fishing can be nearly as productive as boat fishing, because this is a very deep lough and all of the good fishing grounds are close to the shore. The northern, south-eastern and south-western shores are most productive. This is a lough that can give good results when all the others on the system are still too high after heavy rain.

SHANNADULLAGHAUN LOUGH   M 04 38

Permission: The Manager, Costello & Formoyle Fisheries Co., Bridge Cottage, Costello, Co. Galway.
Tel: (091) 72196

This is a small bog lough about ¼ mile east of the stream from Shannawona to Clogher. It holds a fair stock of small brown trout and is reported to have produced a 2-pounder from time to time. It is very weedy and only worth a few casts on the way past if conditions happen to be right.

ROSSAVEEL LOUGH   L 96 25

Permission: Not usually required

This lough lies to the east of the road at Rossaveel. It holds brown trout only and they are very small but plentiful. Small standard lough fly patterns will do well.

LOUGH NAGRAVIN (Ballynahown Lake)   L 98 21

Permission: Mr M. Bolustrim, Ballynahown, Inveran, Co. Galway.

Situated west and south of the junction of the Costello and Rossaveel roads, this is the largest lough in this area and is surrounded by roads on three sides. It is known to have produced brown trout up to 5½ lb, though the average is ¾ lb. It gets occasional salmon as well. The trout are very free-rising and give good lively sport – this lough can produce very big bags. It is very shallow and rocky, with many bays and islands. Boats are available for hire and visiting anglers are welcome. Fly fishing is the rule and useful patterns are Mallard and Claret, Sooty Olive, Butcher, Black Pennell, Invicta and Silver Invicta.

LOUGH ASTICKEEN   L 97 23

This lough is to the east of the Ballynahown–Rossaveel road. Pass it by because there are no fish of any kind in it.

LOUGHAUNEVNEEN   L 98 22
LOUGH NAHOGA   L 99 24

Permission: Mr M. Bolustrim, Ballynahown, Inveran, Co. Galway.

Loughaunevneen involves a walk of 400 yards approximately, west from the Ballynahown–Costello road, or it can be reached by the stream from Lough Nagravin. Fishing is from the bank only and the trout are small but very lively. The average is about 3 to the pound and you may be lucky to get one of ½ lb.

Nahoga is to the east of the Ballynahown–Costello road and involves a short walk. It too holds very small brown trout and they are not very plentiful.

LOUGH NASKANNIVA (Lough Scannive)   M 00 22

Permission: Mr M. Bolustrim, Ballynahown, Inveran, Co. Galway.

Scannive and the small lough to the south of it lie to the north of the main road at Ballynahown. They hold brown trout and occasional sea trout. They can get a very good sea-trout run in high water. There is one boat for hire. Successful fly patterns are Peter Ross, Butcher, Silver Doctor, Bibio, Black Pennell and Watson's Fancy.

LOUGH OUGHTERAGLANNA   M 00 25

Permission: Not usually required

This is a small lough approximately 2 miles east of the Costello–Ballynahown road. It is approached via a bog road. It has a fair stock of nice brown trout, averaging ¾ lb.

LOUGH ADOORAUN   M 01 24

Permission: Not usually required

Adooraun is approached by a bog road off the Ballynahown–Costello road. It is quite remote and holds a small stock of small brown trout.

LOUGH FADDA   M 02 25

Permission: The Manager, Crumlin Lodge Fisheries, Inveran, Co. Galway.
Tel: (091) 93105

This lough is remote but nevertheless easily accessible by a road that runs north off the L100 Inveran–Ballynahown road about a mile west of Inveran. It is a long, narrow, rather shallow lough and looks more like a river. It gets a run of sea trout from July and some consider that it is underfished for the stocks that it holds. This may be because of its location, for it can only be fished comfortably from a boat in a north or a south wind. It is a lovely lough and perfect for two anglers for a day's fishing. Standard sea-trout fly patterns will do.

LOUGH UGGA MORE   M 04 24

Permission: The Manager, Crumlin Lodge Fisheries, Inveran, Co. Galway.
Tel: (091) 93105

Ugga More is right beside Crumlin Lodge and is easily accessible. It gets a fair run of sea trout from July and the north-west shore and around the inflowing and outflowing streams are considered the best areas. One boat is available. All the usual flies work well, though some of the regulars find that a Green Olive can be the most effective pattern.

LOUGH UGGA BEG   M 03 24

Permission: The Manager, Crumlin Lodge Fisheries, Inveran, Co. Galway.
Tel: (091) 93105

This lough is also known as Crumlin Lake Lower. It is a shallow lough that gets a run of sea trout and occasional salmon from late June and can fish well, especially in a south-south-west wind, until the end of the season. It is fishable all over and the trout can be free-rising and good sport. Fly fishing and dapping only, and there are two boats available. This fishing is mostly let with Crumlin Lodge.

LOUGHAUNBEG   M 07 24

Permission: Not usually required

This is a small lough lying to the north of the L100 Spiddal–Inveran road. There is a road right up to it and at present the lough holds only small brown trout. There is a possibility that it may be stocked in the future with large browns and rainbows.

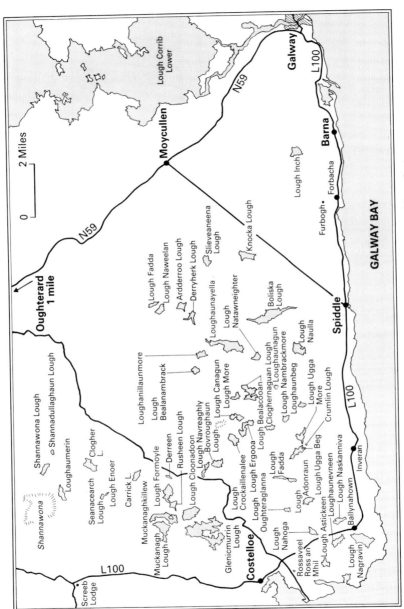

33   The Costelloe, Formoyle, Crumlin and Spiddle Fisheries

LOUGH NAMBRACKMORE   M 06 25

Permission: The Manager, Crumlin Lodge Fisheries, Inveran, Co. Galway.

Tel: (091) 93105

Take the same road as for Loughaunbeg and continue on to a farmhouse by the lough shore. This is a shallow lough holding sea trout from July but one or two good floods are needed to get them up. It is really an August–September lough and can be fished from the boat in any wind. It has the reputation of having once been a great lough with big trout, but now you are likely to find the sea trout sluggish and slow to take after having been such a long time in fresh water before getting this far. They are more likely to be active in short periods after a flood.

CLOGHERNAGUN LOUGH   M 05 26
LOUGH ERGORA   M 05 28
LOUGH CROCKAILLENELEE   M 04 28
TULLYNASHEAY LOUGH   M 05 29

Permission: The Manager, Crumlin Lodge Fisheries, Inveran, Co. Galway.

Tel: (091) 93105

These loughs are very inaccessible. They hold small brown trout and may get a run of sea trout in a season with high floods to get the fish up.

LOUGHAUNAGUN   M 07 26
LOUGH CANAGUN   M 07 27
LOUGH BEALACOOAN   M 07 27
LOUGH MORE   M 07 28

Permission: The Manager, Crumlin Lodge Fisheries, Inveran, Co. Galway.

Tel: (091) 93105

These loughs hold small brown trout and they get a small run of sea trout and occasional salmon. They are very remote.

LOUGH NAULLA   M 10 24

Permission: Not usually required

This lough holds small brown trout and is accessible off the L100 west of Spiddal. The trout come about 3 to the pound.

BOLISKA LOUGH   M 12 25

Permission: Free

This is a fine big lough lying to the north of Spiddal with good access to the shore. It is regarded as free fishing and any angler may put a boat on it with local permission. It is a shallow lough that holds a good resident stock of brown trout averaging ½ lb. Being the first lough on the once famous Spiddal River, it gets a run of salmon and sea trout from early July. It fishes best in a south or south-west wind and all legitimate methods are allowed. The average weight of the Boliska sea trout is nearly 1 lb and it frequently produces sea trout to 2½ lb. The usual sea-trout flies are Bibio, Claret Bumble, Silver Doctor, Black Pennell, Butcher, Green Peter, Daddy and Sooty Olive.

LOUGHANILLAUNMORE   M 10 28

Permission: (west side) The Manager, Crumlin Lodge Fisheries, Inveran, Co. Galway.
Tel: (091) 93105;
(A permit is not usually required for the east side.)

This lough can be approached via a secondary road off the L100 at either Spiddal or Knock. It is a big lough – well over a mile long and half a mile wide. It is on the Spiddal River system and gets sea trout and occasional salmon. It can be fished in any wind and September is the best month to visit it. There is no boat, but the banks are fairly good. The average catch of brownies could be as high as 20 for a day, but it is the chance of a few good sea trout that brings most anglers and these are most likely to be taken from the west side at the mouth of the four inflowing streams.

LOUGH NATAWNEIGHTER   M 09 27

Permission: (west side) The Manager, Crumlin Lodge Fisheries, Inveran, Co. Galway.
Tel: (091) 93105;
(A permit is not usually required for the east side.)

This small lough lies to the south of Loughanillaunmore (above) and can be approached by the same routes. It holds nice brown trout to ¾ lb and gets occasional sea trout in September. It is not much fished before September and a good day should give you 5–6 trout off the bank. Useful patterns are Claret Bumble, Connemara Black, Butcher, Silver Doctor, Bibio, Black Pennell, Daddy and Green Peter.

LOUGHANNAYELLA   M10 30
LOUGH BEALANAMBRACK

Permission: The Manager, Crumlin Lodge Fisheries, Inveran, Co. Galway.
Tel: (091) 93105

These two loughs lie to the north-west of Loughanillaunmore on the edge of the forest. They are very remote and are best approached from Spiddal and up the secondary road by the east side of Boliska Lough. They both hold small brown trout and get a run of sea trout. It is generally September before the sea trout get up in sufficient numbers to warrant fishing for them and both loughs are fished from the bank.

DERRYHERK LOUGH   M 12 31

Permission:
The Manager, Crumlin Lodge Fisheries, Inveran, Co. Galway.
Tel: (091) 93105;
Patrick Curran, Derryherk.

Derryherk is a small lough high up on the Spiddal system at a point where two tributaries and a smaller stream all meet. It is approached via the Derryherk road off the Moycullen–Spiddal road about 3 miles from Moycullen and along by the north side of Ardderroo Lough. It holds small brown trout and sea trout and occasional salmon from July. It is in a delightful setting and, while the largest brown trout will be about 10 inches, the sea trout can run up to 3 lb and there is always the chance of a salmon. It is best fished off the west bank and so the most suitable winds are from the west or south-west. This is definitely a lough for sea-trout patterns and a Silver Doctor, Delphi, Bibio, Watson's Fancy, Black Pennell, Claret Bumble and Green Peter are all worth a try.

LOUGH NAWEELAN   M 12 32
LOUGH FADDA   M 12 33

Permission: The Manager, Crumlin Lodge Fisheries, Inveran, Co. Galway.
Tel: (091) 93105

These loughs are best approached off the N59 Moycullen–Oughterard road. Take the car as far as Letter Lodge and then walk 1 mile in a south-westerly direction. Naweelan holds small brown trout and occasional sea trout from September. Lough Fadda holds brown trout with an average weight of 10 oz but larger trout up to

1½ lb are taken from time to time. In fact, this is an exceptional little lough that can fish well from April and, while you may have to work hard for your fish, you will be surprised at the size of them. The west and north-west shore is sandy and shallow, while the east side is quite deep. Try a Mallard and Claret, Connemara Black, Blue Dun, Greenwell's Glory, Black Pennell and Butcher.

SLIEVEANEENA LOUGH   M 15 30

Permission: The Manager, Crumlin Lodge Fisheries, Inveran, Co. Galway.
Tel: (091) 93105

This lough is approached off the Moycullen–Spiddal road. Turn off to the north-west at Laughil. It holds small brown trout and about 70 per cent of the bank is fishable.

KNOCKA LOUGH   M 15 27

Permission: The Manager, Crumlin Lodge Fisheries, Inveran, Co. Galway.
Tel: (091) 93105;
Mrs Curran at lough shore.

This is a fair-sized lough to the north-west of the Spiddal–Moycullen road. Turn off 4 miles from Spiddal and the lough is only half a mile away. It holds small brown trout and gets a run of sea trout when sufficient rain falls in July to swell the outflowing stream. It has not fished well in recent seasons, but can always produce a surprise for someone lucky to be there when the fish are in the mood. The best sea trout in recent years was 4 lb.

LOUGH INCH   M 21 24

Permission: Not usually required

This lough can be approached off the N59 Moycullen road by taking the road signposted to Barna or off the L100 at Barna. It is about 6 miles from Galway City. The lough holds brown trout averaging about 7 inches, though you will nearly always get a couple up to ¾ lb. This is a good, lively lough and perfect for beginners. Catches vary according to the weather conditions, but you can nearly always be sure of a catch of 6–8 fish. Flies to use include Zulu, Blue Dun, Greenwell's Glory, Black Pennell, Butcher and Wickham's Fancy. Sizes 12 and 14 do best.

16   *Lough Corrib – an early season catch*

LOUGH CORRIB   M 24 30
Permission: Free

The Corrib, as it is affectionately known, has to be one of the world's great game fisheries. It stretches crescent-like around Connemara from Galway City for over 30 miles to Maam Bridge and offers a magnificent variety of angling challenges over a long season. That season begins on 15 February and the first trout are taken on trolled baits, though artificial flies will also give results in sheltered bays, even this early in the season. Serious fly fishing begins in late March with the first fly hatches – large chironomids, known locally as duckfly. This fly hatches in sheltered bays with good weed growth on the bottom and a depth of from 4 to 12 feet approximately. The angler can fish chironomid pupa imitations in calm conditions, but traditional fly patterns in sizes 10–14 are much more productive with a nice breeze blowing. Favourites are Blae Sooty Olive, Red Arrow, Fiery Brown, Mallard and Claret, Connemara Black, Peter Ross, Bibio, Watson's Fancy and Coachman. This fishing can be enjoyed along the west shore from Birchall Bay to Rinneroon Point and on the east side from Rabbit Island almost to Cong, in Carrick Bay to the north of the Doorus Peninsula and on much of Lower Corrib. Depending on weather conditions, the lake olives hatch in late April. The trout again feed freely and can be taken on nymphs, dry fly and wet fly. Popular wet fly patterns at this time are Greenwell's Glory, Blae Sooty Olive, Olive Bumble, Sooty Olive, Cock Robin, Invicta, Green Olive and Claret and Olive. The mayfly hatch begins around 20 May and is undoubtedly the high point of the season, when anglers come from near and far to enjoy its delights. The mayfly fishing lasts for nearly a month. Dapping the natural mayfly – collected and sold by the local schoolchildren – is by far the most successful method and well over 5,000 trout are reported for the mayfly season every year. After mid-June and into early July, the trout can be very difficult to attract, but by mid-August they are back on the move again and a dapped daddy is once more the most successful approach. Natural grasshoppers can also be dapped at this time and, with the onset of autumn and September, wet fly fishing around the islands, along by the shore and across the various headlands will once more get a response from the trout. Useful patterns are Green Peter, Invicta, Black Pennell, Murrough, Bibio, Watson's Fancy, Sooty Olive and Raymond.

Corrib gets a good run of both spring salmon and grilse and the majority of fish taken are caught by trolling. The standard baits are Tobys and copper and silver spoons. The majority of spring salmon are taken in the Cong–Carrick shore area, while the grilse, which are much more numerous when they arrive in June, are likely to take either a fly or a bait in any shallow area. Favourite grilse areas on Lower Lough Corrib are Billybeg, Muckrush, Rabbit Island and the Narrows, while on the upper lough they can be taken anywhere along the west shore from Inishgarraun to the mouth of the Fallomer River. Hot spots in this area are Bog Bay, Oughterard Bay, Inishdawee and along the Glaun shore. Another good area is around Inishdoorus and along the west side of Doorus Peninsula, with special emphasis on Hut Bay. The other good area is the Carrick shore, east past Cong to Inishmicatreer. It is generally agreed that more grilse are taken along the west shore – Inishgarraun to Fallomer River – than anywhere else. They can also be taken on a fly when they come in fresh and favourite patterns are

Green Peter, Silver Doctor, Black Goldfinch, Black Doctor and Thunder and Lightning – sizes 8 and 10.

Access to Upper Corrib is good, with numerous car parks, public quays and slipways. Among the better ones are Derry-moyle, Oughterard Pier, Hackett's Pier, Birchall, Collinamuck, Knockferry, Rinnaknock, Greenfields, Derries, Golden Bay, Lis-loughrey and Cornamona. Access to Lower Corrib is more limited and is easiest from Annaghdown Pier and the Steamers Quay in Galway. There are a number of well recognized angling centres around the lough. Oughterard is probably the best known, but Cong, Cornamona, Headford, Knockferry and Annaghdown are equally well established. There the visiting angler can obtain accommodation and hire boatmen, boats and outboard motors, as well as sharing the company of all those who have come to enjoy the marvellous sport and endless angling variety that is available on Lough Corrib. The salmon fishing season opens on 1 February and the trout season 15 February, and both end on 30 September. There is a statutory 12-inch size limit for trout. A detailed map and angling guide to Lough Corrib is available at a small charge from the Western Regional Fisheries Board, Weir Lodge, Earl's Island, Galway.

LOUGH KIP
M 19 27

Permission: The Manager, Crumlin Lodge Fisheries, Inveran, Co. Galway.
Tel: (091) 93105

Lough Kip lies on a plateau between Moycullen and Spiddal and is best approached off the Moycullen–Barna road at Pollnaclogha. It holds free-rising brown trout and you can count yourself lucky if you get one of ½ lb. The banks are good and it is a good place for beginners to make a start.

LOUGH ATAVAMORE
M 17 31

Permission: Not usually required

Atavamore lies 2 miles west of Moycullen. Take the Polleha road off the N59 north-west of Moycullen. It will bring you within a few hundred yards of the lough, which holds very small brown trout only and is rarely fished.

BUFFY LOUGH
M 13 38

Permission: Not usually required

34   *The Corrib system*

There is a new road up to Buffy from the N59 Moycullen–
Oughterard road or you may walk from the Ross Lake Hotel. The
trout are small, averaging 3 to the pound, but they make up for
their size by their willingness to take a fly. Almost any small fly will
do but try a Butcher, Black Pennell, Greenwell's Glory or Peter
Ross. The banks are good and it helps if there is a ripple on the
water.

LEAD MINE LAKE   M 09 41

Permission: Inquiries to Mr Peter Naughton, Rusheeny, Oughterard, Co. Galway.

This lough of about 10 acres lies approximately 2 miles south-west of Oughterard. One mile out on the Costello road turn right for the village of Rusheeny. Lead Mine Lake holds a resident stock of small brown trout, but it can hold salmon from Lough Corrib as soon as they run the Oughterard River in May and it also gets big Corrib trout from July on their way to the spawning grounds. It can be fished all over. The best areas for salmon are at the inflowing and outflowing rivers. There are hatches of chironomids, olives and sedges and trout up to 4 lb have been taken. The banks are not good and high reeds are a problem, but there is usually one boat for hire.

LOUGH AGRAFFARD   M 06 42

Permission: Inquiries to Mr Jackie Geoghegan, Glengolagh, Oughterard, Co. Galway.

Agraffard lies to the south of the N59 Oughterard–Maam Cross road. It holds a resident stock of brown trout up to ¾ lb and gets a run of salmon from June onwards. It gets Corrib trout from August on their way to the spawning grounds. Fly fishing can be productive and the south-west corner where the river flows in is a likely place for a salmon.

LETTERCRAFFROE LOUGH   M 05 36

Permission: Inquiries to the Manager, Costello and Fermoyle Fisheries Co., Bridge Cottage, Co. Galway.
Tel: (091) 72196

Lettercraffroe lies to the west of the Oughterard–Costello road and about 6 miles from Oughterard. There is a forest road in almost to the southern shore. Kingsmill Moore described it as 'an angler's tragedy, the finest white trout [sea trout] lake that never holds a white trout'. This is quite a large lough by Connemara standards. It is shallow all over with islands and rocks everywhere. The banks are quite good and there is usually no boat available. It holds a very large stock of brown trout and they take freely. The average size is less than ½ lb but it can produce plenty up to ¾ lb. The best catch I know of for the lough was 95 trout taken one afternoon from 3 p.m. This catch was made from a boat. It can fish well from about mid-April and standard lough fly patterns all do well.

SHANNAGHREE LOUGH   M 10 39

Permission: Not usually required

Shannaghree is a small bog lough lying to the west of the

Oughterard–Costello road and about 2 miles from Oughterard. It holds only small brown trout, 3 to the pound. They take freely in the evenings from July onwards, but the banks are soft and difficult to fish.

LOUGH BOFIN   M 02 43

Permission: Inquiries to Screeb Estate Office, Camus P.O., Co. Galway.
Tel: (091) 74110

Bofin is a long, shallow lough running parallel to the N59 Oughterard road. It holds a fair stock of resident brown trout up to ¾ lb, but after the July floods it gets a run of Corrib trout and it also holds salmon from June. The trout have a reputation for being dour and hard to rise. You are most likely to rise a salmon along the shore in the north-east corner and at the western end where the river flows in.

LOUGH APHREAGHAUN   L 99 43
LOUGH CROMLEC   M 01 41

Permission: Inquiries to Screeb Estate Office, Camus P.O., Co. Galway.
Tel: (091) 74110

Both these loughs lie in a remote area south of the N59 Oughterard–Maam Cross road and are approached by a bog road off the L100 Maam Cross–Screeb road. Aphreaghaun is a big lough with rocks and islands and bays and promontories. It holds a good stock of brown trout of ½–¾ lb and is rarely fished. Those who have fished it consider it quite lively and anything up to a dozen trout can be expected in an afternoon. Lough Cromlec is a further 2 miles along the bog road, set on a plateau between two peaks. It has a fair stock of brown trout to 1 lb. Small lough patterns are most likely to get a response in this remote and peaceful area.

TANAGH LOUGH   L 99 45

Permission: Mr H. D. Hodgson, Currarevagh House, Oughterard, Co. Galway.
Tel: (091) 82313

Tanagh Lough is nearly ½ mile long and 400 yards wide. It lies to the north of the N59 near Maam Cross. It is a shallow lough with soft margins and high reedbeds along the shore. These make it hard to fish unless you bring your own boat. It holds a stock of good brown trout up to 1½ lb. Use standard lough fly patterns.

LOUGHAUNIERIN
M 01 45

Permission: Mr H. D. Hodgson, Currarevagh House, Oughterard, Co. Galway.
Tel: (091) 82313

Loughaunierin is adjacent to the N59 2 miles east of Maam Cross. It is easily accessible but the fishing can be difficult, with reeds and high banks in places. It holds a big stock of small brown trout up to ½ lb. However, being at the head of one of the tributaries of Lough Corrib, it gets much larger trout after a good flood in August. Use a Mallard and Claret, Connemara Black and Black Pennell early in the season and a Wickham's Fancy, Green Peter, Soldier Palmer, Butcher and Invicta later on.

LOUGHANILLAUN
L 97 46

Permission: Col. Chavasse, Maam Cross, Co. Galway. (The fishing is not usually let.)

This delightful lough lies to the east of the L100 Maam Cross–Maam road and holds brown trout and salmon from Corrib late in the season.

MAUMWEE LOUGH
L 97 48

Permission: Mr Michael Keogh, Peacock's, Maam Cross, Co. Galway.

Maumwee is to the east of the L100 and adjacent to it about 1½ miles from Maam Cross. The trout are small and come about 3 to the pound. The banks are boggy and difficult to walk but fishable.

LOUGH REA
M 60 14

Permission: Mr Colman Shaughnessy, Hon. Secretary, Lough Rea Anglers' Association, 11 Lakeside Park, Loughrea, Co. Galway.
Tel: (091) 41436

Lough Rea is a fine lough, 1½ miles long by over 1 mile wide. It is situated beside the town of Loughrea and managed by an excellent local angling club. The season runs from 17 March to 15 September and there is an 11-inch size limit and a daily bag limit of 6 trout. Fly fishing and dapping are the angling methods allowed. Access to the lough is good with two boat jetties on the town side. There is a remarkable honesty in this area and it is possible to leave an outboard or even a rod on a boat and come back the following day and find it untouched. The same used be true of most Irish loughs, but regrettably things have changed in recent years. Lough Rea is a spring-fed lough with poor spawning facilities and the club does a great job by cropping the fry from the small streams and transplanting them into the lough. The average size of the trout is 1¼ lb and lovely pink-fleshed, firm fish they are too. It is a well stocked lough, but, because it is so clear, the fish can be quite difficult to rise and you can consider that you have done well if you get 3 in a day. There are good hatches of chironomids, olives and sedges in season. An Olive Nymph, fished properly, can work wonders and dapping the daddy is great fun and very productive in August and September. Some who fish the lough put all their faith in a Muddler Minnow and a Bibio – an unusual combination. This is one of those loughs where you can fish all day without rising a fish and then, at dusk and into the darkness, the water boils with feeding fish. One of the better areas is by the bog along the east shore, keeping to a depth of between 3 and 9 feet. Visitors are welcome and day tickets are available.

LOUGH MASK   M 10 60

Permission: Free

Mask is a limestone lough of some 20,000 acres. It is 10 miles long by about 4 miles wide. It is noted for its beautiful free-rising brown trout. The average size is 1 lb 3 oz but 3-lb fish are common and it holds a big stock of ferox trout to over 20 lb. These big fish are taken by trolling in depths from 10 to 30 feet, usually around the islands in the middle of the lough. The area in question stretches from Carrigeendauv in the north to Ram's Island in the south. There is excellent wet-fly fishing and dapping the mayfly in late May and June is most productive. Dapping the natural grasshopper takes a lot of good fish in August–September. Dry-fly fishing with a lightly dressed Green Drake works well when the trout are feeding on mayfly and shore fishing is possible in a number of places. One such place is the mouth of the canal, where dry Sedges are fished off the shore, and Olive Spinners will take good trout in the summer evenings along many of the bays on the eastern shore. There are good hatches of chironomids from early April and later in that month the lake olives appear and continue into early May. Popular wet fly patterns at this time are Fiery Brown, Sooty Olive, Blae Sooty Olive, Black Pennell, Connemara Black, Peter Ross,

17   *A fine ferox from Lough Mask – 17³⁄₄ lb*

Watson's Fancy, Greenwell's Glory, Mallard and Claret and Cock Robin. The Mayfly dominates the fishing from mid-May to late in June and dapping mayfly and yellow Mayfly patterns work well; the Invicta, Teal and Yellow and Golden Olive are also useful. There is good night buzzer fishing. Trout fishing slows down in July but picks up again in August and September. The best killing patterns from August onwards are Claret Murrough, Green Peter, Bibio, Watson's Fancy, Invicta, Daddy, Golden Olive, Peter Ross and Black and Peacock Spider.

Mask offers the angler enormous variety with vast areas of productive water. To help the angler find the best fishing grounds, the following is a guided tour of the lough, starting at Cushlough Bay and working north in an anticlockwise direction.

Cushlough Bay
Cushlough Bay is shallow and its heavy weed growth in summer makes fishing difficult. It holds a good stock of trout and has hatches of duckfly, olives and sedges. It offers particularly good Buzzer fishing at dusk in May and June
Carrigeennawalla Island, Castle Hag Island, and across to river mouth There are extensive shallows in all of this area with good mayfly and sedge hatches and a sparse olive hatch.
Burnthouse Bay There are some nice deep holes holding good trout. Fish along both shores and around the rocks. The dap can pull up a big trout in any of the inner corners.
Farragher's (Keel) Bay Start drifting well out in the lough in a south-west wind. It fishes best along either shoreline.
Golden Bay This bay has good olive and mayfly hatches. It is shallow and fishes best in a north or south-west wind, starting at least ½ mile out in the lough.
Ram's Horn Bay There are extensive fishing shallows outside the bay and there are two good drifts inside where the dap can work particularly well in August and September.
Lively Bay This bay does not always live up to its name. There are extensive fishing shallows outside the bay and the bay itself is then fished in and around to the right.
The Rocky Shore This is the vast area of shallows and rocks stretching from Lively Bay to Ballygarry Bay. It has good hatches of mayfly, olives and sedges and can be fished with wet fly or dap.
Ballygarry Bay Access from the main lough is from the west and around by the headland, rather than from the south. It is dotted with islands and reefs. It has olives, chironomids, mayfly and sedges. It is an ideal place for fishing dry Buzzers and Olive

Spinners in the evening. The open water can be fished with wet fly and dapping the grasshopper in autumn is frequently very productive.

Bay of Islands (also known locally as Tra na Greine)   There is really excellent trout fishing available all over this vast area at all times in the season. It holds an excellent stock of very big trout and tactics vary from buzzer pupae to dapped grasshoppers.

Mouth of Cloon River   The fishing is limited and the drifts are close to both shores down to the mouth of the river.

Tourmakeady to Annagh Point   There is about 4 miles of shoreline fishing here and the drifts are easiest in a south-west or north-east wind. It is a comparatively safe area and free of rocks but very exposed in a strong wind. It holds very good stocks of trout and the mayfly hatch is generally a week later than on the east side of the lough.

Annagh Point to Foxhill Point and Maamtrasna Bay   There is good fishing in all of this area but the fishing on the south shore of the bay is very close to the shore.

Kilbride Shore   There is good fishing off the shore and around the islands and there is a mayfly hatch.

Upper Mask Bay   Upper Mask is really a lough in its own right, being almost completely cut off from the main lough at the Ferry Bridge. It is over 4 miles long and too deep up the middle for trout fishing, most of which is done at the Ferry Bridge end and around the islands. It holds an excellent stock of trout that rise well during duckfly, mayfly and sedge hatches. There are several boats for hire at the Ferry Bridge.

Ferry Bridge to Big (Red) Island   The fishing is mainly along the shore. This area has an excellent mayfly hatch and fishes best in a west or north-west wind.

Rosshill Bay   The fishing is very limited and the water is too low in summer.

White Island to Inishgleasty   This area offers really excellent trout fishing. There is a good hatch of duckfly off the south point of Inishgleasty and trout concentrate in big numbers in this area in April. The bays along the shore are very good for the dap.

Dringeen Bay   This bay holds a stock of large trout. It gets cut off from the main lough in summer. It is noted for its good shore fishing – with local permission – on summer evenings.

Inishgleasty to the mouth of the canal   Excellent fishing with good sedge and mayfly hatches. This area is noted for its big trout. Bank fishing to trout feeding on sedges and olive spinners is very popular. An 18-lb trout was taken here by an angler spinning off the shore.

The Cuts   These are long, narrow rocky bays to the south-east of Inishowen. They are only the width of a drifting boat in some places and can best be fished in a south wind. Great places for big trout to either wet fly or dap.

Castle Bay   This bay lies to the north of the mouth of the canal but is inaccessible by boat from the main lough in summer. It holds very good trout.

Inishowen   The shallows extend to the west and south. This whole area offers really excellent wet-fly fishing and has a good mayfly hatch.

Caher Bay   This bay is noted for its wet-fly fishing and dapping. There is a small bay to the north of Lamb's Island that gets a great rise of trout to buzzers and olives on summer evenings.

Ballinchalla Bay (also called Ballahalla Bay)   This is a large shallow bay to the south-east of Caher Bay. It gets a great hatch of olives in April and the fish appear to migrate into the bay to feed on them. There is frequently great fishing at this time which anglers do not always take advantage of. It again provides great buzzer fishing late in the evening in May and June. It does not have a mayfly hatch.

Lamb's Island to Curramore Point   All of this area, and out to Martin's Island and beyond to Rialisk, is a mass of fishing shallows.

Ram's Island   Fish along both shores; there is a mayfly hatch.

Corrigeenagur   The best fishing is along both shores. There is a mayfly hatch.

Corrigeennaweelaun   Fish along the shore and the shallows around.

Inishowel north to Devenish   This is a vast fishing area, nearly 3 miles long by 1 mile wide. There is an island and shallows to the west of Inishowel and to the south-west and north. Then continue fishing all the way up to Shintilla and to the west of Devenish as far as the Black Rocks.

Inishoght   There is excellent fishing along both shores and on the shallows to the west. This is a great area for mayfly fishing.

Carrigeendavoe   The fishing along both shorelines is very good. There are good shallows to the north. This is an area where the angler will always rise a fish even when the fishing is quiet in other areas.

Carrigeendauv   Fish along both shores. The 30-foot contour around this island is a noted place for taking a big ferox trout.

Ballinrobe is the major angling centre for Mask, but anglers also stay at Cushlough, Partry, Srah, Tourmakeady, Trean, Ferry Bridge, Clonbur and Ballinchalla. Access to the lough is very good with safe moorings and slipways in most areas. The chief points of access are Cushlough – where there is a large car park, anglers' shelter, public toilets and a number of excellent guest-houses – Cahir Bay, Ballinchalla Bay, Roshill, Ferry Bridge, Annagh, Churchfield, Tourmakeady, Srah, Ballygarry and Aughinish. Anglers should check, as local permission is required at some of the above. A limited number of boats and boatmen are available for hire right around the lough. The newcomer to Mask would be well advised to avail himself of the services of an experienced boatman. Mask is a dangerous place with extensive reefs, capable of splitting a boat wide open, lying just under the surface. There is another factor that visitors should bear in mind and that is that the level of the lough varies by as much as 8 feet from summer level to winter. The Western Fisheries Board has a development and information centre at Cushlough. For information on the availability of boats, boatmen, accommodation, etc., telephone (092) 41562. There is a statutory 12-inch size limit for trout on the lough.

LOUGH NAFOOEY
L 95 59

Permission: Not usually required

Nafooey lies in a deep valley to the west of Lough Mask. It can be approached off the L100 halfway between Leenane and Maam or from the L101 at Clonbur. It holds a limited stock of resident trout but come the September floods and a lot of Lough Mask trout move into the lough on their way to the spawning streams. Even then, it is a dour lough that does not give up its trout easily.

COOLIN LOUGH
M 06 55

Permission: Not usually required

Coolin Lough lies about 2 miles west of Clonbur in the shadow of Benlevy. It is approached off the Clonbur–Ferry Bridge road via a small secondary road that goes within a field of the water's edge. It holds a limited stock of really fine trout with an average weight of 1¾ lb and some of over 4 lb. They are pink-fleshed but seem to put on most of their condition by feeding on small perch. They don't give themselves up easily, so don't be disappointed if you don't get a response. If you do succeed, you will most surely have caught a fine trout in a magnificent setting.

LOUGH CARRA
M 18 70

Permission: Free

Lough Carra has an area of 4,000 acres. It is approximately 6 miles

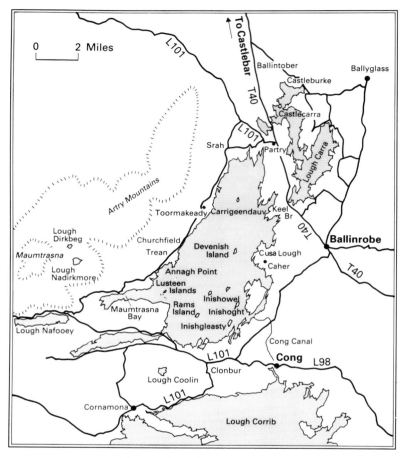

35   *Lough Mask and Lough Carra*

long and varies in width from 400 yards to 1 mile. It lies to the
north-east of Lough Mask and is often overshadowed by it, but
Carra is a great brown-trout lough in its own right. The average
size of the wild trout is greater than in any of the other great
western loughs and it once produced an 18-lb trout. Anglers
believe it still holds trout into double figures and the best chance of
taking one is during the mayfly season. It is heavily fished and the
Fisheries Board augments the wild stock with several thousand
adult brown trout annually to maintain attractive and lively fishing.
The water is crystal-clear, much of it over a white marl bottom,

and it is one of those places where the trout can be clearly seen swimming up to take the fly. Public access to the lough is good and the chief access points are at Brownstown, Moorehall and Castle-burke. There are good hatches of duckfly – chironomids – from late March and lake olives appear in April. The best fly patterns at this time are Fiery Brown, Peter Ross, Red Arrow, Sooty and Blae Olive, Connemara Black, Bibio, Watson's Fancy and Greenwell's Glory. The lough gets a wonderful mayfly hatch all over and this is one of its great attractions. The hatch begins about 25 April, peaks by 12 May and tapers off by the end of May. The trout will take most Green Drake patterns, but it is the superb Spent Gnat dry-fly fishing that is the chief attraction and brings up the very best trout. In warm, balmy weather, the fly wait until about 7.30 p.m. before returning to the water, but in cold weather they will often go out during the day and the angler with the patience to sit, watch and wait will be well rewarded. The principal fly hatches in June and July are lake olives, claret duns, murroughs, silverhorn sedges and various other small sedges. During August and September, the lake olives, murroughs and small sedges are all plentiful and the most successful artificial fly patterns are Daddy, Claret Murrough, Invicta, Bibio, Sooty Olive, Silver Invicta, Dunkeld and Watson's Fancy. The nearest towns are Ballinrobe (3 miles), Castlebar (8 miles) and Partry (1 mile).

CLOON LOUGH   M 14 73
Permission: Not usually required

Cloon lies north of Lough Mask and gets a run of migratory trout in September on their way to the spawning grounds. It holds mainly pike for the rest of the season, but it witnesses an unusual occurrence in that a big stock of pike moves in from Mask to feed on the trout as they pass through the lough.

LOUGH NADERKMORE   L 99 63
DIRKBEG LOUGH   L 99 65
Permission: Not usually required

These two loughs lie in deep valleys to the north-east of Maumtras-na Mountain. They look to be very inaccessible, but there is a secondary road to the larger one and a bog road most of the way to Dirkbeg. For the most part, they only hold small trout coming at 3 to the pound, but from early September, after the first floods, they get a good run of Mask trout. The banks are reasonably good.

LUOGH LOUGH

R 06 93

Permission: Free

This is the most southerly lough in the Western Fisheries Region. It is situated on a plateau to the east of the L54 Liscannor–Lisdoonvarna road and about 2 miles north of O'Brien's Tower at the Cliffs of Moher. Access to the lough is good and it is easily fished from the bank. It holds a fair stock of good trout and fish to 3½ lb have been recorded.

36   *Eastern Fisheries Region*

6 Eastern Fisheries Region

The Eastern Fisheries Region covers the east coast from north Monaghan to Carnsore Point in Co. Wexford. It is an area that is better known for its rivers – the Boyne, the Liffey and the Slaney are household names for game fishers. Dublin, the capital city, is set right in the middle of the area and the anglers amongst its 1 million-plus population may consider themselves hard done by where trout loughs are concerned. The topography of the region does not lend itself to lough formation and anglers must travel for their sport. Some of the best of it is provided artificially in the various reservoirs that serve the towns and cities in the area, and it is none the worse for that. The smaller stocked waters give excellent sport and such is the vastness of waters like Polaphuca and Roundwood that one might as well be on a great western lough. The fishing, too, can be just as challenging and even a little more rewarding at times. The basic fly hatches such as chironomids and sedges are the same all over the country and trout stocked as fingerlings soon become naturalized and grow just as clever and sometimes a lot bigger than their wild cousins. Wicklow has its granite mountains and wild places, while further north few anglers will argue about the quality of the wild fishing on Emy Lough.

LOUGH ANTRAWER   H 54 41
LOUGH APORTAN   H 54 42
LOUGH MEENISH   H 57 41
Permission: Not usually required

These three little loughs lie on the slopes of Slieve Beagh on the Monaghan–Tyrone border. They are about 5 miles north-west of Scotstown. There is a small road to within a short distance of Lough Meenish and Lough Aportan involves a walk of over a mile, while Lough Antrawer is a further mile to the south-west. Each of these loughs holds good stocks of trout up to ½ lb. All can be fished from the bank and Aportan and Antrawer are beautifully situated. Useful fly patterns are Black Pennell, Bibio, Hare's Ear, Fiery Brown, and Butcher. Lough Gullnane – the Stick Lough – is further to the north, but don't bother to go there. It does not hold fish and I have no knowledge of any in Lough Bradan either.

STATUTORY OPEN SEASON FOR ROD AND LINE FISHING IN THE EASTERN FISHERIES REGION

District/Area	Salmon	Sea trout	Brown trout
Dublin			
River Liffey, its lakes and tributaries	1 Jan.–30 Sept.	1 Jan.–30 Sept.	1 Mar.–30 Sept.
River Dodder and tributaries except Bohernabreena Res.	1 Jan.–30 Sept.	1 Jan.–30 Sept.	17 Mar.–30 Sept.
Rest of District	1 Feb.–30 Sept.	1 Feb.–30 Sept.	1 Mar.–30 Sept.
Dundalk			
All lakes, rivers and their tributaries flowing into the sea between Clogher Head and that point where a straight line from the Protestant Church at Drumiskin through the White House, seapoint meets the coast of Co. Louth	1 Feb.–30 Sept. (Freshwater)	1 Feb.–30 Sept. (Freshwater)	12 Feb.–30 Sept. (Freshwater)
Rest of District	1 Mar.–30 Sept.	1 Mar.–12 Oct.	1 Mar.–12 Oct.
Orogheda			
River Boyne, its lakes and tributaries	1 Feb.–15 Sept.	1 Feb.–15 Sept.	15 Feb.–15 Sept.
Rest of District	12 Feb.–15 Sept.	12 Feb.–15 Sept.	15 Feb.–15 Sept.
Wexford			
River Slaney and tributaries southward of its junction with the River Bann to the mouth of the Slaney	26 Feb.–15 Sept.	26 Feb.–15 Feb.	15 Feb.–15 Sept.
Remainder of R. Slaney and tributaries including River Bann	26 Feb.–30 Aug.	26 Feb.–30 Aug.	15 Feb.–15 Sept.
Rest of District	15 Mar.–30 Sept.	15 Mar.–30 Sept.	15 Feb.–15 Sept.
River Slaney and tributaries downstream of Enniscorthy Bridge to mouth of Slaney	15 Mar.–30 Sept.	15 Mar.–30 Sept.	26 Feb.–15 Sept.
River Slaney and tributaries upstream of Enniscorthy Bridge	15 Mar.–30 Sept.	15 Mar.–30 Sept.	26 Feb.–30 Sept.
Rest of District	15 Mar.–30 Sept.	15 Mar.–30 Sept.	15 Mar.–30 Sept.

LOUGH MORE   H 59 48

Permission: A permit is not usually required. There was a report that development work was to be carried out on this lough and so inquiries should be made locally about permission.

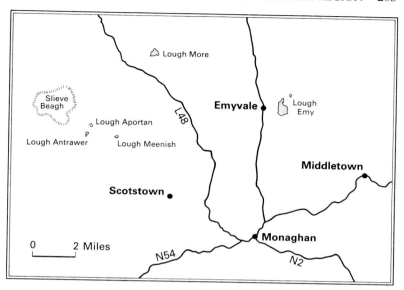

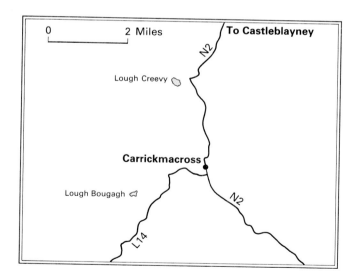

37   *North Monaghan and Carrickmacross Area*

This is one of the most northerly loughs in Co. Monaghan, midway between Emyvale and Clogher in Co. Tyrone. It is not a big lough – maybe 100 acres – and the border runs through it from south-west to north-east. It holds quite a good stock of brown trout averaging 1 lb and you might even be surprised by a 2-lb or 3-lb beauty. There is a good hatch of chironomids in May–June and pupa patterns or a Grey Duster at dusk can take a few fish. It has a good sedge hatch, too, with Murrough in June and again in late July and August. Most of the fly hatches at dusk and evening is the best time to fish here. There is a road to the shore on both the southern and northern sides and space to park a car. Perch have become a problem here in recent times and it remains to be seen what effect they will have on the trout stock.

EMY LOUGH   H 69 44

Permission: A Regional Fisheries Board Permit

Emy is situated a little over a mile east of Emyvale in north Monaghan. The access is good with a road to the shore and ample car parking facilities. This fishery is developed by the Eastern Fisheries Board and the season runs from 1 March to 30 September. There is an 11-inch size limit and a bag limit of 6 trout. Fishing methods are strictly artificial and by fly only. This marvellous fishery of some 140 acres has a fine stock of wild trout and takable trout are stocked occasionally. You will rarely fish Emy without seeing a few fish moving and there is nearly always the chance of a couple of trout. It gets a duckfly hatch in April and the natural fly is unusually small. A Bibio, Black Gnat and a Black Pennell work particularly well early in the season. Later on there is a good hatch of chironomids and the apple-green midge is prominent among the species hatching. Chironomid pupa patterns work well fished nymph-style from the bank and a Sooty Olive, Green Olive and Watson's Fancy can get results too, especially when fished from a boat. There is a mayfly hatch that occurs spasmodically from late May until September. When these appear on the water, it is time to put up a Gosling Mayfly (as for Lough Melvin) or a Green Drake pattern. This is a lough that can be fished all over, though the local preference is to stay within 30 or 40 yards of the shore. It is therefore ideally suited to bank fishing and while this may be somewhat restricted in the early season due to the high water level there is adequate space later on with more than half the banks fishable. Anglers may not put their own boat on Emy Lough. Four boats are available for hire from the waterkeeper, Mr Patrick

McMahon and, these should be booked in advance by phoning (047) 87598. Outboard motors are not allowed.

CREEVY LOUGH   H 83 06
Permission: A Regional Fisheries Board Permit

Creevy Lough is approximately 2 miles north of Carrickmacross and is signposted off the N2 Carrickmacross–Castleblayney road. It holds a small stock of wild trout and is stocked with rainbows. The season runs from 1 April to 30 September and all legitimate angling methods are allowed. There is a 10-inch size limit and a bag limit of 6 trout. This fishery is managed on a 'put and take' basis and is heavily fished by young people from the area. It is bank fishing only and boats are not allowed.

LOUGH BOUGAGH   H 81 02
Permission:
Mr Gordon Sweetnam, 57 Main Street, Carrickmacross, Co. Monaghan.
Tel: (042) 61319;
The Sports Den, Carrickmacross, Co. Monaghan.

Lough Bougagh is nearly 3 miles from Carrickmacross, off the L14 Kingscourt road. Parking facilities are limited. There is a 10-inch size limit and a 4-trout bag limit and all legitimate angling methods are allowed. The lough holds stocked brown and rainbow trout and the stocks are maintained by Carrickmacross Anglers' Club. The shore fishing is difficult due to soft banks and high reedbeds.

LOUGH BRACKAN   N 87 88
Permission: Drumconrath Trout Anglers' Association stocks this lough and day tickets are available from local guest houses or from Mr L. Ward, Drumconrath, Co. Meath.

This is a small lough in a lovely wooded setting, 2 miles south-west of Drumconrath and just off the Nobber road. It is well signposted. The season runs from 1 March to 30 September and there is a 10-inch size limit and a 4-trout bag limit. Fishing is strictly by artificial fly only. The fishing is entirely dependent on stocked trout and both rainbows and brown are stocked each season. The average size is 1 lb, but trout to over 2 lb are taken frequently. The banks are reasonably good and can accommodate about 20 anglers. Standard lough fly patterns all take fish and a Green Peter or a

Murrough fished dry at dusk in July and August can often take a good fish. Don't expect a big catch. Brackan can be slow at times, possibly due to its location with forest on two sides. It is a pretty place, nevertheless.

LOUGH ACURRY (Grousehall Lake)   N 58 98

Permission: Mr Brendan Cooney, Carrickacroman, Tunnyduff, Cootehill, Co. Cavan.
Tel: (042) 60187

Laragh Anglers' Association has obtained permission to fish from the majority of the riparian owners around this lough. It is better known as Grousehall Lake and lies to the south of the L24 Bailieborough–Cavan road, 4 miles from Bailieborough. Access to it is good with a small road to the shore at the east end and more than half of it is fishable from the bank. This is a remarkable lough in that it has always held a stock of trout even though the spawning facilities would appear to be very limited. Over the years, the stock appears to fluctuate between a small stock of very big trout and a reasonable stock of fair-sized trout. The stock is now augmented by the local club with hatchery-reared fish. Trout of 4 and 5 lb are taken every season and the average size of the wild fish is nearly 1½ lb. These trout are slow to come to a fly and persistence is required to get one. The best time appears to be the evening, particularly in June, when there is a good hatch of murrough and a big Sedge fished dry can take a fish or two. The big sedges hatch again at dusk in late July and early August and Green Peter or Murrough patterns fished dry are the surest way of getting the big trout's attention.

WHITE LAKE   N 50 72

Permission: A Regional Fisheries Board Permit

White Lake lies in a secluded valley off the L49 Castlepollard–Oldcastle road. There is a road to the shore at Sallymount House and car parking space is limited. It is not advisable to take the car all the way down to the shore. This lake is noted for its white marl bottom and the clarity of the water. More than half of it is fishable from the shore and there are boats for hire from Mr William Dunne, Sallymount, Castlepollard. The open season is from 1 May to 30 September and there is a 10-inch size limit and a 6-trout bag limit. This lough is stocked with rainbow trout and some browns and it is delightfully situated, surrounded by hills, some of which

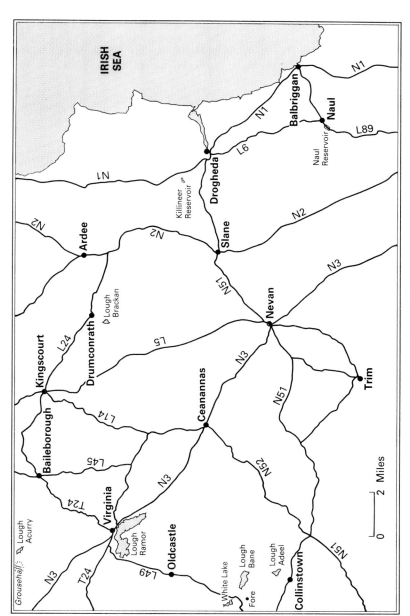

38 The Boyne and Dee systems

are wooded. Trout of up to 3 lb and over are taken every season. Standard lough fly patterns work well when there is a ripple, but the use of a dry fly representing either a chironomid or a sedge should not be discounted. Small brown sedges work well, both during the day and at dusk. There is a hatch of large sedges in late July and August at the opposite end of the lake to where the boats are moored. A Green Peter or a Murrough fished dry can often take a very big trout at this time. This is a lovely lough and well worth a visit.

LOUGH RAMOR   N 57 85

Permission: Not usually required

Ramor is a big lough, nearly 4 miles long, just south of the village of Virginia in Co. Cavan. It is in a lovely attractive setting with many wooded islands. It is highly eutrophic and trout stocks are sparse. The average weight of the trout is about 2 lb but they are rarely taken on the fly except at mayfly time – from mid-May to mid-June. Even then the fishing can be slow. The best fishing is usually around the islands and bays at the north-west end of the lough. Fish are sometimes taken on the dap and the lough was once famous for its Spent Gnat fishing. A small number of trout are still taken by that method.

LOUGH BANE   N 54 70

Permission: Not usually required

This is another of the gin-clear loughs on the border of Counties Meath and Westmeath. It holds a very small stock of good-sized trout, and the most important flies are the sedges that hatch on summer evenings. Fly fishing is possible off the shore at some points, with riparian owners' permission, and Mr Matthew Hand will allow boats to be launched from his land on the north shore. This is a most beautiful lough situated among lovely wooded hills.

LOUGH ADEEL   N 66 55

Permission: Not usually required

Lough Adeel lies over 2 miles due east of Collinstown and about 4 miles north-west of Delvin in Co. Westmeath. There is no public access to the shore and one route is off the by-road to the south-west with the permission of the farmer, Mr P. Burke. This is a very deep glacial lough with deep water right up to the shore and anglers should be very careful not to fall in. It shallows off in the small bay to the east. This lough holds a good stock of big trout, but it is not fished seriously. Most of the trout are caught by spinning and fish to 7 lb have been reported. It has good hatches of buzzers and a big hatch of sedge, and good numbers of trout have been observed feeding on silverhorns on summer evenings. It is possible to fish part of it from the shore and it may be possible to hire a boat from a local angler.

KILLINEER RESERVOIR   O 06 77

Permission:
Mr Frank Smyth, Sports Shop, 30 Shop Street, Drogheda, Co. Louth.
Tel: (041) 37100;
Mr Jim Donegan, Sports Shop, Stockwell Street, Drogheda, Co. Louth.
Tel: (041) 32063;
Mr G. Kelly, St Enda's, North Road, Drogheda, Co. Louth.

Killineer is a small reservoir stocked with brown trout. It lies to the west of the N1 Drogheda–Dunleer road, 2 miles from Drogheda. It is fly fishing only and there is a bag limit of 2 trout. Trout do well in this water and grow fast, and consequently there is a 12-inch size limit. The average size is just under 1 lb and trout to over 3 lb have been taken. Killineer is about 10 acres in area. It holds what might be called educated trout. They rise freely but always a little further away than the angler can cast. There are hatches of caenis, buzzer and sedges. To be successful, the angler must fish fine and small and Green Midge and Black Spider patterns dressed on size 16 and 18 hooks are often necessary to get a response from these discerning trout.

NAUL RESERVOIR   O 12 60

Permission: Mr Chris Byrne, Lecklinstown, Naul, Co. Dublin.

This is a reservoir of about 20 acres to the south of the L85 just west of Naul. It is stocked with brown trout by the Balbriggan and Skerries Angling Club and there is a 12-inch size limit and a bag limit of 2 trout. In addition to the stocked fish, it holds a natural stock of brown trout and, while the average weight is 1 lb, trout have been taken over 7 lb. Useful fly patterns are Connemara Black, Bibio, Sooty Olive, Mallard and Claret and Invicta and 12s and 14s appear to be more effective than the larger sizes. It has a buzzer hatch and gets a hatch of silverhorn sedge. It can be fished all around the shore but the south end is more shallow and tends to hold a better stock of trout.

BOHERNABREENA UPPER RESERVOIR   O 09 20
BOHERNABREENA LOWER RESERVOIR   O 08 22

Permission:
Dublin Corporation, Castle Street, Dublin 2.
Tel: Dublin (01) 776811, ext. 327.
Members of Dublin Trout Anglers and Dodder Anglers Association may fish the Reservoirs and membership cards for these associations may be purchased in most Dublin tackle shops.

Bohernabreena Reservoirs are situated south of Tallaght in Co. Dublin and access to them is off the L199 Firhouse–Brittas road beyond the Fort Bridge. The reservoirs are set in the lovely Glenasmole valley and this is a grand place to spend a summer evening – close to the city and yet far removed from the rush of city life. The gatekeeper must inspect all permits and parking is never a problem because this is one fishery that is rarely crowded. Fishing on both reservoirs is by fly only and this is by ministerial order. The average size of the trout in the lower reservoir is just over ½ lb, with plenty of fish to 1 lb. The feeding here is reasonably rich and the water has produced fish to 4½ lb. This water is no longer stocked and the fish are entirely wild. There are hatches of black chironomids right through the season (which runs from 1 March to 30 September) and there are small olives, caenis in June and a good hatch of sedge from July onwards. Evening fishing usually produces best results and a Greenwell's Glory, a small Hare's Ear and a Hare's Ear Nymph, a Connemara Black, a Black Pennell and an Invicta in small sizes are all worth a try. For dry-fly fishing, a small Black Gnat, Red Spinner or a Brown Sedge are about the most popular patterns. There are no boats available and the best fishing area is along by the dam and part of the west bank. The east bank is unfishable.

The upper reservoir is much bigger and is nearly a mile long. The same angling regulations apply. Here the trout are much smaller and much more plentiful and they come 4 to the pound. But it is a great place to teach someone to fish and the big chironomid hatches often bring on a good rise. The upper reservoir also holds quite a few trout in the 1–1½ lb range and ferox trout to 7 lb. The reservoir has a big stock of minnows and the larger trout feed on them. A useful tactic for getting at the larger fish is to fish a Green Peter or a Muddler Minnow on the surface late at night.

39 *Dublin, Wicklow*

POOLAPHUCA RESERVOIR

N 98 10

Permission:
Electricity Supply Board, Lower Fitzwilliam Street, Dublin 2.
Miley's Bar, Main Street, Blessington, Co. Wicklow.
Day tickets and season tickets are available from some tackle shops in Dublin.

This is the largest reservoir in these islands and is over 6 miles long, stretching from Blessington on the N81 to Valleymount. There is good public access to the water at Russellstown Amenity Park (across from Russborough House), at Featherbed Lane and at Tulferris. Access may also be gained at all the bridges, and this is recommended since local farmers object strongly to anglers crossing their land to the water. The season runs from 1 March to 30 September, there is a 6-trout bag limit and fish under 10 inches must be returned. All legitimate angling methods are allowed except maggot fishing. This water holds a small stock of natural trout but it is heavily dependent on artificial stocking and the average size is ¾ lb. These trout take well and the big bay at Poolaphuca appears always to hold a good stock, while the Valleymount area appears to produce the largest trout. There are good seasonal hatches of duckfly, buzzers and sedges and the water sometimes gets a big fall of terrestrial flies during the summer, the most important of which are daddies. A wide range of traditional flies work well and deep lure fishing is particularly effective, with large Dunkelds, Black Lures and Baby Dolls being the most popular. Bank fishing is allowed, and is widely practised and can be very productive. Anglers may put their own boat on the water after obtaining a boat permit and a number from the ESB. The boats are moored at Russellstown Amenity Park. Outboard motors of not more than 4 hp only are allowed. This is a well stocked fishery that takes a lot of getting to know and these trout do not give themselves up easily.

LOUGH BRAY LOWER	O 13 16
LOUGH BRAY UPPER	O 13 15
LOUGH TAY	O 15 07
LOUGH DAN	O 14 02

These loughs are private and the fishing is not let except on Lough Bray Lower, where a local angling club has fishing rights, but there are no day tickets.

LOUGH OULER   O 08 02

Permission: Free

Ouler lies deep in the Wicklow Mountains, 1,800 feet up on the side of Tonelagee. It is best approached from the Military Road. About 6 miles south of the Sally Gap, cross the Gleninacnass River at the ford which is half a mile above the waterfall and be prepared for a very rough walk of over 1½ miles. The trout are very pretty with big red spots and come about 4 to the pound. There are some bigger fish in there too. These are probably ferox trout and are quite ugly with large heads that are completely out of proportion to the rest of their bodies. Useful flies in small sizes are Bibio, Zulu, Black Pennell, Connemara Black, Mallard and Claret and Butcher.

VARTRY RESERVOIR (Roundwood Lakes)   O 19 02

Permission: Dublin Corporation, Castle Street, Dublin 2.
Tel: Dublin (01) 776811, ext. 327

Dublin Corporation issues tickets for bank fishing and the boat fishing is let to the Wicklow Anglers' Association. Fishing methods are by artificial fly only – a statutory regulation – the size limit is 8 inches and the hours of fishing are from 8 a.m. to one hour after sunset. Bank fishing is not allowed on the north reservoir. The season runs from 1 March to 30 September. The reservoirs hold a stock of brown trout. The trout in the upper reservoir are entirely wild in origin and the average size is around 9 oz. The wild trout stock in the lower reservoir is augmented by stocking occasionally with fingerlings and these become naturalized and are indistinguishable from the wild stock. The average size here is ¾ lb. Wicklow Anglers' Association has boats on both lakes for use by members, but there are none for hire to the public. The trout feed heavily on chironomid pupae and all stages of the sedge from caddis larva to adult. The sedge population has decreased in recent years due to the drought of 1984–5 and the big hatch of Green Peter at Knocktemple is almost gone. Traditional flies and nymph patterns both work well and the Coch-y-bondhu is probably the most important fly pattern. After that come the Bibio, Mallard and Claret, Black Pennell, Bog Fly, Peat Bug, and various caddis larva imitations. Bank fishing is not easy on the lower lake until the water drops in summer time.

GLENDALOUGH LOWER LOUGH   T 11 96
GLENDALOUGH UPPER LOUGH   T 09 96

Permission: Not usually required

Glendalough Lower holds a very poor stock of small trout and is not worth fishing. The upper lough has a fair stock of trout coming 4 to the pound, but it holds some nice trout too and fish to 1 lb have been reported. Near the car park and along the north shore is one of the favourite areas and a Daddy fished in August can often tempt a couple of the better trout.

KELLY'S LOUGH

T 05 90

Permission: Free

This is one of the most inaccessible loughs in Wicklow and probably the best of them all. It lies on the north side of Carrawaystick Mountain and should be approached off the Glenmalure road. Ford the Avonbeg River 1½ miles north of Drumgoff Bridge and be prepared for a long walk. It can take up to 3 hours to get there, up the steep face and across the moor, and it is exactly 2 miles from the roadside to the lough. It is advisable to attempt the journey only in dry weather because the bog can become almost impassable when wet. You should tell someone where you have gone and when to expect you back. The lough holds a good stock of lovely golden trout and the average weight is nearly ¾ lb. Small wet flies work well. Try a Bibio, a Black Pennell, a Mallard and Claret, a Watson's Fancy and a Bloody Butcher.

40 *The Shannon Fisheries Region*

7 Shannon Fisheries Region

The Shannon Region is the largest fisheries region in the country. It consists of the entire catchment of the River Shannon – the longest river (240 miles) in Ireland or Britain – together with part of north Kerry and the coastal area of south Co. Clare. It drains the Central Plain of Ireland, an area rich in limestone. Its loughs are rich and fertile, like the land that surrounds them. I tend to visualize the Shannon loughs as falling into the following categories. First, there are the loughs on the River Inny system to the north-east. Here we have Loughs Sheelin, Owel, Ennell and others, highly developed trout fisheries, where no effort was spared in the past by the Inland Fisheries Trust to ensure that they held bountiful stocks of trout. This work is continued today by the Shannon Fisheries Board. Then there are the loughs on the main river itself – Allen, Ree and Derg – great expanses of water and great mixed fisheries where the trout survive side by side with myriads of coarse fish. These are fertile waters, capable of sustaining big fish populations. The trout are well fed and tend to come to the surface only in mayfly time. The same conditions apply to numerous smaller loughs along the way, though there are more free-rising developed trout loughs on the River Suck system to the west. Developed fisheries and lakes that are managed by a Regional Fisheries Board and where trout stocks are monitored, nursery and spawning streams are developed and pike, perch and roach stocks are culled. In the event of the trout stocks becoming seriously depleted by over fishing or otherwise (e.g., drought, pollution, etc.) trout stocks are maintained by artificial stocking – generally with takable (adult) trout. The third group are the loughs of Co. Clare, where we have a mixture of developed trout loughs on rich limestone and wild hill loughs where the stocks are sometimes augmented with hatchery-reared trout. Wherever you fish in the Shannon Region, you are certain to find quality trout. This is the region that produced the Irish record lough trout – 26 lb 2 oz. It came from Lough Ennell. The season opens for trout fishing on 15 February on the Shannon loughs downstream of Portumna, and on the Co. Clare loughs upstream of Portumna and on the midland loughs it opens on 1 March. The closing date is 30 September, except on the developed loughs of the midlands – Sheelin, O'Flyn, etc. – and on the Co. Clare developed loughs, where it was extended in 1986 to 12 October.

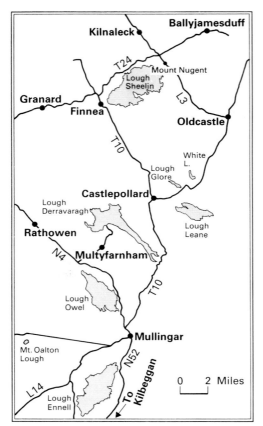

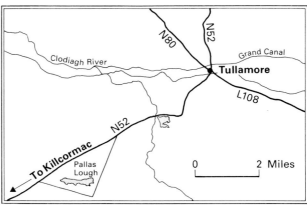

41   *The Midland Lakes*

MONEEN LOUGH   G 98 28
Permission: Free

This little lough is a little over 1 mile due north of the village of Dowra. It is best approached off the L43 Dowra–Belcoo road via a series of small country roads. There is a road all along the west shore and the lough is fishable from the bank on this side only. It holds a fair stock of hard-fighting trout that average about ½ lb. Dark fly patterns work best – Bibio, Connemara Black, Black Pennell and Butcher.

ARDLOUGHER LOUGH   G 97 27
Permission: Free

This is another small lough to the north-west of Dowra. It is best approached off the L50 Dowra–Drumkeeran road and contains trout that average ½ lb, with much better fish taken sometimes. This lough gets a run of trout from Lough Allen via the Owennayle River. The banks are soft with high reeds and it is difficult to fish.

LOUGH ALLEN   G 96 16
Permission: Free

Lough Allen is the first of the big loughs on the River Shannon. It is a great, wild lough, 8 miles long by about 3 miles wide, and lies between the Slieve Anierin Mountains to the east and the Arigna Mountains to the west. It is liable to blow up in windy conditions and a strong north-westerly wind can give rise to particularly squally conditions of which boat anglers should beware. The water level on the lough is controlled by sluice gates and can fluctuate by as much as 8 feet. This is because the Electricity Supply Board uses the lough as a reservoir. The southern portion of the lough from Gobcormongan southwards is relatively shallow, while the wide part is very deep even close in to the shores. The northern portion from Fahy Point, across by the mouth of the inflowing River Shannon and across by Corry Point, is again shallow and provides a suitable habitat for trout. The L43 Drumshanbo–Dowra road and the T54 Drumshanbo–Drumkeeran road run parallel to the shore on either side of the lough for almost its entire length. There are a number of public access points. There is a slip and pier at Cormongan on the east shore and a similar facility is being developed at Corry at the northern end of the lough. There are less developed access points with limited car parking facilities at Cleighranmore and Fahy on the east shore and at Spencer Harbour,

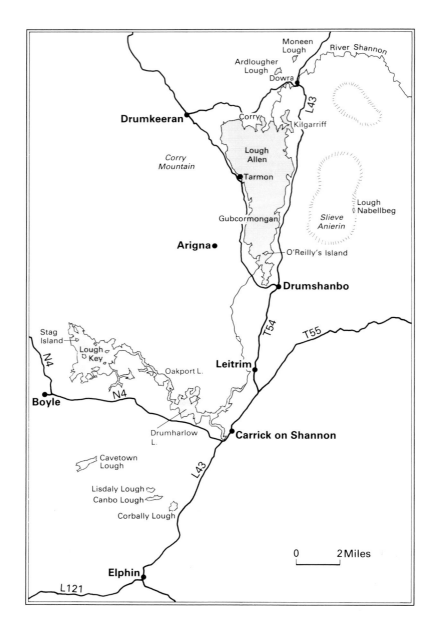

42   *Lough Allen and the Upper Shannon Area*

Strabragan School and Ballintra Bridge to the west and south. Lough Allen is a mixed fishery; it is noted for its pike fishing and holds many other species besides. What is less well known is that it has a good stock of trout, averaging 1 lb with the best one known to have been taken on rod and line weighing in at 16½ lb. There is a small mayfly hatch, though it is maintained that the best trout fishing is in April, August and September. The area from Gobcormongan to the mouth of the Stoney River, on the east shore, is a noted area for trout and is often referred to as 'Murder Mile' by anglers trolling for pike because of the number of trout that come to the baits. Another noted area is across the northern end from the mouth of the River Shannon to Corry Point, while the trout fishing is also good along the western shore by Termon Point, around the islands and shallows at the power station, and in the area of O'Reilly's Island. When the sluice gates are open and water is being drawn off, there can be a considerable current of water between O'Reilly's Island and the shore to the west, a feature which seems to attract considerable numbers of trout to that area. All the standard wet flies work well, according to season, and Bibio, Butcher, Mallard and Claret, Green Peter, Murrough and Daddy are all highly favoured. Dapping can be very good in August and September, with the natural daddy and the grasshopper both effective. Boats are available for hire from Mr P. J. Reynolds, Barrack Street, Drumshanbo, Co. Leitrim, Tel: (078) 41157, and from Mr R. O'Dwyer, Lakeside House, Cormongan, Drumshanbo, Co. Leitrim, Tel: (078) 41112. Outboard motors are also available by prior arrangement.

LOUGH NABELLBEG (Loughaun)   H 03 16
Permission: Free

This small lough is known locally as Loughaun. It is only really a pond 100 yards long by about 50 yards wide. It is approached off the Aughacashel road from Drumshanbo. Turn off at Gallagher's shop and be prepared for a long walk – nearly 2 miles – up the south-east slopes of Slieve Anierin, for this lovely little lough lies at 1,400 feet. It holds brown trout only and small standard wet flies work well. The trout are said to average ½ lb and the size has increased in recent years. The bank is fishable all round.

LOUGH KEY   G 82 04
Permission: Free

Lough Key, just over a mile north-east of Boyle and 6 miles

north-west of Carrick-on-Shannon, is, with its wooded islands and Forest Park, one of the most beautiful loughs in these parts. There are three major access points – at Doon Shore, at the Drum Bridge and from the Forest Park. In each case, there is ample car parking and it is possible to launch a boat. The lough holds a fair stock of brown trout with a big average weight – probably near to 2 lb – but they do not come freely to the fly. In fact Lough Key is only fished at mayfly time, which generally commences about 15–20 May. Every season many fine specimens are taken on the dapped mayfly, but more especially on the Spent Gnat imitation fished dry. This is challenging and rewarding fishing, calling for great skill in boat handling and good angling technique. The careless splash of an oar or a clumsy cast can spoil what may well be the only opportunity that may occur all day. Wet-fly fishing is considered to be unproductive. Favourite areas for Gnat fishing are around by Stag Island, Orchard Island, Hogs Island and Church Island. There are boats for hire from Mr James Egan, Deer Park, Boyle, Co. Roscommon; Mr Thomas Egan, Deer Park, Boyle, Co. Roscommon; and Mr P. Walsh, Rockingham, Boyle, Co. Roscommon.

LOUGH DRUMHARLOW   G 90 01

Permission: Free

This lough lies a little over a mile west of Carrick-on-Shannon. The two main ways of getting to it are down the Boyle River from Cootehall and up the river from Carrick-on-Shannon. It holds a good stock of brown trout with a big average size – probably close to 2 lb. They are mainly taken at mayfly time. It also gets hatches of lake olives and some sedge. The trout fishing here is attractive enough to tempt discerning anglers to do their mayfly fishing on Drumharlow every year. The best areas are in the vicinity of the big island, across the shallows of the numerous points that jut out into the water, and in the bay where the river flows in and again where it leaves the lough. Bank fishing is possible and there are good areas of clean stony shoreline. Useful fly patterns in sizes 8–12 are Sooty Olive, Golden Olive, Mallard and Claret, Fiery Brown, Green Peter, Connemara Black and, of course, Mayfly patterns. Boats and outboards can be hired from Mr Michael Lynch, The Bridge, Carrick-on-Shannon, Co. Leitrim, Tel: (078) 20034. It is worth recording that this was once a good spring salmon fishery and the average catch for a week's fishing was 4 fish. Now alas no more!

CAVETOWN LAKE   M 82 96
Permission: Mr Francis Beirne, Hon. Secretary, Cavetown Anglers' Association, Croghan, Co. Roscommon.

This lough lies 5 miles south of Boyle and 6 miles west of Carrick-on-Shannon. Access to it is good with a road running along the south shore. It holds a fair stock of wild brown trout and is occasionally stocked by the local angling association. The trout average ¾ lb but it has been known to produce fish to 3½ lb. The trout are notoriously dour except at mayfly time. The fishing picks up considerably in May and the Spent Gnat fishing is reported to be as good as is to be found anywhere. The lake is best fished from a boat, but there are no boats available for hire. Local anglers put a boat on it occasionally. There is a wood and high reeds along part of the shore, but there are good clear areas and much of the fishing is done from the bank.

LOUGH CANBO (Knockroe Lake)   M 87 94
Permission: Free

Lough Canbo is known locally as Knockroe Lake and is situated approximately 5 miles south-west of Carrick-on-Shannon. It is best approached by taking a by-road west off the L43 road between Carrick-on-Shannon and Elphin and turning off for the lough past Barrett's farmhouse. The average size of the trout is ½ lb and you can expect to get half a dozen. The most successful fly patterns in sizes 12 and 14 are Golden Olive, Cow Dung, Hare's Ear, Sooty Olive, Butcher, Mallard and Claret, March Brown and Bluebottle. This is a shallow lough and gets heavily weeded from June, especially on the east side. There are reeds all around the shore and a boat is necessary to fish it. A local angler sometimes puts a boat on the water and it may just be possible to hire it if inquiries are made locally.

LISDALY LOUGH   M 87 95
Permission: Free

This small lough lies a few hundred yards to the north of Lough Canbo. While it is not in the same category for trout stocks, the average size may be slightly bigger. The banks are soft and boggy, with high reeds, but a number of fishing platforms have been erected for the coarse fishermen.

CORBALLY LOUGH   M 89 93

Permission: Free

While the fishing is free on this lough, anglers should seek the permission of the local farmer before crossing over his land. Corbally Lough lies approximately 4 miles south of Carrick-on-Shannon off the L43 road from Carrick-on-Shannon to Elphin. Take the same by-road as for Lough Canbo (above) and approach the lough in a southerly direction. The average size of the trout here is ½ lb, with fish to 1½ lb. They are there in quite reasonable numbers. There are good hatches of chironomids and sedges – including murroughs – and there can be an excellent evening rise from June. This is a lough that can produce a few trout at any time in the season, for they can be very free-rising and will restore lost confidence and offer encouragement to a young angler. The north shore is free of reeds and firm underfoot. Useful fly patterns are Hare's Ear, Golden Olive, Sooty Olive, Invicta, Mallard and Claret, Butcher and Watson's Fancy in sizes 12 and 14.

LAKE O'FLYNN   M 58 78

Permission: A Regional Fisheries Board Permit

This limestone lough of approximately 600 acres lies about 1 mile due north of the village of Ballinlough on the N60 Castlerea–Ballyhaunis road. There is good public access with a car park and small boat harbour. The trout average just over 1¼ lb and there is a size limit of 10 inches and a 6-trout bag limit. Fishing methods are restricted to fly fishing, dapping and spinning, with trolling allowed under oars only. This lough was developed as a trout fishery by the Inland Fisheries Trust and development work continues under the Shannon Regional Fisheries Board. It has

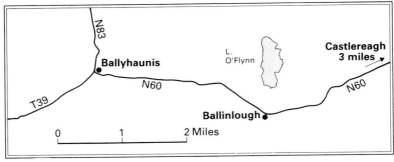

43   *Lough O'Flynn*

prolific hatches of duckfly, chironomids, lake olives, mayfly and sedges. The Mayfly and Spent Gnat fishing is as good here as anywhere in the country. There is an enormous fall of daddies in August and dapping the daddy – which can be collected in the rushes by the shore – and the grasshopper is almost guaranteed to produce a few trout. The lough has a good stock of wild trout and this stock is supplemented with takable stocked fish to maintain adequate stocks. The results of this policy have been very favourable for anglers and in recent years Lough O'Flynn has had the highest average rod catches in the country – the trout coming about fifty-fifty wild and stocked. The lough is fishable all over, with the exception of the northern end, which is very shallow. There are six boats for hire and these can be booked through Mr Padraig Campbell, Lough O'Flynn Bar, Ballinlough, Co. Roscommon, or by telephoning John Gaffney, Ballinlough, Co. Roscommon, Tel: (097) 40003. Outboard motors are not supplied but are very desirable because this lough is a little too big to have to row all day. Lough O'Flynn can be highly recommended. Best flies include Sooty Olive, Fiery Brown, March Brown, Connemara Black, Invicta, Mayfly patterns – including Spent Gnat imitations – Murrough, Green Peter and Daddy.

CLONFREE LOUGH   M 90 79
Permission: Free

This is a lough of about 300 acres, 2 miles south-west of Strokestown. Take the N5 Tulsk road out of Strokestown and turn off to the left opposite the chapel. Follow this by-road for nearly 1½ miles until you come to a bridge where there is a slip and jetty where the boats are kept. It can be difficult to get down the river as it sometimes becomes overgrown. This lough holds an excellent stock of wild trout with an average size of 1½ lb. In 1985, a 12½-lb trout was taken here by an Englishman. There are good hatches of duckfly, lake olives, claret duns, mayfly and sedges. The western end of the lough is considered to be the best fishing area. The banks are soft with high reeds, but there are two places where bank fishing is possible. Boats and outboards are available for hire from George Geraghty, Corner House, Bridge Street, Strokestown, Co. Roscommon, Tel: Strokestown 40.

LOUGH CREEVIN   M 81 69
Permission: Free

This small lough lies over a mile north of the N60 Roscommon-

Ballymoe road. Take the by-road at Rockfield; the lough is to the left over a mile along it. The trout average ¾ lb and the water has been known to produce fish over 3 lb. This lough is rarely fished but holds a really good stock of trout and is very attractive. The bank is soft in places, but at least half of it is fishable. There is no boat available.

LOUGH FERGUS   M 80 68

Permission: Free

This is a deep little lough ½ mile to the north of the N60 Roscommon–Ballymoe road. Take the small road on the Ballymoe side of Rockfield and the lough is by the roadside. It holds a fair stock of trout averaging ¾ lb. The banks are soft with high reeds and you will need a small boat to fish it.

LOUGH REE   N 00 50

Permission: Free

This is the second of the great loughs on the River Shannon and stretches for 16 miles from Lanesborough in the north to Athlone in the south. It is 7 miles wide at its widest point, but the average width of the northern half is 2 miles and the southern half averages 4 miles. Access to the lough is fairly good. At Lanesborough to the north there is a tarred road from the Anchor Hotel with a boat slip and moorings. Then there is a pier north of the town bridge with a boat slip and there is also a small harbour to the east of the town with a small slipway. Coming south along the east shore, there is a tarred road to the shore at Elfeet Bay with a harbour and slip and similar facilities at Barley Harbour, which is to the west of Leveran Point. There is limited access at Saints Island. There are good berthage facilities for anglers' boats and a natural slip at Portlick Castle; the best route to this very central access point is off the N55 Ballymahon–Athlone road past Ballynakill church. There is a car park and entry to the lough at Coosan Point and at both Barry More and Hodson's Bay. There are good mooring facilities and anglers' boats are kept at both places. The road down to Kilmore Bay is narrow and mooring facilities are limited. Galey Bay has a slipway and moorings and an amenity area in the process of construction. There is an excellent shoreline for boats at Portrunny Bay, but it is very exposed to east winds.

Lough Ree is a mixed wild fishery with a good stock of trout. Incidentally, it is the only lough in the country where draught

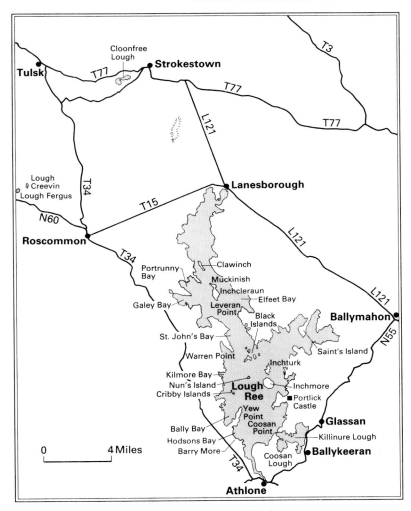

44   *Lough Ree and the Middle Shannon*

netting for trout still continues. This practice does not appear to affect the trout stocks to any great extent. There are many who claim that the lough is completely underfished. There may be a good reason for this shortage of anglers (mayfly time is an exception). The trout are very much bottom feeders and huge shoals of them have been located at depths between 20 and 30 feet during fisheries survey work. Otherwise they are slow to come to the fly and wet-fly fishing is rarely practised and considered a waste of time. At mayfly time – from mid-May – the fish move into shallower water along the shores and around the numerous islands and shallows. Anglers on Lough Ree all have their favourite fishing grounds in mayfly time. Some consider that the area around the Black Islands, southwards to Inchturk and on to Inchmore, gives the best fishing. Another good area is southwards along the Portlick shore into Rinardoo Bay and on to Hare Island. Much of this area is shallow and boats should proceed with care. The large expanse of water known as the Inner Lakes – Coosan Lough and Killinure Lough – is coarse-fish water and trout anglers should not waste time there. On the west shore, there are excellent fishing grounds from Yew Point, Bally Bay to the Cribby Islands and all the way northwards along that shore to Galey Bay. The area between Clawinch and Inchcleraun (Quaker Island) was found to hold a very high trout population when Fisheries Board staff carried out a survey of the lough. The mayfly season is the time to go for the Lough Ree trout. The average weight must be near 2 lb and fish up to 16 lb have been taken by trolling. Trout from 5 to 7 lb are frequently taken on the dap and there are many stories every season of big trout lost. When conditions are right, the trout will take a Green Drake imitation and there are many anglers who go there just for the thrills and excitement of the Spent Gnat fishing. Ree is also famous for its sedge hatches. The sedge fishing is very localized and the same is true of the buzzer fishing. A limited number of boats are available for hire around the lough and inquiries should be made with S. G. S. Marine, Ballykeeran,

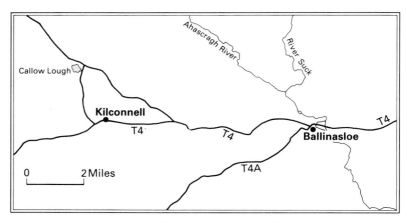

45   *Callow Lough (Lough Acalla)*

Athlone. Tel: (0902) 85163; or to Harry Waterstone, Griffith Street, Athlone. Tel: (0902) 72896.

CALLOW LAKE (Lough Acalla)   M 71 34
Permission: A Regional Fisheries Board Permit

This is a small gin-clear limestone lake of some 30 acres that has been cleared of coarse fish and stocked with rainbow trout. The open season is from 1 May to 31 October, with a bag limit of 4 trout and an 11-inch size limit. The artifical fly only is allowed. The lough is 2 miles north of Kilconnell and 8 miles from Ballinasloe. This is an extremely rich lough and the fingerling trout which are stocked annually grow quickly into perfect full-finned specimens. It undoubtedly produces some of the finest rainbow trout in the country. In some seasons the trout overwinter in great numbers and the following year fish between 4 and 7 lb are quite common. The trout feed heavily on freshwater shrimp (*Gammarus*) and there are huge hatches of chironomids and large sedges, including murroughs and Dark Peters. Nymph fishing, lure fishing and dry-fly fishing are all methods that are practised, depending on fly hatches and weather conditions. Late evening dry-fly fishing with a big Sedge can be particularly good. More than half of the bank is clean and can be easily waded, though this practice is discouraged. This is a lough that tends to get heavily weeded in summer. There is a car park by the lake shore.

LOUGH DERG   R 70 83
Permission: Free

This is the largest lough on the Shannon, stretching for 22 miles from Portumna in the north to Killaloe in the south. It is a great mixed fishery, with salmon, trout, pollan and coarse fish. Public access is good and (in a clockwise direction from Portumna) the following access points should be noted. There is public access at Portumna and a slip and berthage at Terryglass. At Kilgarvan, south-west of Ballinderry, there is a fine slip, moorings and car park. The access at Dromineer is excellent, and there is a pier equipped with navigational lights. The main access to the Youghal Bay area is at Garrykennedy, where there is a sheltered harbour. There is excellent access at Ballina and Killaloe and a lot of angling boats are kept at Tinorana Bay. Scarriff and Mountshannon are both major access points with boat slips and berthage, and there is a small pier and a slip at Knockaphort opposite Holy Island. The

18   *Lough Derg on the Shannon – showing Saint's Island*

access at Church Bay, south of Whitegate, is good, Slaghty has limited access, while Rossmore Pier is not considered suitable for small boats.

Historically, this has been one of the great trout fisheries, though the fishing was mainly concentrated on mayfly time. The fishing has dropped off considerably in recent times, particularly in the northern half of the lough. Water clarity has deteriorated and increasing eutrophication has given rise to an algal growth, particularly during the summer months. Notwithstanding that, there are many anglers who make it their mayfly destination every season, for Derg is mainly a mayfly lough. The fly is usually up by 10 May and has been known to appear at the end of April. The average weight of the trout is 2 lb and some very large fish, even into double figures, are taken every year on both dapped mayfly and Spent Gnat. Without doubt, the Grey Wulff is the most favoured artificial Mayfly pattern. Wet-fly fishing is not widely practised, but has gained in popularity recently, especially in late April and September. There are big localized hatches of chironomids and the apple-green, ginger, red and orange varieties are most common. The lough has very notable hatches of sedge of both the black and brown variety and the trout frequently take the dry fly freely along by sheltered shores and in the lee of islands. This has been described as Rolls Royce fishing, stalking the big golden trout with fine tackle and small flies – sometimes down to size 16. Local Sedge patterns used in this area are quite unusual. They are hackled patterns with no wings.

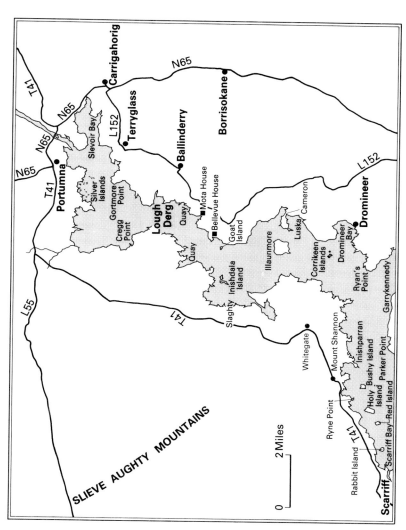

46 *Lough Derg*

The trout fishing from Slevoir Bay south along the shore to Gortmore Point can only be described as fair, and the fishing from Kilgarvan Bay at Mota down to Goat Island is somewhat similar. The first hatch of mayfly generally occurs at Luska Bay, which is fairly shallow, and the trout are smaller than average but plentiful. Dromineer Bay is a popular fishing area but catches seem to have dropped off in recent times. Good trout stocks are to be found around the Corrikeen Island to the north and Ryan's Point to the south. Youghal Bay can produce big trout to the spent gnat. Parker's Point to Castlelough is good trout water and is reported to have given the best fishing in recent times. The fishing is equally good across by the Scilly Island, Aughinish Point, the Lushag Rocks and the Middle Ground – a shallow area to the east of Holy Island. This is a favourite area, even for wet-fly fishing. The area from Scarriff to Mountshannon is all fished for trout. The flooded area between Killaloe and O'Brien's Bridge is dangerous for boats, with a lot of underwater hazards, but holds a good stock of trout.

Boats, and on occasions outboard motors, are available for hire from J. Bottcher, Mountshannon, Co. Clare, Tel: Mountshannon 25; Arthur Monaghan, Shannon Road, Portumna, Co. Galway; Tony Cunningham, Dominic Street, Portumna; Jackie Keane, Middle Line, Mountshannon; James Minogue, Middle Line, Mountshannon (boat and gillie); and The Sail Inn, Dromineer, Co. Tipperary. There are also a number of boats available for hire in both Whitegate and Scarriff.

LICKEEN LOUGH   R 16 90

Permission: Free

This lough has easy access, lying approximately 3 miles north-east of Ennistimon. There is a road to the shore at either end and the lough holds trout, char and rudd. The trout are small, averaging 3 and sometimes 4 to the pound. The lough is used as a water supply. There is a good shoreline for fishing and boats are available for hire from Bill O'Brien, Lickeen, Co. Clare.

MOOGHNA LOUGH   R 13 83

Permission: Free

This is a small 10-acre lough about 2¼ miles south of Ennistimon. The water is quite acid and poor, but it was stocked in 1986 with 1-lb brown trout. The banks are quite good and standard lough fly patterns should be effective.

THE INAGH LAKES

DRUMCULLAUN LOUGH	R 18 82
CURTINS LOUGH	R 20 81
CLOONMACKAN LOUGH	R 19 80
DRUMINURE LOUGH	R 21 84
GARVILLAUN LOUGH (Carthy's Lough)	R 24 83
MORGAN'S LOUGH	R 25 83

Permission: No permit is required to fish, but it is necessary to cross farmland to reach Druminure and the local farmer should be consulted.

The Inagh Lakes are spread around the village of Inagh, which is 7 miles south of Ennistimon and approximately 9 miles west of Ennis on the T70. Access to Drumcullaun and Druminure is not good, while the others have small roads running close to the shore. Druminure, which is about 20 acres, and Garvillaun, 11 acres, each holds a good stock of wild trout with an average weight approaching ¾ lb. The other loughs have smaller brown trout, but all are stocked annually with brown trout averaging 1 lb. Traditional fly patterns work well and information on the fishing is always available in Garvey's public house, Inagh.

AILLBRACK LOUGH R 09 83

Permission: Kevin Duffy, Main Street, Ennistimon, Co. Clare. *Tel:* (065) 71061

Aillbrack is about 3 miles south of Lahinch and a similar distance north-east of Milltown Malbay. It is not easy to find in a maze of backroads. It does not have a native stock of trout and is stocked annually with brown trout of about 1 lb.

LOUGH KEAGH (Rockmount Lake) R 10 80

Permission: Kevin Duffy, Main Street, Ennistimon, Co. Clare. *Tel:* (065) 71061

This lough, known locally as Rockmount Lake, lies on a plateau nearly 3 miles north-east of Milltown Malbay. It holds a fair stock of wild trout to 1½ lb and is stocked annually with 1-lb brownies. This is a remote and peaceful place and 80 per cent of the bank is fishable.

DOO LOUGH   R 11 72
Permission: Free

This is the largest lough in the hills of west Clare and is nearly 1½ miles long. Access to it is good, off the small road that runs parallel to the south shore. It holds a big stock of small trout and if you get one ½ lb you can consider yourself lucky. If the trout are lacking in size, they make up for it in their eagerness to take a small fly and you may expect at least a dozen in a couple of hours. The banks are good. This lough is now used as a reservoir and the water level has been raised, which just might help to increase the size of the trout.

KNOCKALOUGH   R 13 63
Permission: Free

This lough lies off the N68 Ennis–Kilrush road alongside the small road to the village of Kilmihil. There is good access to it off the road and the banks are firm with quite a bit of fishing space. The trout are normally free-rising and average just under ½ lb. It has produced trout in the past up to 1½ lb and, if there is a boat available, dapping in September usually tempts out a few of the better trout. Otherwise, try small wet flies; and occasionally a small Grey Duster or a Black Gnat will also take a trout or two.

KILKEE RESERVOIR   R 89 60
Permission: Mr Francis Meaney, Hon. Secretary, West Clare Anglers' Association, Kilrush, Co. Clare.

This small reservoir, 1 mile north of the town of Kilkee, is stocked annually with takable brown and rainbow trout. It is an ideal place for stocking because the feeding is rich and the trout put on weight quickly. This water produces some lovely trout, firm and pink-fleshed. It is liable to run low in a dry summer. There is a car park close by.

KNOCKERRY LOUGH   R 05 57
Permission: Free

This small lough lies high on a hill 4 miles north-east of Kilrush and can be approached off the N68 Ennis road or the L51 Labasheeda road. It holds a good stock of nice brown trout averaging 1 lb and fishes well in April and May. For the rest of the season, it can be notoriously dour. It is bank fishing only and 70 per cent of the bank is fishable.

EFFERNAM LOUGH
R 21 55

Permission: Free

This is a small hill lough holding a fair stock of 6-oz trout. It lies 2½ miles south-west of Kildysart and access is very difficult.

GORTGLASS LAKE
R 21 59

Permission: Free, but anglers are invited to join the local angling club; contact Mr J. Carroll or Mr J. Ringrose, Kildysart, Co. Clare. The club recommends that anglers observe a 10-inch size limit and bans trolling, worms and maggot fishing.

This small lough lies about 2 miles north-west of Kildysart. It has a limited stock of wild trout and is stocked annually – usually with fingerlings that grow into beautifully marked, full-finned, plump trout. The average size is about 1 lb and there are plenty of fish up to about 2 lb. The lough has good hatches of duckfly and lake olives and a fair hatch of sedges. The fishing can be very lively in April and May and this is one of the few loughs I know where the trout take the Lake Olive well. After May, the trout become more selective and you have to work hard for them. There is ample space for bank fishing. Boats are sometimes available and inquiries should be made to the local club.

CLOONSNAGHTA LOUGH
R 21 59

Permission: Free

This small lough is a couple of hundred yards upstream from Gortglass Lake (above). It is now used as a reservoir and a dam has been built at the outflow. This has affected the natural recruitment and the lough is now almost entirely dependent on stocked trout. The average size of the trout here is ¾ lb and they are more free-rising than in Gortglass. It always seems to hold a good stock of trout. It has a good duckfly hatch and the Buzzer fishing towards the end of May can be particularly lively with the trout taking both pupa and adult imitations. Useful fly patterns in small sizes are Peter Ross, Sooty Olive, Fiery Brown, Mallard and Claret, Greenwell's Glory and Grey Duster.

LOUGH NAMINNA
R 17 70

Permission: Free, but the lough is stocked by Kilmaley Anglers' Association and anglers fishing it are requested to join. Contact Alan Aswell, Hon. Secretary, Kilmaley, Co. Clare.

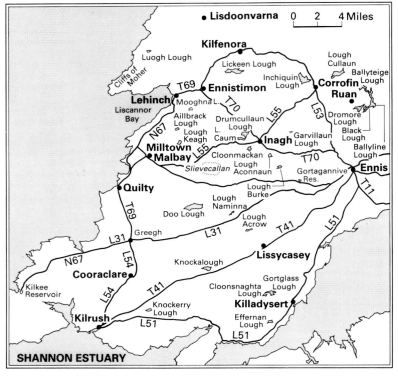

Map labels:
Lisdoonvarna 0 2 4 Miles
Kilfenora
Luogh Lough
Lickeen Lough
Lough Cullaun
Inchiquin Lough
Ballyteige Lough
Cliffs of Moher
T69
Ennistimon
Corrofin
Ruan
Lehinch
Mooghna L.
T70
Liscannor Bay
Aillbrack Lough
Drumcullaun L.
L. Lough
Dromore Lough
Black Lough
Garvillaun Lough
Lough Keagh
Caum
Inagh
Milltown
Ballyline Lough
Malbay
Cloonmackan Lough
Slievecallan
Lough Aconnaun
Gortagannive Res.
Ennis
Quilty
Lough Burke
T41
T70
L51
Lough Naminna
Doo Lough
Lough Acrow
T69
Greegh
L31
L31
L54
N67
Knockalough
Lissycasey
Cooraclare
Gortglass Lough
Kilkee Reservoir
L54
T41
Cloonsnaghta Lough
Killadysert
Kilrush
Knockerry Lough
Effernan Lough
L51
SHANNON ESTUARY

47 *Milltown, Ennis*

This is a lough of some 60 acres lying to the north of the L31 Ennis–Creegh road. It holds a large stock of small free-rising trout and is stocked occasionally with big trout of fish farm origin. It is bank fishing only, there is adequate fishing space and the condition of the bank is fair.

GORTAGANNIVE LOUGH   R 26 75
GORTAGANNIVE RESERVOIR   R 27 74

Permission: Alan Aswell, Hon. Secretary, Kilmaley Anglers' Association, Kilmaley, Co. Clare.

These two small waters lie either side of the L52 Ennis–Milltown Malbay road about 4 miles from Ennis. Both are stocked with brown trout with an average size of around 1 lb. They are easily accessible and fishing is from the bank only. The reservoir is in a beautiful secluded setting.

DROMORE LAKE
BALLYLINE LAKE

R 34 84
R 36 96

Permission: Not required

Dromore Lake is a rich limestone water lying about 6 miles north of Ennis and 4 miles east of Corofin. It is difficult to find in a maze of by-roads near Ruan village and there is a forest road from the north right to a car park at the shore. It holds a good stock of wild trout with an average size of 1½ lb and it has been known to produce trout up to 5 lb. It fishes best early in the season and has a terrific duckfly hatch, which begins to appear in some seasons in early March. The water level on Dromore tends to fluctuate a lot and the lake fishes best in low water conditions. The best fishing months are March, April, May and September. Standard early-season wet flies work well and the lake can be fished all over. Bank fishing is not really possible but the Shannon Fisheries Board can arrange for a boat on this water, for a fee, if prior notice is given to Michael Cleary, Corofin, Co. Clare, Tel: (065) 27675.

Access to Ballyline Lake is by boat, up the river from Dromore Lake and through the Black Lake. This is a distance of about 1 mile. Ballyline holds an excellent stock of good-quality wild trout and it is even possible to pick up a salmon from the River Fergus. It fishes at much the same time and to the same flies as Dromore and some of the best drifts are along by the north and east shores and into the secluded bay to the east known as the Bull Hole.

BALLYTEIGE LOUGH

R 34 88

Permission: Not required

Access to Ballyteige is difficult and involves a walk of over half a mile down by the inflowing stream from the road bridge. This is another rich limestone lough 2 miles north-east of Ruan with a small stock of quality brown trout. The fish are short and fat, the average weight must be close to 2 lb, and trout to 7 lb have been caught. The lough has good hatches of duckfly, lake olives and sedges and fishes well up to the end of April. Again in late June and July there can be spectacular rises to sedges and buzzer late in the evening – from 10 p.m. until after midnight. The water level fluctuates a lot and the inflowing stream dries up nearly every summer, which must be the limiting factor for trout stocks. This is a lough on which a boat is necessary because the bank fishing is limited and difficult and the amount of fishable bank available depends very much on the water level. Useful fly patterns are Hare's Ear, Cock Robin, Mallard and Claret, various nymphs and a long-shanked Jungle Cock and Silver lure.

INCHIQUIN LAKE

R 26 89

Permission: Free

This is a limestone lake of some 260 acres with good public access, car park and boat pier, less than a mile from the village of Corofin. It holds an excellent stock of wild brown trout averaging 1¼ lb, with many fish to 3 lb and better. The nursery streams and their stocks suffer greatly in dry seasons and this appears to be the limiting factor on the trout size in the following years. A dry season is followed by fewer, larger trout and a wet season by a big population of smaller fish. But one thing is certain – Inchiquin

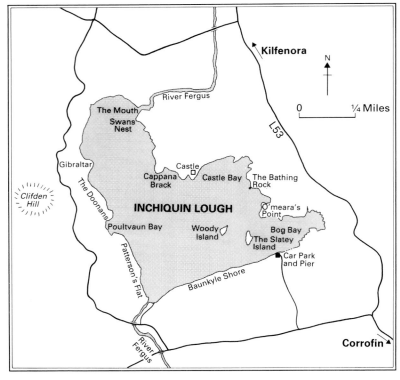

48   *Inchiquin Lough*

always holds an adequate stock to satisfy even the most demanding angler. Getting them out is the problem, for while they can come freely to the fly early in the season you will have to work hard for your fish over the summer months. It fishes particularly well to the Duckfly in April, has a good hatch of lake olives in May, and a big hatch of large olive buzzers (*Campto* chironomids) in late May and early June; this fly brings on a frenzied rise at dusk and sometimes at dawn. This is one of the few Irish loughs that gets a hatch of the sedge known as the Welshman's Button and the trout take the pupa in preference to the adult fly. The bay at the mouth of the inflowing river is a very productive area all season, as is the Wood Shore and Bog Bay. Small flies generally work best and the Cock Robin, which was invented for Inchiquin, is still a popular pattern. After that come the Hare's Ear, Mallard and Claret, Fiery Brown and varius nymph and pupa patterns, together with adult chironomid and sedge imitations. Boats are available for hire from Burke's Shop, Main Street, Corofin. This is an exciting and challenging trout fishery and well worth a visit. It can be highly recommended from April to June and in September.

LOUGH CULLAUN (Monanagh Lake)   R 30 90
Permission: Free

This lough, known locally as Monanagh Lake, can be reached off the Corofin–Tubber road. It is not really regarded as a trout fishery, as there are so many other fine trout loughs in the vicinity of Corofin. It nevertheless holds quite a good stock of big trout and anglers sometimes go trolling for them. The average size is 2 lb. This is a beautiful lough, shallow, with very clear water, and the access to it is good, with a road to the shore and a car park. A boat is necessary and this can be arranged for a fee by the Shannon Regional Fisheries Board, through Mr Michael Cleary, Corofin, Co. Clare, Tel: (065) 27675.

MUCKANAGH LOUGH   R 36 92
(Tullymacken Lough)
Permission: Free

This lough is known locally as Tullymacken Lough. There is good access to it off the Corofin–Tubber road. It is quite large – 300 acres – but very shallow and has a fair stock of good trout. It has hatches of chironomids, lake olives, mayfly and sedges. It can be fished all over with the wet fly, and a boat can be arranged as for Lough

Cullaun through Mr Michael Cleary, Corofin, Co. Clare, Tel: (065) 27675. The banks are soft with high reeds and it is not possible to fish from the shore.

LOUGH OWEL   N 40 56

Permission: A Regional Fisheries Board Permit

Lough Owel is a spring-fed lough, 4 miles long by 2 miles wide, and lies just over 2 miles north-west of Mullingar. It is approached off the N4 Mullingar–Longford road and there are two public access points – both at the south-east end – at the yacht club and at Tullaghan. At the former point, known as Mullaly's, there is a gently sloping shoreline where the boats are pulled up. There is adequate car parking space here and there are similar facilities at Tullaghan, which is of more recent origin with a modern boat slip. The size limit is 12 inches and there is a bag limit of 6 trout. All legitimate trout fishing methods are allowed. The average size of the trout can vary from 1¼ to 2 lb, depending on the time of the season; the largest rod-caught trout weighed 7½ lb, and the lough definitely holds trout up to 12 lb. Unlike other loughs, this one fishes best in a settled northerly wind – possibly because it reduces the clarity of the water. The lough holds a good stock of wild trout but they can be sometimes slow to come to an angler's fly, except at the peak of a fly hatch, and so it is stocked annually with about 5,000 takable brown trout to make the fishing somewhat easier. The chief fly hatches are duckfly in April, lake olives in late April and May, followed by a localized mayfly hatch, with some buzzer fishing and a big hatch of Green Peter in late July and early August. Most of the early season trout are taken by trolling. The trout at this time prey heavily on sticklebacks and a grey Lane Minnow, fished close in to the shore and around by the shallows, is by far the best bait. Bank fishing is not practised very much, but fishing from the railway embankment can be productive in March. The duckfly hatch begins around the second week of April and, while some anglers have success fishing standard traditional flies and drifting all over the shallower areas, the best fly hatches occur at the Mount Murray end of the lough and west of Sruddorra Island. There is a big hatch of lake olives in late April and into May. This really brings up the stocked fish and an occasional wild trout is taken at this time too. All the standard wet flies work well and a small Sooty Olive is especially good. The mayfly hatches along the north-east shore – Brabazon's Point – and, when the buzzer hatch occurs, the most effective fly is without doubt a Grey Duster dressed with a good quality white-tipped badger hackle and fished mainly at dusk.

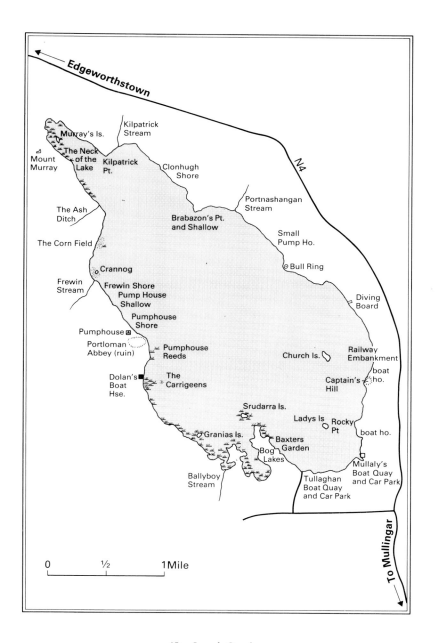

Edgeworthstown

Murray's Is.

Kilpatrick
Stream

Mount
Murray

The Neck
of the
Lake

Kilpatrick
Pt.

Clonhugh
Shore

N4

The Ash
Ditch

Brabazon's Pt.
and Shallow

Portnashangan
Stream

The Corn Field

Small
Pump Ho.

Frewin
Stream

Crannog

Frewin Shore
Pump House
Shallow

Bull Ring

Pumphouse
Shore

Diving
Board

Pumphouse

Portloman
Abbey (ruin)

Pumphouse
Reeds

Church Is.

Railway
Embankment

boat
ho.

Dolan's
Boat
Hse.

The
Carrigeens

Captain's
Hill

Srudarra Is.

Ladys Is

Rocky
Pt

boat ho.

Granias Is.

Baxters
Garden

Bog
Lakes

Mullaly's
Boat Quay
and Car Park

Ballyboy
Stream

Tullaghan
Boat Quay
and Car Park

0   ½   1 Mile

To Mullingar

49   *Lough Owel*

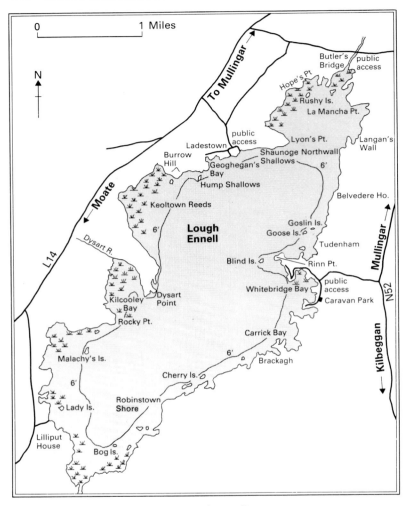

50   *Lough Ennell*

June and early July is a quiet period on the lough. The Green Peter fishing is the climax of the Owel trout season. Now the big wild trout come to the surface to feed on the huge sedges after dusk. In a hot summer, the hatch can occur as early as 14 July but it can be as late as 27 July. The fly hatches soon after 10 p.m. each evening and sometimes continues until after midnight. It generally lasts for two weeks and the best areas are from Sruddorra Island to the Cornfield on the west shore and around Church Island and in by the Bull Ring on the north-east side. Daytime fishing can be moderately good at this time to standard wet flies. The dapped grasshopper is very effective and the naturals can be caught on the shore at the Captain's Hill and at Portloman. Standard wet flies work well in September. Rowing boats are available for hire from Mr Jack Doolan, Levington, Mullingar, Co. Westmeath, Tel: (044) 42085.

19   *A nice pair from Lough Sheelin*

LOUGH SHEELIN   N 41 82

Permission: A Regional Fisheries Board Permit

Sheelin has always been one of my favourite loughs. Its attractive-
ness lies in the size and quality of its trout, the many and varied
challenges they offer, the range of fly-fishing techniques that may
be used and, above all, the great spirit of friendship among the
anglers who fish it regularly. It has had its problems with eutrophication in recent years and the great mayfly hatches of the sixties
are but a memory. They have been replaced by other fly species
and other methods, and the 1986 angling season demonstrated that
Sheelin still holds one of the finest stocks of trout of any lough in
the country. Trout up to 4 lb were not uncommon and at least one
angler had 4 trout totalling over 16 lb for one outing. That the
lough continues to offer such superb sport is a great tribute to the
tenacity of the local angling association, together with the fisheries
authorities and the local authority, in the face of tremendous
pressure from factory farming. Fishery scientists estimate that it
has the largest trout-carrying capacity of any lough of comparable
size in Ireland – over 100,000 trout, with at least 40,000 of them
between 2 and 4 lb. The season runs from 1 March to 30 September. The size limit is 30 cm (11·82 inches) and there is a bag limit of
6 trout. The fishing methods are artificial fly only until 30 April,
spinning and trolling (under oars only) from 1 May, and all legitimate methods from 16 June. The lough is well served with public
access points and car parks. There are free mooring facilities at
Kilnahard Pier, at Crover Pier and in the River Inny at Finea. The
Department of Forestry provides mooring for a fee at Rusheen Pier
and boats may also be kept at various private access points, for
example the Sheelin Shamrock Hotel. The lough is 4,500 acres in
area, 5 miles long and about 2 miles wide.

    This is a high-pH limestone water with extensive shallow bays.
The best fishing in March and early April is mainly along rocky
shores and exposed points, and favourite areas are Chambers' Bay,
Kilnahard Shore, Merry Point, Arley Point, Curry Point, Ross Bay
and the south shore of Derrysheridan. Useful fly patterns at this
time are Sooty Olive, Mallard and Claret, March Brown, and
Watson's Fancy, sizes 8 and 10, and a Sweeney Todd dressed on a
long-shank 6 or 8. The duckfly hatch begins about 15 April –
depending on weather conditions – and lasts for about two weeks.
It is confined mainly to the area from Merry Point to Stony Island
and there are usually two hatches per day – one about 11 a.m. and
the other after 8 p.m. Useful fly patterns are Blae Winged Sooty,
Sooty Olive, Fiery Brown, Mallard and Claret, Dunkeld, Con-

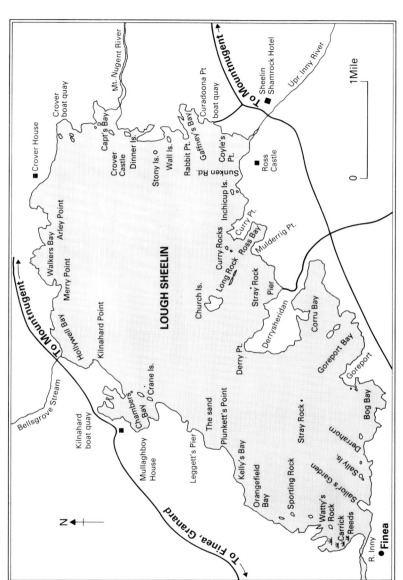

51 *Lough Sheelin*

LOUGH SHEELIN

To Mountnugent →

To Mountnugent →

To Finea, Granard →

N

Crover House

Crover boat quay

Mt. Nugent River

Capt's Bay

Crover Castle

Dinner Is.

Stony Is.

Wall Is.

Rabbit Pt.

Gaffney's Bay

Curadoona Pt.

Coyle's Pt.

boat quay

Sheelin
Shamrock Hotel

Upr. Inny River

Sunken Rd.

Ross Castle

Walkers Bay

Arley Point

Merry Point

Curry Rocks

Inchicup Is.

Curry Pt.

Ross Bay

Mulderrig Pt.

Church Is.

Long Rock

Stray Rock

Pier

Hollywell Bay

Kilnahard Point

Derrysheridan

Corru Bay

Bellsgrove Stream

Kilnahard boat quay

Mullaghboy House

Chambers Bay

Crane Is.

Leggett's Pier

The sand

Plunkett's Point

Derry Pt.

Goreport Bay

Goreport

Kelly's Bay

Stray Rock

Bog Bay

Orangefield Bay

Sporting Rock

Sallor's Garden

Derrahorn

Sally Is.

Watty's Rock

Carrick

Reeds

Finea

R. Inny

1 Mile

0

20   *A fine catch from Sheelin*

nemara Black and Blae and Black in sizes 10 and 12. Chironomid pupa patterns can get good results too in calmer conditions. The fishing is generally quiet in early May and the most prolific period in the whole season begins around 15 May when the action switches to the south side – roughly south of a line from Kilnahard Point to Inchicup Island. It is then that areas like Chamber's Bay, Rusheen Bay, Goreport Bay, Bog Bay and the Watty's Rock area start producing fish. The fly hatches of importance during the day are lake olives, chironomids, alders and reed smut, with mur-roughs after dusk. There may be a few mayfly too. The chirono-mids are the most important species for the trout, which feed on them in huge quantities. Small traditional flies such as the Blae Winged Sooty, Sooty Olive, Golden Olive and Greenwell's Glory can work well in a good wave but chironomid pupa patterns probably take more trout in calm conditions. It is important to have some dry Buzzer and Murrough patterns for evening fishing, which can continue until 1 a.m. The importance of fishing in sheltered bays and at the back of points and islands at this time must be emphasized. The period from mid-June to mid-July sees the advent of perch fry – and now roach fry. Trout can be taken on bright flies, for example the Dunkeld, especially in the Plunketts Point–Kilnahard area. There can be marvellous fishing to the Caenis at this time, too, particularly in sheltered areas around 7 a.m. Late July and early August brings a hatch of Green Peter, silverhorns and other sedges in Chamber's Bay, Rusheen Bay, Goreport Bay, Bog Bay and Derrahorn. The fishing is generally best in the evening and chironomids may be hatching too. Dapping the grasshopper brings best results during the day. September sees a return to traditional-style fishing and a team of wet flies – which can include a Green Peter or Murrough, Invicta, Connemara Black, Sooty Olive, Greenwell's Glory, Dunkeld and a Fiery Brown – fished in front of a drifting boat can get results almost anywhere in the lough.

A boat and outboard motor are necessary to fish Sheelin. Anglers may put their own boats on the lough and boats are for hire from Stephen Reilly, Finea, Co. Cavan, Tel: (043) 81124; The Sheelin Shamrock Hotel, Mountnugent, Co. Cavan, Tel: (049) 40113; Crover House, Mountnugent, Tel: (049) 40206; and at Kilnahard Pier.

LOUGH GLORE   N 48 71
Permission: A Regional Fisheries Board Permit

This small lough lies to the north of the L49 Castlepollard–Oldcastle road, 2½ miles from Castlepollard. Access to it is from the eastern side. The banks are soft, with high reeds, and bank fishing is not possible. Inquiries about boats for hire should be made to Mr Fergus Dunne, Chapel Road, Castlepollard. I have often stopped and admired the trout feeding on this lough as I went on my way to fish some of the other loughs in the area. Glore holds a good stock of wild brown trout and the average size must be well over 1½ lb. It has produced trout to 9 lb to the fly and can be fished all over, though it tends to get a bit weeded up late in the summer. It has an excellent hatch of lake olives, *campto* chironomids, murroughs and sedges, and a magnificent hatch of Green Peter in late July. Wet-fly fishing is best in April and September and useful fly patterns are Sooty, Green and Golden Olives, Fiery Brown, March Brown and Orange and Grouse. A dry fly can work well at times and Greenwell's Glory, Red Spinner, Murrough and Green Peter are all effective. The size limit is 10 inches and there is a 6-trout bag limit.

LOUGH LENE   N 49 68

Permission: Mr Michael Kelly, Hon. Secretary, Lough Lene Anglers' Association, 52 Glenview Heights, Mullingar, Co. Westmeath.

Tel: (044) 41358

Lough Lene – not to be confused with Lough Leane at Killarney – is a rich, gin-clear limestone water nestling among the hills of Westmeath, just a couple of miles south of the historic village of Fore with its seven wonders. There are extensive shallows all over the lough and particularly in the middle around the islands. There is good access at a number of points, but the chief access point is at the car park to the east where the river flows out. There are no boats for hire and it is not safe to leave a boat at the car park. Lough Lene holds a small stock of very big trout. The average size must be close on 3½ lb – one of the biggest in the country – and it has produced trout to 12 lb. Most of the trout are taken by trolling, but it has good fly hatches – chironomids, and sedges in particular. It gets a massive hatch of duckfly in April and a big hatch of murrough in June. Green Peter hatch in big numbers in late July and August and it is then that some magnificent trout are taken on the fly, particularly after dusk. You may not catch many on Lene, but should you be lucky enough to get one of these monsters it could be the fish of a lifetime. An unusual feature of this lough is that most of the trout spawn not in the streams but along the shore.

LOUGH DERRAVARAGH   N 40 65

Permission: A Regional Fisheries Board Permit

This lough lies 8 miles north of Mullingar and the best access to it is at Donore Shore near Multyfarnham or at Coolure, which is 3 miles west of Castlepollard off the T10 Mullingar road. This is a high-pH limestone lough that has suffered greatly as the result of arterial drainage and excess eutrophication. Trout stocks have decreased dramatically in recent years. This was once a famous mayfly fishery with super catches to both dap and dry fly. It now holds a small stock of quite large trout and most of these are taken trolling. There are good hatches of chironomids from May and right throughout the summer. Boats are available for hire from Mr Peter Goldsbury, Multyfarnham, Co. Westmeath.

LOUGH ENNELL   N 38 44

Permission: A Regional Fisheries Board Permit

Ennell lies 2 miles south of Mullingar. The season runs from 1 March to 30 September, and there is a 6-trout bag limit and a 30 cm (11·82 inches) size limit. It is nice to be able to report a success story relating to trout fishing, as is the case with Ennell. In the late seventies, Ennell was dead as far as trout fishing was concerned. Thanks to the good work done by the fisheries board and the local authority, Ennell is today a fishery of note and produces some of the finest brown trout in the country. They don't give themselves up easily and the angler who comes away with even a couple of these beautiful fish should feel just as pleased and satisfied as if he had taken a pair of salmon – and pound for pound the trout fight harder. Ennell has many claims to fame. On the shore is Belvedere

21   *A pair of beauties from Lough Ennell*

House with its Jealous Wall, but the fact that it holds the record for Ireland's largest brown trout – 26 lb 2 oz – is the one that will appeal most to anglers. This fish was taken in 1894 along by the Belvedere Shore by William Mears. The average size of the trout today is 1¾ lb.

In March and early April, the best of the fishing is in Kirlcooley Bay, from Burrow Hill to Hump Island shallow, along by Bog Island, the Robinstown shore, Brackagh and Carrick Bay, and between Blind Island and River Point. Bibio, Sooty Olive and March Brown, sizes 10 or 12, are probably the most effective flies. The duckfly hatch reaches its peak between 18 and 25 April. The lough gets a particularly heavy hatch and the species that hatches here is very large. It hatches over deep water around noon and again about 8 p.m. The best area is from Dysart Point across the middle of the lough to Blind Island and northwards from Dysart to Geoghegan's Bay. Useful fly patterns are Blae Winged Sooty, Fiery Brown, Mallard and Claret (with claret hackle), Connemara Black, Blae and Black and various chironomid pupa patterns in rather large sizes. The lake olive hatch comes early in May and lasts for three weeks. It occurs mainly along the shore from Robinstown to Bog Island, to Lady Island to Malachy's Island and by Keoltown Reeds – there may be a hatch of alder at this time too. Fly patterns worth trying are Greenwell's Glory, Golden Olive, Sooty Olive, Mallard and Claret and an Alder. The apple-green midge and the *campto* species of chironomid begin to hatch about 20 May and continue until mid-June. The fishing can be very good from around 9.30 a.m. until noon and again from 10 p.m. A Sooty Olive, Blae Sooty, Black & Peacock Spider (size 12) and claret and apple-green nymphs are probably the most useful patterns and a dry buzzer can be deadly in the evening along by the Keoltown Reeds and around Bog Island. Other areas with lots of action are north of a line from Lyon's Island to Northwall, from Dysart to Burrow Hill and from Lady Island to Malachy's Island. There is a small hatch of mayfly at this time in Carrick Bay, in Whitebridge Bay and from Blind Island to Belvedere. The trout occasionally feed on the pupa of the Welshman's Button at this time, a dark brown sedge that sits on the water for ages after hatching. A lot of small black terrestrial flies fall on the water in early June, which is why the small Black and Peacock Spider or even a Black Pennell (size 12 or 14) will take fish. From mid-June until the end of July the lough is stuffed with perch fry and the trout are very difficult to tempt. August is the month for the sedges – silverhorns, murroughs, etc. – and the trout love them. The apple-green midge makes a return and the trout come up for them, particularly at dusk. The lake olives make a return in early August and last until the season ends. Useful flies at this time are Green Peter, Golden Olive, Black Pennell and various nymphs and pupae. It is now time to start thinking about dapping the grasshopper and the daddy. The last week in August and the first two in September often give the best fishing of the whole season. From River Point to Northwall is a particularly good area and a small Black Pennell is a must as a point fly. Other good flies at this time are Green Peter, Green Olive, Invicta, Bibio, Raymond, Daddy, Mallard and Claret and Black and Peacock Spider. You must fish Ennell some time, feel the power of its trout and admire their graceful lines.

Boats are available from Mr Kit Raleigh, Whitebridge Bay, Mullingar, Co. Westmeath, Tel: (044) 40955; Mr Myles Hope, Lake View, Lough Ennell, Mullingar, Tel: (044) 40807; and from Bloomfield House Hotel, Mullingar, Tel: (044) 40894. There is public access to the lough with good car parking facilities at Ladestown, Butlers' Bridge and Whitebridge Bay.

MOUNT DALTON LAKE   N 30 51
Permission: A Regional Fisheries Board Permit

This beautiful little fishery is situated in lovely parkland in the grounds of Brabazon Hall. Access to it is off a by-road off the L121 Mullingar–Ballymahon road and in the avenue to the big house (Brabazon Hall). The open season is from 1 May to 30 September and there is a 6-trout bag limit and a 10-inch size limit. Boat fishing with artificial fly only is allowed. Mount Dalton holds only brown trout – and sticklebacks. The trout are stocked as fingerlings and grow naturally, thereby showing none of the signs of stocked trout. This lough is very rich in feeding and you have to work for your trout. Useful fly patterns are Greenwell's Glory, Sooty Olive, Connemara Black, Silver Invicta, Dunkeld, Peter Ross, Green Peter, Murrough and Daddy. There is one boat for hire, which should be booked in advance; call Mrs Gibson-Brabazon on (044) 55102. This is a super little fishery and well worth a visit, if only to savour the peace and quiet. It is also a safe refuge when one is blown off some of the bigger midland loughs.

PALLAS LAKE   N 26 19
Permission: A Regional Fisheries Board Permit

Pallas Lake is situated 8 miles south-west of Tullamore off the N52 Tullamore–Birr road. The open season is from 1 May to 30 September and there is a 6-trout bag limit with an 11-inch size limit. The lake is stocked with both rainbow and brown trout and gives good sport right through the season. The trout average 1 lb and since this is a very rich limestone lake fish that overwinter can grow very big. Only the western end of the lake is fishable and wading is particularly dangerous, so anglers are advised to use the fishing stands provided. There are good hatches of olives, chironomids, sedges – including murrough – and damselflies. There is a big corixid population. Most traditional flies work quite well. Lures can be especially effective and the Muddler Minnow is probably the favourite. Fishing methods are restricted to artificial fly only.

Derry

Belfast

Sligo

Galway

Dublin

Athy

Limerick

Thurles

Kilkenny

Cashel

Carrick on Suir

Tipperary

Waterford

Dungarvan

Cork

52   *The Southern Fisheries Region*

8 Southern Fisheries Region

The Southern Fisheries Region covers the catchments of the four big southern rivers – Barrow, Nore, Suir and the Munster Blackwater. It is an area rich in trout and salmon fishing, nearly all of which is done in the rivers and streams for this part of Ireland has very few decent trout loughs and none holding either salmon or sea trout. The reservoirs offer some reasonable-sized trout and if you feel energetic enough you can fish the loughs high in the Comeragh and Monavillagh Mountains where the water is gin-clear and the trout are small and careful and fight like tigers. Your alternative is to fish the rivers, always with the thought at the back of your mind that you might hook and land a bigger fish than Michael Maher, whose 57-lb salmon, taken from the Suir on a fly called the Mystery in 1874, is still an Irish record.

BAY LOUGH   S 02 11

Permission: Not usually required

This small mountain lough is situated in very beautiful countryside off the L34 Clogeen–Lismore Road. It lies in a valley less than half a mile from the road at The Gap at Sugarloaf Hill in the Knockmealdown Mountains. There is parking space at a lay-by a short distance from the lough. As you can well imagine, this is a mountain water with a low pH and the trout are very small – coming 4 to the pound. Bay Lough is fishable from the north and east banks only. Flies to use are Butcher, Black Pennell, Peter Ross and Wickham's Fancy. The season runs from 1 March to 30 September.

BALLYSHUNNOCK RESERVOIR   S 45 08

Permission: Inquiries to the caretaker, Tom Sullivan, Minaun, Cheekpoint, Co. Waterford.
Tel: (051) 82259

This water is situated 1 mile off the T12 Portlaw–Kilmacthomas road at Carroll's Cross Roads. The season runs from 15 March to the 30 September and there is a 9-inch size limit with a bag limit of 4 trout. The water holds a big stock of small brown trout averaging

½ lb with some to 1½ lb, though they have a reputation for being dour and difficult to catch. The main fly hatches are chironomids and sedges. Bank fishing only, and this is restricted as the banks are overgrown in places.

KNOCKADERRY RESERVOIR   S 49 05

Permission: Inquiries to Jackie Connolly, Knockaderry, or to Tom Sullivan, Miraun, Cheekpoint, Co. Waterford.
Tel: (051) 82259

This reservoir holds a stock of wild brown trout averaging 1 lb with trout up to 3 lb. It is occasionally stocked with brown trout. It is located 4 miles off the T12 Waterford–Cork road, 6 miles from Waterford, and the parking space by the roadside is limited. The trout can be fairly free-rising early in the season and Peter Ross and Silver Invicta are useful patterns at this time. There are weed problems in some areas in low water conditions and the fish tend to feed on the bottom, but will take an artificial fly again in September. Only fly fishing is permitted, and there is a 9-inch size limit and a 4-trout bag limit. Bank fishing is not allowed and boats are for hire from Jackie Connolly at the house by the dam.

BALLYSCANLAN LOUGH   S 53 02

Permission: This lough is leased by a private syndicate and the fishing is by invitation only.

CARRIGAVANTRY RESERVOIR   S 54 01

Permission: Tom Deegan, Chairman, Waterford City and District Anglers' Association, Engineering Works, Bridge Street, Waterford.
Tel: (051) 74258

This is a totally artificial trout fishery of some 30 acres, 3 miles off the Tramore–Dungarvan road at Fener village. It is stocked with both brown and rainbow trout and the average size is ¾ lb. The trout are free-rising and there are good hatches of olives, chironomids and damselfly.

COUMSHINGAUN LOUGH   S 32 11

Permission: Free

The lough can be approached by a rough pathway north of

Kilclooney Wood from the T56 Dungarvan–Carrick-on-Suir Road. The water is very clean, with small trout of 4–6 oz which are difficult to catch. A beautiful lough set in a corrie with a magnificent view of Co. Waterford and right out to the sea.

COUMDUALA LOUGHS   S 29 14
Permission: Free

There are three small mountain loughs here with trout averaging 6 oz in two of them. The best approach is a long walk over rough ground from Curragheen townland, near Rathgormuck in Co. Waterford. The trout here are slow to take. The banks are good.

CROTTYS LAKE   S 32 12
Permission: Free

This lake is approached from the minor road at Coolnalingady. The trout are very small – 4 oz – and slow to take a fly.

LOUGH MOHRA   S 28 18
Permission: Free

Mohra is only about 8 acres in area and is approached off the forest road at Cloondonnell. It has a good stock of trout averaging 5 oz and the banks are good.

SGILLOGE LOUGHS   S 29 12
Permission: Free

These two small loughs are approached from the Nier valley. The trout here average 6 oz, with the bigger trout in the lower lough. They are very slow to take a fly unless conditions are good.

COUMALOCHA   S 28 09
Permission: Free

These loughs are at the source of the River Nier and reaching them involves a long walk. They are three in all and the trout average nearly ½ lb.

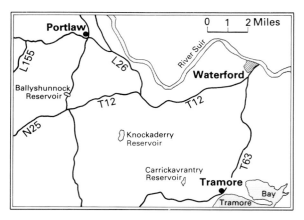

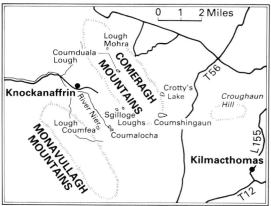

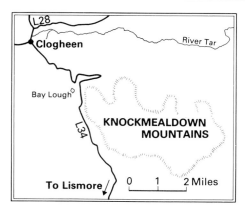

53 *Loughs of the Southern Fisheries Region*

LOUGH COUMFEA

S 27 09

Permission: Free

This small mountain lough is approached from the Nier valley. The trout average 6 oz and you might be lucky to get one up to 10 oz.

54   *The South-Western Fisheries Region*

9 South-Western Fisheries Region

Words are quite inadequate to describe the beauty of the Cork and Kerry countryside, with its mountains, lakes and forests. The lakes of Killarney are among the most beautiful in the world. Glencar, Waterville and the Kenmare area cannot be far behind. The quality of the lough fishing too can often match the magnificence of the surroundings and you are more likely to encounter a specimen sea trout in the Waterville lakes than anywhere else in Ireland. Loughs Caragh, Leane and Currane produce a high percentage of the country's lough-caught spring salmon to rod and line. Here, too, you are likely to encounter a frisky grilse in the month of June, and in many others besides.

Brown trout are everywhere – maybe not the largest in the country, but certainly the south-west holds some of the most numerous stocks. Rainbow trout can be found here too in small, well managed fisheries and the average catch per rod day must surely be amongst the highest in these islands. Be careful when boat fishing on loughs which lie deep in the mountains. A sudden storm can cause an emergency, so don't take chances. When fishing the mountain loughs, make sure someone knows where you are going and when you expect to return. With that bit of advice, enjoy your fishing in a part of Ireland renowned worldwide for its scenery.

LOUGH GILL   Q 60 13

Permission: Not usually required

This large (1½ miles by ½ mile) lough lies west of Castlegregory. It is very shallow and bank fishing is not possible. There is a pier and car park and boats are available for hire from Mrs Kelleher's guest-house. This lough has an excellent stock of brown trout averaging ½ lb and can give good lively fishing. A good day's fishing should produce 6 or 8 trout. Local information on the fishing is important and there are reports that the trout stocks can fluctuate wildly from season to season. Try a Greenwell's Glory, Sooty Olive, Olive Quill, Golden Olive, Bibio and Connemara Black.

LOUGH ADOON   Q 52 06

Permission: Not usually required

Adoon lies in the shadow of Slievenagower and it is possible to bring a car within a short distance of the shore. It holds small brown trout and gets a nice run of sea trout after the first flood in August. The banks are good and it is fishable all round. It is necessary to wade the river to fish the south bank and waders are useful as it is possible to wade out and fish off the island, which is one of the best taking spots on the lough. The other good taking place is where the river flows in. Try a Bibio, Butcher, Devil and Alexandra.

LOUGH ANSCAUL   Q 58 05

Permission: Inquire locally

This lough lies 2 miles north of the village of Anscaul on the Dingle Peninsula. It is reported to hold excellent stocks of sea trout in August and September and inquiries about the fishing should be made locally.

LOUGH LEANE   V 90 86

Permission: Free

Lovely Lough Leane, the largest (4,500 acres) of the lakes of Killarney, is noted among anglers for its trout and salmon fishing every bit as much as it is famous worldwide for the beauty of its scenery. The salmon fishing season runs from 17 January to 30 September and the trout season from 14 February to 12 October. The lough produces hundreds of spring salmon and grilse to trolled baits every season and it is not unusual for half a dozen spring salmon to be taken on opening day. The best salmon-fishing months are January to June. The lough has a really excellent stock of brown trout with an average size of just over ½ lb. It holds large ferox trout too, and a 16-lb specimen was taken in 1985. The trout fishing can be very good from early March and right through April, with enormous hatches of duckfly. The fly hatch in fairly deep water and drift in, and the trout feed extensively on drowned adult flies. The local anglers' answer to this is to fish three small Blae and Blacks on the leader. Later in the season there are hatches of olives, a small mayfly hatch and big hatches of small dark sedges. A lot of woodland insects get blown onto the water in summer. A short list of fly patterns for trout would include Blae and Black, Straw Grouse, Green Devil, Watson's Fancy, Mar Lodge, Black

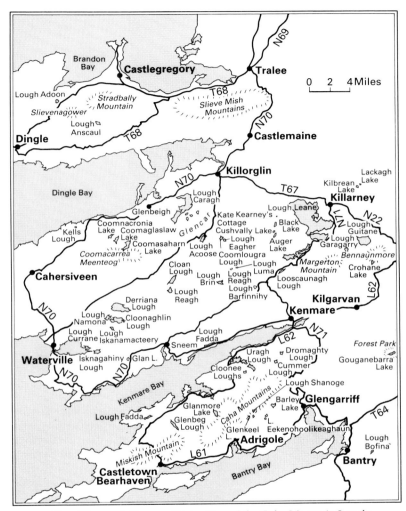

55   *Glencar, Killarney, Waterville and the Caha Mountain Loughs*

Jungle Cock, Bibio, Alder, Matt Gorman, Green Grouse, Orange
Grouse, Hardy's Favourite, Olive Quill, Ginger Quill and Red
Quill, and Soldier Palmer. Lough Leane affords good, lively
fishing, and favourite areas are mainly along the north shore – for
example, The Wash (along by the golf course), Mahony's Bay,
Victoria Bay and around Lamb Island, Heron Island, Brown Island
and Innisfallen. There are numerous boatmen, boats and outboards

for hire and Henry Clifden at Ross Castle, Killarney, Co. Kerry, Tel: (064) 32252, or Alfie Doyle, Tel: (064) 33652, will look after the angler's needs.

KILBREAN LAKE   W 00 93
Permission: Inquire locally

Stocking on this lough has ceased in recent times. There is a possibility that stocking with rainbow trout may recommence and anglers should telephone the Fisheries Inspector, Noel Hackett, on (026) 41222, for details.

LACKAGH LAKE   W 00 93
Permission: Not usually required

This is an easily accessible little lough of about 6 acres, 3½ miles north-east of Killarney. The road runs along one side and access is good. About one-third of the bank is fishable and the trout come 3 to the pound. Use small traditional lough fly patterns.

MUCKROSS LAKE (The Middle Lake)   V 93 84
Permission: Free

This very beautiful lough lies along the N71 Killarney–Kenmare road, 3½ miles south of Killarney. It gets a great run of spring salmon and some anglers regard it as better for spring salmon than Lough Leane. The trout are small, averaging 4 to the pound, but better fish are usually taken in September, when the bigger fish move up from Leane. There are dozens of boats available for hire from private operators at Muckross House and bank fishing is allowed. The fishing can be lively, especially if there is a nice breeze. This is a lovely place to bring the family. They can spend several hours visiting Muckross House, Muckross Abbey and Muckross Gardens, while the angler in the party gets in a bit of fishing.

THE UPPER LAKE, KILLARNEY   V 89 81
Permission: Free

This is a long, rocky and very beautiful lough at the bottom of Killarney's Black Valley. The trout here average 6 oz, but it is really as a salmon fishery that the lough is of most interest to anglers. A lot of salmon are caught here up to the end of June and

2 or 3 per day is quite common. The fish here are fickle. Often on a day with lovely conditions you get nothing and on a day when you least expect success 2 or 3 will oblige. Boats are available from John O'Donoghue, The Black Valley, Killarney, Co. Kerry, and from private operators at Derrycunnaghy. You will fish here in very beautiful and majestic surroundings and it can be highly recommended – if only for the scenery.

CUMMEENDUFF LOUGHS   V 82 80
Permission: Not usually required

These loughs lie near the head of the Black Valley in the middle of the Kerry mountains. They can be approached on foot via the Gap of Dunloe, or by car by turning off the N71 Killarney–Kenmare road near Moll's Gap. The brown trout here average 4 oz, but these loughs get a fair run of spring salmon and a big run of grilse. There is a lovely story told of how the young local anglers used to dread the arrival of the grilse in June. This was in the days before monofilament leaders and these lads – who would be fishing for trout – would frequently have their tackle smashed and possibly lose all three flies to a powerful fresh-run grilse. The salmon can still be taken here – on fly, by spinning or on worms – and the angler who drags a dry Daddy across the surface here may well get the fright of his life as a salmon lunges at it with a noisy splash. Boats are available from John O'Donoghue, The Black Valley, Killarney, Co. Kerry. This is a peaceful and lovely place in the shadow of MacGillycuddy's Reeks.

LOUGH REAGH   V 81 80
Permission: Not usually required

Reagh lies at the top of the Black Valley. There is a road to within a few hundred yards of the shore. The trout are very small but there is a chance of a salmon late in the season.

LOOSCAUNAGH LOUGH   V 88 79
Permission: Free

Looscaunagh Lough is on the scenic N71 Killarney–Kenmare road, a mile north-east of Moll's Gap. It is a small lough with reasonably good banks, a bit rocky, that are about 90 per cent fishable, with the road running along one side. It has a big stock of small trout – 4 or 5 to the pound – and is just the place to stop at to get the younger members of the family interested in fly fishing. The trout come 3 to a cast when they are on the move.

COOMLOUGHRA LOUGH   V 78 84
LOUGH EAGHER   V 78 84
Permission: Not usually required

These loughs are now one, having been converted into a reservoir. They are approached off the Killorglin–Waterville road and there is now a roadway nearly to the shore. They lie right at the western side of Carrauntoohil – Ireland's highest mountain – and this is about the highest place where you could possibly fish in Ireland. This is magnificent country with breathtaking views out over Dingle Bay. The water is crystal clear; the rocks are bare with no moss and no lichens; the midges will eat you on a calm day; and the trout are about 8 to the pound.

BLACK LAKE   V 87 87
CUSHVALLEY LAKE   V 87 86
AUGER LAKE   V 87 85
Permission: Not usually required

22 *Looscaunagh Lough*

These three small, narrow lakes lie in the famous Gap of Dunloe, near Killarney and to the south of Kate Kearney's Cottage. Access is gained to them off the T67 Killarney–Killorglin road. Motor vehicles may only be brought as far as Kate Kearney's and the angler may then proceed on foot, on horseback, or by bicycle. Two of the lakes are close to the road. They all hold large stocks of small trout – 3 to the pound – with big square tails. They fight like terriers. Two are frequently hooked at the same time and they will put up a much better fight than a 1-lb stocky. Useful patterns are Bibio, Peter Ross, Butcher and Alexandra in small sizes.

LOUGH GUITANE   W 01 83
Permission: Not usually required

Lough Guitane lies 4 miles south-east of Killarney and can be approached off the Muckross road or from Glen Flesk. It holds a big stock of brown trout and sea trout from July, but the latter rarely take. The brown trout are free-rising, a lot of them are about 3 to the pound, while there are plenty of ½-lb trout and better. On occasions, Lough Guitane can produce good trout up to 3 lb. It has good hatches of chironomids and sedges, including the odd mur-rough, and gets a big fall of terrestrials. Useful fly patterns are Blae and Black, Bibio, Straw Grouse, Raymond, and Claret Bumble. While conditions are ideal for shore fishing, a boat is necessary if this beautiful lough is to be enjoyed to the full. Boats are for hire along the road by the north shore.

LOUGH GARAGARRY   V 99 82
Permission: Not usually required

This lough lies to the south-west of Lough Guitane. It is approached off the road to the west of Guitane and the last mile is on foot, with a good climb of maybe 300 feet, but the ground is easy to walk. This is a deep lough – 260 feet – and the trout are about 4 to the pound and tend to be close to the shore. The banks are easy to fish and this place is a useful alternative if the weather happens to be too nasty to go out on Lough Guitane. Try Blae & Black, Black Jungle Cock, Straw Grouse and Watson's Fancy in small sizes.

LOUGH CARAGH (Glencar Lake)   V 71 90
Permission: Free

Lough Caragh, sometimes referred to as Glencar Lake, is at the

23 *Lough Caragh*

mouth of the beautiful Glencar valley and is noted especially for its spring-salmon and grilse fishing and to a lesser extent for its brown trout and sea trout. The season opens for salmon on 17 January and the boats are out in strength from opening day. The majority of the fish are taken by trolling or spinning and this holds true throughout the season. There is no reason why they should not take a fly, but the tradition is for trolling and spinning. Access to the lough is very restricted, but there is a public access at the outflowing river. There are lots of boats and boatmen available for hire along the north and west shores, or a boat and boatman can be arranged through Mr Carl Daly, Glencar Hotel, Glencar, Co. Kerry, Tel: (066) 60102. The best salmon fishing is at the southern end along the west and east shores and along by the mouth of the inflowing river. The early-season fish average 14 lb and the record for the lough is 24 lb. The sea trout arrive in the lough in July and the bay at the outflowing river is probably the best area to find them. The brown trout are to be found on all the shores. They come 3 to the pound and a day's fishing should produce at least a dozen keepable trout, of which a few should weigh at least ½ lb with perhaps one near to 1 lb. The trout at the southern end are bigger than elsewhere and can average nearly ½ lb at the mouth of the inflowing river. A fast retrieve is recommended for the brownies and any bright fly stripped across the surface should bring a response. Try Black Jungle Cock, Alexandra, Peter Ross, Butcher or Delphi in small sizes. Lough Caragh is remote yet well serviced, and the scenery is superb. Beware of sudden squalls if you are out on your own on windy days.

LOUGH CUMMERNAMUCK   V 74 89

Permission: Not usually required

This lough lies nearly 5 miles south of Killorglin and to the east of the Glencar road. The brownies are small here and a Peter Ross, Teal, Blue and Silver or Butcher in small sizes should get a quick response.

LOUGH CAPPANALEA   V 72 89

This lough is used as a centre for outdoor pursuits and the angler should give it a miss.

LOUGH NAKIRKA   V 73 89

Permission:

A Regional Fisheries Board Permit, available from Cappanalea Outdoor Education Centre, Co. Kerry.

Tel: (066) 69244;

Dermot Foley, The Bridge, Killorglin, Co. Kerry.

Tel: (066) 61193

Lough Nakirka is a small lough by the roadside to the east of Caragh Lough. Three-quarters of the bank is fishable and the lough has an excellent stock of small brown trout and, in addition, is stocked regularly with rainbow trout, some of which weigh over 4 lb. This is definitely a lough for the tourists during the day, particularly in July and August, but can give good fun late in the evening when all the day trippers have gone. A small sedge (size 14) fished dry can drive the rainbows crazy and is almost certain to get you a few trout.

LOUGH NAMBRACKDARRIG   V 72 88

Permission: Not usually required

The trout in this lough are small and come about 5 to the pound, though it is reported to hold better ones. The lough is in the middle of a solid bog, which is probably what gives them their reddish hue. The easiest way to this water is up the hill from Nakirka. Try a Peter Ross, any of the Butchers, or a small Watson's Fancy.

LOUGH ACOOSE   V 75 84

Permission: (For the southern part) Mr Carl Daly, Glencar Hotel, Glencar, Co. Kerry.
Tel: (066) 60102

This is a fine lough conveniently situated along the Killorglin–Waterville road, 7 miles south of Killorglin. It is fished mainly for its brown trout, but gets a run of grilse from July and upwards of 30 fish are taken annually – mostly by anglers fishing for trout. The trout come 4 to the pound and are taken mostly on very small flies – mainly size 14. Useful patterns are Bibio, Claret and Jay, Claret Bumble, Black Pennell, Peter Ross, and Butcher. The southern part of the lough between the inflowing and outflowing river is the most productive area and can produce up to 50 trout in a day. This is certainly a good place to teach the children. There are boats and outboards and boatmen available.

CLOON LOUGH   V 70 77

Permission: Mr Carl Daly, Glencar Hotel, Glencar, Co. Kerry.
Tel: (066) 60102

Cloon is situated deep in the Kerry mountains between the Craggy Peaks of Knocknacusha and Mullaghanattin. It holds salmon from early April and the grilse run up in June. They take a fly well, particularly along the west shore and at the southern end. The most favoured salmon fly patterns are Lemon and Grey, Garry Dog, Blue Charm, Claret Bumble and Connemara Black. The trout come 3 to the pound and a day's fishing should produce several half-pounders and the odd one to ¾ lb. Trolling is widely practised for the salmon, with a copper spoon the most popular bait, and very small flies work best for the trout, for example Black Pennell, Orange & Grouse, Butcher, Bibio and Watson's Fancy in sizes 12 and 14. There are two boats for hire, with outboard motors and boatmen, and bank fishing is allowed.

LOUGH REAGH   V 69 75

Permission: Mr Carl Daly, Glencar Hotel, Glencar, Co. Kerry.
Tel: (066) 60102

Lough Reagh is south of Cloon Lough and is overshadowed by the high ridge to the south-east. You can take the car as far as Cloon and then walk the last ¾ mile across the bog. Reagh holds numerous small trout and occasional salmon towards the end of the season. Bank fishing only.

COOMNACRONIA LAKE
COOMAGLASLAW LAKE
COOMASAHARN LAKE

V 60 85

V 60 84

V 61 83

Permission: Not usually required

These three glacier loughs lie to the north of Teermoyle Mountain and about 5 miles south-south-west of Glenbeigh. Coomnacronia is well over a mile from the nearest road and a climb of 700 feet as well. The trout are very small and not very plentiful. It can produce a very occasional trout to ¾ lb.

Coomaglaslaw has a road to within ½ mile of the shore, but the trout are just as small as in Coomnacronia and every bit as scarce.

Coomasaharn has a road almost to the shore. The trout here are again very small but an occasional sea trout can make its way in, late in the season. This lough holds a big population of char averaging 6 inches. The banks are steep with steep cliffs and the lake itself is over 150 feet deep. A peaceful, quite place.

KELLS LOUGH

V 54 87

Permission: Not usually required

This lough is land-locked and percolates out through the sand into Dingle Bay. It lies midway between Glenbeigh and Caherciveen and is about 200 yards from the end of a cul de sac. It has a plentiful stock of wild brown trout and the average weight must be close to ½ lb – good for these parts. Useful fly patterns are Bibio, Butcher, Peter Ross and Daddy. In all these parts, there are large white moths that sometimes fall on the water after dusk and the trout love them. A Heather Moth – fished dry – is just the thing when the moths are about. Kells Bay is nearby. It has a lovely strand, and you may even decide to do a little mackerel fishing off the rocks.

LOUGH CURRANE

V 51 65

Permission: Free

Mention Lough Currane, Waterville, Co. Kerry, and images of spring salmon and huge sea trout together with shining grilse and brown trout flash across the imagination. For this must surely be

24   *Lough Currane, boulders and lichen, sunshine and cloud*

one of Ireland's greatest game fishing loughs – one that draws anglers from all over Europe and further afield too, and where, with the help of an experienced and competent local boatman, many a novice landed his or her first salmon. There is public access at the Bog, the Bridge and Water Lily Bay, and numerous private access points too. Anglers may launch their own boats on the water and moor them at private or public jetties where, for a small fee, they will be cared for for the season. The spring salmon fishing opens on 17 January and the early-season fish – which average 14 lb – are taken mainly by trolling, but quite a few are taken on fly too and it is not unknown for the first fish of the season to fall to the fly. A double-handed rod, floating line and strong leader (20 lb BS) are recommended for the spring fishing and the favourite flies in sizes 4, 6 and 8 are Hairy Mary, Shrimp Fly, Garry Dog, Blue Charm, Jack Scott, and Thunder and Lightning. The Hairy Mary is probably best of all. The grilse run begins in June and 350 salmon were reported taken on the lough in 1986. The salmon lie by rocks and islands and at headlands jutting into the lough. A boatman will hold the boat over a known lie for hours while the angler teases the salmon with the fly. While this is a free fishery and all legitimate methods are allowed, certain local customs and conventions are observed. It is fly fishing only at the mouth of the two rivers and at

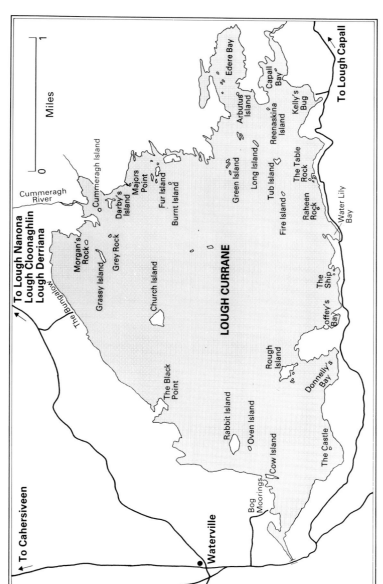

To Cahersiveen

To Lough Nanona
Lough Cloonaghlin
Lough Derriana

Waterville

Cummeragh
River

The Bungalow

Miles

0   1

To Lough Capall

Morgan's Rock
Grassy Island
Grey Rock

Church Island

Cummeragh Island
Darby's Island
Majors Point
Fur Island
Burnt Island

Green Island
Long Island

Edere Bay
Arbutus Island
Capall Bay
Reenaskina Island
Kelly's Bug

LOUGH CURRANE

Tub Island
Fire Island
Raheen Rock

The Table Rock

Water Lily Bay

The Ship

Coffey's Bay

Rough Island

Donnelly's Bay

The Black Point

Rabbit Island
Oven Island

Cow Island

Bog Moorings

The Castle

56   *Lough Currane*

Morgan's Rock, and the first boat up to a known lie each morning may fish that lie for as long as the anglers wish.

The big sea trout arrive in April and Lough Currane produces several Irish specimens every season. It is usually the second week of June before the sport hots up, and then the fishing can remain good until August – depending on weather conditions. The next marker for good sea-trout fishing is around the second week in September and it often remains good until closing date – 12 October. Sea trout lie all over the lough. It is accepted that there are certain favoured drifts but these are sometimes overfished and the angler who experiments with new ground can sometimes meet a lot of trout. Trout flies in sizes 8–14 are essential, and of all the flies tied by anglers the Bibio is probably the most consistent fly on Currane and no leader should be without one. The other patterns the angler should bring are Claret Bumble, Claret and Jay, Claret and Blue, Mallard and Claret, Fiery Brown, Raymond, Watson's Fancy, Black Pennell, Sooty Olive, Bog Fly, Kingsmill, and Wickham's Fancy. Dapping can pull up a big trout on a dour day and they don't seem to mind whether it is a daddy or a grasshopper.

Currane is a lovely lough with the potential to satisfy even the most demanding angler. There are few who have fished it who do not have a yearning to try their luck there again. The very active Waterville Anglers' Association aims to maintain the lough as one of the country's premier game fisheries and has embarked on an extensive spawning stream enhancement programme. The construction of a hatchery was begun in 1986. Boatmen, boats and outboards can be arranged through the Secretary of the Waterville Anglers' Association, Michael O'Sullivan, The Lobster Bar, Waterville, Co. Kerry, Tel: (0667) 4183, and a similar service can be supplied by Brod O'Sullivan, Stella Maris, Waterville, Tel: (0667) 4249; Vincent O'Sullivan, Waterville, Tel: (0667) 4255; Terence Wharton, Ballybrack, Waterville, Tel: (0667) 4264; Frank Donnelly, Lake Road, Waterville, Tel: (0667) 4303; John M. Donnelly, Lake Road, Waterville, Tel: (0667) 4139; and Michael Donnelly, Raheen, Waterville, Co. Kerry.

LOUGH NAMONA   V 59 71

Permission:
Butler Arms Hotel, Waterville, Co. Kerry.
Tel: (0667) 4156;
Waterville Lake Hotel, Waterville, Co. Kerry.
Tel: (0667) 4310

Namona is one of the first loughs up the system from Lough Currane. It holds plenty of brown trout averaging 7 oz with quite a few to ¾ lb, but it is for its sea trout that it is fished most. This lough holds some of the really big sea trout for which all these Waterville lakes are famous. It can be fished all over – even right down the middle – though some anglers have little faith in the bay at the extreme east side. There is a boat available and the same flies work here as on Lough Currane.

CLOONAGHLIN LOUGH   V 60 70

Permission:
Butler Arms Hotel, Waterville, Co. Kerry.
Tel: (0667) 4156;
Waterville Lake Hotel, Waterville, Co. Kerry.
Tel: (0667) 4310

This lough is on the same tributary as Namona and is another sea-trout lough with small brownies and occasional salmon. It is set deep in the mountains above Waterville and requires a nice south-west breeze to get the trout going. It can be a slow lough where the sea trout are concerned and the best bet for action is probably along by the southern shore.

DERRIANA LOUGH   V 60 72

Permission:
Butler Arms Hotel, Waterville, Co. Kerry.
Tel: (0667) 4156;
Waterville Lake Hotel, Waterville, Co. Kerry.
Tel: (0667) 4310

This lough, with its magnificent mountain scenery, can produce fishing of an exceedingly high standard. This is the top lough on this part of the system as far as angling is concerned, and holds good brown trout and plenty of sea trout and salmon from early in the season, even as early as March. The best fishing is on the shallows and by the shore and particular hot spots are the bay at the mouth of the outflowing river, along by the north shore where the three little rivers flow in, and the bay to the east. Boats are available and an outboard motor is essential. This lough is 2 miles long and anglers should beware of getting caught in a storm – they can be particularly nasty in this mountainous spot.

LOUGH ISKANAMACTEERY V 60 69

Permission: Waterville Lake Hotel, Waterville, Co. Kerry.
Tel: (0667) 4310

This relatively small lough on the Waterville system has a resident stock of very small brown trout and gets a run of sea trout late in the season. There is one boat available and the lough can be fished all over, though particular attention should be given to the north shore if conditions are suitable. It is a great favourite in September and October. The same flies as for Currane are recommended.

ISKNAGAHINY LOUGH (Capal Lough) V 57 65

Permission: Butler Arms Hotel, Waterville, Co. Kerry.
Tel: (0667) 4156

Capal Lough, at the top of the short Capal River out of Lough Currane, is noted for its big sea trout, particularly at the end of the season. This is a typical sea-trout lough with numerous islands and headlands and rocky bays and has a character all of its own. A very attractive place indeed, where good sport can be expected when conditions are suitable any time from mid-June. Similar flies to Lough Currane.

GLAN LOUGH V 62 62

Permission: Inquire locally

This lough lies west of the Ring of Kerry N70 road from Sneem to Caherdaniel. It holds a fair stock of brown trout averaging 6 oz and about half of the bank is fishable.

LOUGH FADDA V 75 65

Permission: A Regional Fisheries Board Permit, available from Hussey's Shop, Sneem or from Liam Sheehan or Mrs O'Sullivan on the Kenmare side of the lough.

This attractive little lough is midway between Kenmare and Sneem by the side of the N70. It is intensively stocked with mainly rainbow trout and the average weight is 1 lb, though some fish are stocked up to 4 lb. The water is gin-clear and all methods are allowed except groundbait and maggots.

LOUGH BRIN V 78 77

Permission: Keith Johnson, Estate Office, Park Street, Kenmare, Co. Kerry.

This is a fair-sized lough lying deep in the Kerry mountains and about 10 miles north-west of Kenmare. Access is good with a small road running along one side, and it holds good brown trout up to 1 lb and the sea trout make their way up about August. The trout are relatively free-rising and it would be difficult to find a more beautiful setting, with mountains rising up on every side. There is one boat available and the banks are very good, except on the north side, where they become too steep. Useful fly patterns on this lough are Kingsmill, Bibio, Peter Ross and Alexandra.

LOUGH BARFINNIHY   V 84 76

Permission: A Regional Fisheries Board Permit, available from:
John O'Hare, Kenmare, Co. Kerry.
Tel: (064) 41499;
Cremins Tourist Shop, Moll's Gap, Co. Kerry.

This is a super lough both for the beauty of the scenery and the quality of the fishing. It is situated near Moll's Gap along the Killarney–Sneem road, 5 miles north-west of Kenmare. It has a nice stock of brown trout averaging 6 oz and is intensively stocked with rainbow trout by the South-Western Regional Fisheries Board. This is really a holidaymakers' lough and a lovely place for a

25   *Lough Barfinnihy*

26   *Capal Lough, Waterville*

picnic. Bright flies work best, while a small sedge fished dry in a quiet corner by the edge of the ripple can often account for a limit bag. It is possible to wade out on a gravel bank at the southern end and this area produces some nice red-spotted brownies. Expect to get at least 3 or 4 for the afternoon. The banks are fishable all round and the season runs from 1 June to 31 August.

THE DOO LOUGHS (The Humphry Lakes)   W 06 76
Permission: Not usually required

These small loughs are in the mountains of east Kerry and are best approached from the north off the L62 Kenmare–Ballyvourney road. There is a small road to within ½ mile of the water at the north-east side. The trout here are unusually large and average well over 1 lb, and fish to 4 lb have been reported. The loughs fish best in high water, but be warned – they can be notoriously dour and it has been recommended to bring along a few worms, in case everything else fails. Make no mistake, this place can have its good days.

CROHANE LAKE   W 04 80
Permission: Not usually required

Crohane Lake lies in a valley on the southern slopes of Bennaun-more. It is approached through the forest off the L62 Kenmare–Ballyvourney road and up to the farmhouse of the O'Sullivans, who own the surrounding land. It has a stock of brown trout ranging from ½ lb to 6 lb and can be brilliant on its day – I have seen a lovely 4 lb trout from Crohane. It is usually dour and sulky and is known locally as The Mug's Lake, after all the anglers who make the long journey and return empty-handed.

DROMOGHTY LOUGH
V 88 65
Permission: Not usually required

Dromoghty, 4 miles south of Kenmare, is difficult to fish because of the high reeds along the shore. A boat is required. It has small brown trout, sea trout from August and occasional salmon.

CUMMER LOUGH
V 88 63
Permission: Not usually required

Cummer Lough is approached by the same route as Dromoghty Lough, turning south off the L62 3 miles south of Kenmare. There is another small road to the south and this will bring you up the hill to within a few hundred yards of Cummer Lough. The trout here are great fighters and a very respectable size too, ranging from ½–¾ lb. The banks are all fishable, but don't attempt to wade because this lough is like a hole in the mountain, with very deep water close in, particularly at the south-east end. Try a small Invicta, Greenwell's Glory, Light Olive Quill, Butcher, Bibio and Raymond.

CLONEE LOUGHS
V 80 63
Permission: Mrs May O'Shea, Lake House, Clonee, Kenmare, Co. Kerry.
Tel: (064) 84205

These are two attractive and very scenic loughs lying 8 miles south of Kenmare. There is excellent access at the hotel, where anglers are well catered for and half a dozen boats are available for hire. Bank fishing is not allowed. The loughs hold an excellent stock of brown trout with some sea trout from late July and occasional salmon. The brownies average 6 oz, with some up to 1 lb. They take freely – unlike the sea trout – and are terrific fighters, pink-fleshed with big red spots. Favourite fly patterns are Golden Olive, Zulu, Bibio,

Raymond, Black Pennell and Greenwell's Glory. These are shallow loughs. Fishing is all over, not just by the shores, and the east lough is very attractive with its islands, bays and headlands. The best fishing is in April, May and September.

URAGH LOUGH

Permission: John O'Hare, Kenmare Angling Association, Fishing Tackle Shop, Main Street, Kenmare, Co. Kerry.
Tel: (064) 41499

Uragh Lough lies to the east of the Clonee Loughs and the access is good, off the small road by the north shore. It holds good brown trout averaging ½ lb with the occasional one to 1½ lb. The sea trout come in August and they are of a good average size – 1 lb – with some to 3 lb. In fact, you rarely ever get a small sea trout. The lough gets a small run of salmon in July. There is one club boat for hire – from John O'Hare – and bank fishing is allowed. Uragh can be fished all over and in August and September you are just as likely to get a sea trout out in the middle as by the shore. Useful fly patterns are Sooty Olive, Invicta, Connemara Black, Peter Ross, Greenwell's Glory, Fiery Brown and Bibio.

INCHIQUIN LOUGH   V 83 62

Permission: Keith Johnson, Estate Office, Park Street, Kenmare, Co. Kerry.

Inchiquin is about 8 miles south of Kenmare with good and easy access off a small road off the L62. This is a beautiful lough, with mountains on three sides and a primeval oak forest all along the south shore which hinders fishing but adds to the beauty of the place. This lough has char, brown trout, sea trout and salmon, and is fished mainly for its brownies and sea trout. Inchiquin is very deep in the middle, so most of the fishing is done drifting by the shores. There is one boat available for hire, from the estate office. The banks are soft and rocky and the wood hinders fishing off the south shore. The trout here average ¾ lb and the lough has produced some to 4½ lb. They take best in September and you may find them dour and sulky at other times. Flies to bring are Bibio, Zulu, Sooty Olive, Invicta, Connemara Black, Fiery Brown, Daddy and Peter Ross.

CUMMEENALOUGHAN   V 85 61
Permission: Not usually required

Only the fit and agile should attempt to reach this little lough. It is the most easterly of this chain of loughs and those who make it will be rewarded with fantastic views. The route is up the left side of the waterfall – have a few casts in the deep pools of the river near the lough, and be sure to stand well back out of sight. The trout here are 4 to the pound, but the beauty of the place makes up for their lack of size.

CUMMEENADILLURE LOUGH   V 84 61
Permission: Free

Follow the stream up the hill off the small road which runs to the north of the lough. This is an unusual lough in a very peaceful and beautiful setting. The water is gin-clear and the lake bed is carpeted with green vegetation – which gives the lough its name. The trout come 3 to the pound, with some to ½ lb. They are a lovely olive colour and great fighters. They have their days, though, and can be quite temperamental. If you find them in a taking mood, you can have most enjoyable fishing. They take with a bang and dance on their tails like sea trout. Only the north shore is fishable as there is a steep cliff to the south. Flies as for Uragh and Inchiquin.

LOUGH NAPEASTA (of the serpent)   V 82 62
Permission: Not usually required

This lough is so named not because it holds a large reptile but from the ridge of rock to the north, which when wet and viewed from the valley has the appearance of a writhing serpent as it glistens in the sunlight. Follow the old road around by the east side of Uragh Lough and don't bring a car too far. The rest of the way is on foot – up the mountain and across the ridge. This lough looks like a volcano crater filled with water. The trout come 4 to the pound and the north-east side fishes best. They can have their off days, too, and then there is nothing for it but to enjoy the lovely views of Kenmare Bay. Flies as for Uragh or Inchiquin.

GLANMORE LAKE   V 77 54
Permission: Keith Johnson, Estate Office, Park Street, Kenmare, Co. Kerry.

Glanmore Lake is one of the best loughs in this area. It is situated amongst some of the nicest scenery in Kerry and holds brown trout, sea trout and salmon. On its day it can give superb sport. It gets a small run of spring salmon and the grilse come in June. It has a good stock of sea trout by August, and they can give superb fishing. Someone said that there are no small sea trout here. Certainly it can produce plenty in the 2-lb, 3-lb and 4-lb range. This is a lovely lough, shallow and productive, with lots of rocks, islands and bays. There is no bank fishing. There is one boat for hire and anglers must take the estate boatman. Flies to bring are Hairy Mary, Jock Scott, Thunder and Lightning, Dunkeld and Blue Charm for spring salmon and Bibio, Claret and Blue, Claret and Jay, Connemara Black, Invicta, Kingsmill and Watson's Fancy for later in the season.

GLENBEG LOUGH	V 70 52
LOUGH FADDA	V 65 54
DERRYVEGAL LOUGH	V 64 55

Permission: Michael Harrington, Church Gate, Castletownbere, Co. Cork.
Tel: (027) 70011

Berehaven Anglers' Association has a lease on these loughs and a number of other smaller ones in the Ardgroom area. Glenbeg Lough has a big stock of small brown trout and the banks are fishable all round – which is quite a distance, because this lough is over a mile long. The trout come 3 to the pound – but better trout to ½ lb are often taken and larger trout were stocked recently.

Lough Fadda is not very accessible and the trout are very small and black.

Derryvegal Lough is to the south-west of Ardgroom, with a small road close to the shore. It has a nice stock of quite good brown trout averaging ½ lb, with occasional trout to 1 lb. The banks can be fished all round and fly patterns recommended for this area are Orange Grouse, Green Grouse, Claret and Jay, Claret Bumble, Bibio, Jungle Cock, Dunkeld and Alexandra.

GLEN LOUGH   V 83 52
Permission: Mrs Frances Keaney, Glenbrook, Adrigole, Co. Cork.
Tel: (027) 60064

Glen Lough is 2 miles north-east of Adrigole and access to it off the road is quite easy. It holds small brown trout and sea trout from July and an occasional salmon. The banks are soft and boggy and the sandbar at the top of the lough, where the river flows in, offers the best chance of a trout. Try a Bibio, Alexandra, Claret and Jay, Dunkeld, Peter Ross and Watson's Fancy.

THE CAHA MOUNTAIN LOUGHS

GLENKEEL LOUGH	V 83 53
LOUGH MOREDOOLIG	V 84 54
LOUGH BEGDOOLIG	V 84 54
LOUGH SHANOGE	V 84 55

Permission: Mrs Frances Keaney, Glenbrook, Adrigole, Co. Cork.
Tel: (027) 60064

LOUGH EEKENOHOOLIKEAGHAUN	V 86 54
LOUGH DERREENADAVODIA	V 86 54
LOUGH NALACA	V 85 56
BARLEY LAKE	V 87 56

Permission: Generally regarded as free, together with many other unnamed loughs in the area.

As can be seen from a glance at the contour lines on an Ordnance Survey map of this area, these are true mountain loughs, accessible only to the fit and agile. They are all situated high on the Caha Mountains on the Beara Peninsula to the south-west of Glengarriff. The loughs can be approached by several routes. The first way is to set out from Adrigole village for Glen Lough and then make a steep climb up by the left side of the waterfall towards Glenkeel Lough. The next is to set out from Glengarriff and take the Tunnel road from Kenmare. Turn off to the left about a mile from Glengarriff at the sign for Barley Lake, then turn off at the second junction to the left. It is possible to bring a car within about one mile of Barley Lake. For the third route take the same Kenmare–Tunnel road, and take the same left turn about a mile from Glengariff. Now, instead of turning left again as for Barley Lake, continue for approximately 5 miles into the narrow valley until you reach the end of the road. There is a farmhouse a few hundred yards ahead to the right of the valley. You will see a waterfall ahead and the loughs above can be reached by following the pony or goat track, taking care to stay to the right of the waterfall, as you climb. This track leads to the first of the loughs and the journey will take about 1½ hours. The effort involved is well worth while for the angler now has access to nearly twenty loughs, all easily fished from shorelines of slate and sandstone, with nothing to distract him except the wild goats and the grouse.

The trout in Glenkeel are small – about 4 to the pound – and the fine dam at the outfall has been irreparably damaged in the course of the construction of a hydroelectric scheme which was never completed. Moredoolig Lough and Begdoolig Lough hold very few, if any, trout. Lough Shanoge has lovely trout, averaging ½ lb, with many to at least 1½ lb. There is a fine dam at the outflow, built by Lord Bantry at the beginning of the century. Barley Lake is a fine sheet of water, well over 100 acres, and lies under the steep cliffs of the Cahas. Part of the shoreline is soft and marshy with high reeds, but at least half of it is fishable. The average size of the trout is ½ lb, with plenty to 1 lb and some to 2½ lb. The best fishing here is in April, May and September, and it can be very dour in June, July and August. A good plan in fishing the rest of the loughs higher up is to concentrate on those waters which drain into Bantry Bay. They were stocked with trout by Lord Bantry early in this century, while those draining into Kenmare Bay were not, and some of the latter hold no trout at all. On reaching the top of the waterfall, as you climb up from the farmhouse at the Glengarriff approach, you will see the streams feeding it. The stream to the right will bring you the ruins of Lord Bantry's shooting lodge, and at this point these loughs come into view. All of them offer good fishing, with free-rising trout averaging nearly ¾ lb. Lough Nalaca and some of the others hold exceptionally big trout up to 6 lb. These trout seldom take a fly, but are frequently taken on worms and sometimes on a small spinner. The most successful fly patterns in this area are Jungle Cock, Mar Lodge, Invicta, Conwell's Pride, Black Pennell, Claret Bumble, Greenwell's Glory, Matt Gorman, various Olives and the Grouse series of patterns in sizes 12 and 14.

Cloud and fog are hazards encountered from time to time at this altitude. The correct procedure in the event of such weather is to remain on the mountain and wait until it disperses, no matter how long this may take. To do otherwise is extremely dangerous and attempts to follow streams, etc., can have disastrous consequences because of the numerous sheer cliff faces all over this range of mountains. Before setting out for the mountain, always advise someone when you expect to return.

Fishing the loughs of the Cahas on the historic Beara Peninsula is an experience the angler will long remember. On a pleasant day, it can be close to paradise – or at least the Garden of Eden.

AVAUL LOUGHS   V 90 52

Permission: A Regional Fisheries Board Permit, available from:
Con Sullivan, Upper Lough Avaul, Glengarriff, Co. Cork.
Bernard Harrington, Glengarriff, Co. Cork.
Tel: (027) 63021
(Boat permits for the upper lough available from the same sources)
These two loughs lie about 2 miles south of Glengarriff on the L61

road. Each is about 10 acres and both hold good stocks of wild brown trout averaging ½ lb. In addition, they are intensively stocked with rainbow trout averaging 1 lb, with some to nearly 4 lb. The season runs from 1 June to 31 August. Bank fishing is allowed and all legitimate methods go except maggots and groundbait.

LOUGH BOFINNA W 03 48

Permission: A Regional Fisheries Board Permit, available from:
Jerry Spillane, Waterkeeper, Lough Bofinna, Bantry, Co. Cork.

Bofinna lies 3 miles east of Bantry and, with a road on two sides is very accessible to the tourist angler. It is stocked regularly with rainbow trout and the average rod catch per day is 3 trout. It has produced trout up to 6 lb. The bank fishing facilities are excellent and boats are available from the waterkeeper, Jerry Spillane.

SCHULL RESERVOIR V 94 33

Permission: A Regional Fisheries Board Permit, available from:
Tom Newman, Schull, Co. Cork.
Tel: (028) 28223

Schull Reservoir is situated overlooking Schull Harbour. It is about 5 acres in area, mainly shallow and with an excellent shoreline for angling. The angling season runs from 1 May to 31 August and the reservoir is stocked regularly with rainbow trout throughout the season.

SHREELANE LAKES (Shepperton Lakes) W 16 35

Permission: A Regional Fisheries Board Permit, available from:
Michael O'Driscoll, Shepperton Lakes, Skibbereen, Co. Cork.
Tel: (028) 33291

These two loughs lie midway between Skibbereen and Leap off a by-road and close to the N71 Skibbereen–Leap road. The two lakes – 15 acres and 35 acres – are linked by a canal. There is good bank fishing off the eastern shore of the larger lough, and six boats are available for hire from Michael O'Driscoll. The lakes are regularly stocked with rainbow trout and the average return is 3 trout per angler per rod day. The season runs from 1 April to 30 September.

DRIMINIDY LAKE   W 15 43
Permission: A Regional Fisheries Board Permit, available from:
Christina Crowley, The Pharmacy, Drimoleague, Co. Cork.
Tel: (028) 31116;
Christina Crowley, The Pharmacy, Dunmanway, Co. Cork.
Tel: (023) 45471;
Con O'Donoghue by the lakeside.

This is an attractive 6-acre pond holding small wild brown trout
and it is regularly stocked with rainbow trout averaging 1 lb. It
is conveniently situated by the roadside, 3 miles south-east of
Drimoleague and 7 miles north-east of Skibbereen.

LOUGH CLUHIR   W 20 32
Permission: Inquire locally

This attractive lough, surrounded by roads on all sides, is 3 miles
south of Leap and holds a small stock of good wild trout averaging
1 lb but with some as much as 4 lb. Shore fishing is limited due to
reeds and soft banks.

BALLIN LOUGH   W 19 39
Permission: James Maxwell, Leap-Ross Carbery Angling Association, Leap, Co. Cork.

Ballin Lough is by the roadside 2 miles north of Leap. It holds a
small stock of wild brown trout and is stocked with takable brown
trout by the angling association. Fly fishing only and the banks are
fairly good. Day tickets available.

LOUGH ATARRIFF   W 25 45
Permission: Not usually required

This is a small hill lough, 5 miles south of Dunmanway. It has a fair
stock of brown trout averaging 6 oz and about one-third of the
bank is fishable.

GARRANES LAKE   W 17 46
Permission: A Regional Fisheries Board Permit, available from:
Christine Crowley, The Pharmacy, Drimoleague, Co. Cork.
Tel: (028) 31116;
Christine Crowley, The Pharmacy, Dunmanway, Co. Cork.
Tel: (023) 45471;

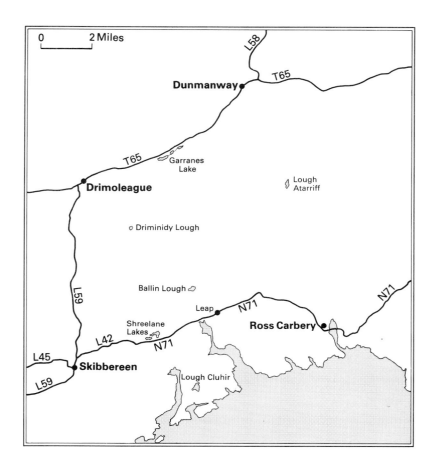

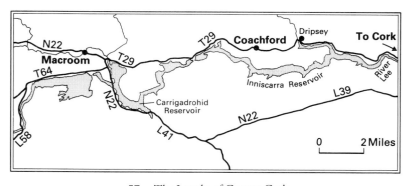

57   *The Loughs of County Cork*

J. Lucey, Waterkeeper, Garranes Lake, Drimoleague, Co. Cork. *Tel:* (028) 31330

Garranes Lake lies to the south of the T65 Drimoleague–Dunmanway road, about 3 miles from Drimoleague. It holds an excellent stock of small brown trout averaging 6 oz and was stocked with adult trout for the first time in 1986. It gave excellent angling returns. This is a lake of about 25 acres and the banks are soft and boggy. There are four boats for hire, available from the waterkeeper, J. Lucey.

GOUGANEBARRA LAKE   W 08 65
Permission: Not usually required

This lovely lough is set in the hills of west Cork, 2 miles west of the T64 Macroom–Bantry road. The trout average 4 to the pound and large baskets are caught. The lough may be fished from the bank or boats are available from the Gouganebarra Hotel, Tel: (026) 47069. This is a really beautiful area and the Gouganebarra Forest Park was the first established in Ireland.

THE LEE RESERVOIRS (Iniscarra Reservoir)   W 35 70
Permission: Not usually required.

Inniscarra Reservoir, to the west of Cork City, holds a fair stock of wild brown trout and trout stocks are supplemented each season by the Lee Trout Restocking Committee, the South-Western Fisheries Board and the Electricity Supply Board. These bodies stock substantial numbers of trout, averaging 1 lb, into the system annually. The best trout fishing areas are the north arm at the mouth of Dripsey River, the wide shallow area east of Carrigadrohid, and along the northern shore east of the mouth of the Dripsey River. Boats are available for hire 1½ miles west of Inniscarra Dam on the north shore. A map of this great mixed fishery and up-to-date information are available from the South-Western Regional Fisheries Board, 1 Nevilles Terrace, Macroom, Co. Cork, Tel: (026) 41222.

LOUGH ADERRY   W 93 73
Permission: A Regional Fisheries Board Permit

This excellent rainbow-trout fishery lies to the south of the N25 Midleton–Castlemartyr road, 2 miles from Castlemartyr. It is a shallow lough of some 30 acres, has good access and is heavily fished. An intensive stocking programme is carried out throughout the angling season, which runs from March to November, and the lough provides first-class fishing. Fishing is from the bank and from boats. Bankside weed tends to create a problem in summer. Six boats are available for hire from the waterkeeper, M. Higgins, Lough Aderra, Castlemartyr, Co. Cork. An excellent fishery where the best trout in 1985 weighed 6 lb 8 oz.

Appendix   Useful Addresses

Central Fisheries Board
Balnagowan
Mobhi Boreen
Glasnevin
Dublin 9.
Tel: (01) 379206

Bord Failte/Irish Tourist
    Board
Baggot Street Bridge
Dublin 2.
Tel: (01) 765871

Department of Agriculture for
    Northern Ireland
Fisheries Division
Hut 5
Castle Grounds
Stormont
Belfast BT4 3TA.
Tel: Belfast 63939

Foyle Fisheries Commission
8 Victoria Road
Derry BT47 2AB.
Tel: (0504) 42100

Northern Ireland Tourist Board
River House
48 High Street
Belfast BT1 2DS.
Tel: Belfast 31221

Shannon Regional Fisheries
    Board
Thomond Weir
Limerick.
Tel: (061) 55171

South Western Regional
    Fisheries Board
1 Nevilles Terrace
Massey Town
Macroom
Co. Cork.
Tel: (026) 41222

Southern Regional Fisheries
    Board
Anglesea Street
Clonmel
Co. Tipperary.
Tel: (052) 23624

Eastern Regional Fisheries
    Board
Mobhi Boreen
Glasnevin
Dublin 9.
Tel: (01) 379209

Northern Regional Fisheries
    Board
Station Road
Ballyshannon
Co. Donegal.
Tel: (072) 51435

North Western Regional
    Fisheries Board
Abbey Street
Ballina
Co. Mayo.
Tel: (096) 22623

Western Regional Fisheries
    Board
Weir Lodge
Earl's Island
Galway. Tel: (091) 65548

Alphabetical Index of Loughs